Price to Book & Replacement
Value Analysis.
Mix of Equities to Fixed Income.

5

SECTOR DECISION:

Growth Industries.
Cyclical Growth Industries.
Cyclical Industries.
Energy and Natural Resources.
Interest Sensitive Industries.

SECTOR ANALYSIS:

Macro Economic Earnings
Determinants.
Relative Earnings Comparison.
Changes in Return on Capital.
Relative Value of Assets, Earnings
and Equity Prices.
Current P/E, Book Value to
Historical Ranges.

6

Revenue Growth.
Cost Analysis.
Leverage Factors.
Relative Earnings Momentum.
Relative ROE Momentum.
Reinvestment Rate Comparisons.

Net Cash Flow Trends.
Relative P/E Ratio to S&P Index.
Investor Attitudes.
Technical Review.

7

Earnings Projections.
Dividend Growth Projections.
Relative P/E Judgment.
Relative and Absolute P/E
Comparison.
Development of Risk/Gain
Expectations.
Estimate of Realizable Asset Value.
Analysis of Quality of Earnings.

8

Maturity Mix.
Classification Mix.
Gov't/Agency vs Corporate.
Quality Ratings.

9

Loss Limitation Review.
Fundamental Changes in
Perception.
Valuation Change.
Technical Deterioration.
Senior Management
Accountability.

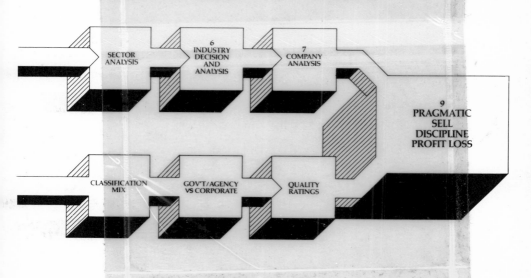

SILENT INVESTOR, SILENT LOSER

Silent Investor, Silent Loser

MARTIN SOSNOFF

RICHARDSON & STEIRMAN
NEW YORK

ISBN 0-931933-30-7

Library of Congress Catalog Number: 86-082395

SILENT INVESTOR, SILENT LOSER is published
by Richardson & Steirman, Inc., 246 Fifth Avenue,
New York, New York 10001.

Designed by: Joseph Ascherl

Production Managed by Pauline Neuwirth

Printed by: Haddon Craftsman

First Edition

Distributed to the trade by:
Kampmann & Company, Inc.
New York, New York

2299118

DEDICATION

For Toni and Jason, who showed me much more than the efficeint mart stocket.

Contents

1   Gun Racks in the 727 3

2   The Perception of La Gioconda 18

3   The Pathology of Representation 30

4   The Search for Reductiveness 45

5   The Anatomy Lesson 66

6   The Unmarked-Door Phenomenon 82

7   The *Efficeint* Mart Stocket 96

8   The Art of Packaging 115

9   Sometimes the Fish Die 127

10   Napoleon, Rubber Tires, and Craps 147

11   David vs. Goliath. 154

12   Stress Cracks in the Marble Pillars 170

13   The Enduring Rape of Shareholders 188

14   The Case against Custodial Management 205

15   The United States of Leverage. 222

16   Red Highways of the Eighties. 235

17   Goodbye, Tanzania 249

18   Silent Investor, Silent Loser 261

      Epilogue. 279

ACKNOWLEDGMENTS

My friend, Jacques de Spoelberch, showed unwavering faith in this manuscript and placed it with Sandy Richardson, my gentlemanly editor. I am indebted to both for the sensitivity of their editorial suggestions and the active interest in all phases of the development of *Silent Investor, Silent Loser.* My associates at Atalanta/Sosnoff Capital were very supportive. Janet Greenberg, my assistant, was a prestidigitator of the word processor. Ann Marie Lewis, our computer analyst, programmed many of the charts, tables, and graphs. Our director of research, Eric Stiefel, was ready with hundreds of answers to hundreds of questions. My partner, Shep Osherow, read chapter after chapter with a good eye for the gut issues of money management. The Comtesse du Mont Alban, Toni, my wife, read the first and last drafts with the loving but unwavering point of view that the work had to radiate clarity with the minimum of Wall Street mumbo jumbo. All points rang true. Thank you all.

Martin T. Sosnoff

Illustrations

		PAGE
1	Barnett Newman, Untitled drawing	8
2	Arakawa, Marx's Desire	12
3	Frans Hals, La Bohemienne	26
4	A. R. Penck, Standart West II	48
5	F. E. Picot, L'Amour et Psyché	61
6	William Bouguereau, Le Ravissement de Psyché	62
7	Thomas Eakins, The Agnew Clinic	64
8	Rembrandt, Dr. Tulp Demonstrating the Anatomy of the Arm	67
9	John Baldessari, Kiss/Panic	93
10	Sol LeWitt, Three Part Variation on Three Different Trends	110
11	Georg Baselitz, Frau am Strand	144
12	Robert Rauschenberg, Able Was I Ere I Saw Elba	148
13	Dario Morales, Woman on Mattress	155
14	Edouard Manet, Olympia	157
15	Darenfort, Contemporary Conception of the Corporation	189
16	Jean-Auguste-Dominique Ingres, Mme. Moitessier	206
17	Alexandre Cabanel, The Birth of Venus	207
18	Henri Matisse, Portrait of Mme. Matisse. Mask, Sira-Puna	247

TELL SERRET that I should be desperate if my figures were correct, tell him that I do not want them to be academically correct, tell him that I mean: If one photographs a digger, he certainly would not be digging then. Tell him that I adore the figures by Michelangelo, though the legs are undoubtedly too long, the hips and the backsides too large. Tell him that, for me, Millet and Lhermitte are the real artists for the very reason that they do not paint things as they are, traced in a dry analytical way, but as they—Millet, Lhermitte, Michelangelo—feel them. Tell him that my great longing is to learn to make those very incorrectnesses, those deviations, remodelings, changes in reality, so that they may become, yes, lies if you like—but truer than the literal truth.

Vincent Van Gogh
Letter to Theo,
July 1885

SILENT INVESTOR,
SILENT LOSER

1 Gun Racks in the 727

NOBODY I know who manages a lot of money has written about what it's like to invest serious money day after day. There are a couple of dozen consistently good operators in the country and they know who's who. Each of us does things a little differently, and there is rarely a day when we don't change a few stones in the never-ending mosaic of our investment schema. The textbooks can tell you about valuation techniques and computer-screening the investment universe, but nobody talks about the need for physical stamina to sift through the daily entrails of economic data. Finally, you need the courage to stand alone. If you find yourself within the band of the consensus forecast, cash in. It's all over.

I recycle some money into the art of my generation and curate shows from time to time. Many of my friends are sculptors and painters, and they are successful because they see the world in a way nobody else sees it. Artists deal in perception. They are good at it. The sculptor controls his materials; the financier does not. To be successful, money managers try to see ahead six months to a year. Few of us made the grade consistently. The most reductive and sound investment concept valid the past five years is that paper assets were better than hard goods. Give it another five years. Art reflects financial and political tensions just as much as securities markets. It is another leading indicator worth listening to—sometimes.

ANNUAL RATES OF RETURN—1981–1985	
Your Home	3.28%
A barrel of oil	−3.88
An ounce of gold	−11.52
90-Day Certificate	11.59
10-Year Bond	23.69
Stocks (S & P 500)	13.50

I am secure about what the financial world will look like for the remainder of the decade. The dialectics of the past has given birth to the future. Except for Japan and Germany, the Western world has lived beyond its means. Everybody knows this. You don't hide budget deficits. What has gone on South of the Border is pure musical comedy. The Western world's banks loaned $500 billion to a coterie of Latin corporations and countries which threw it away on steel mills and railroads that don't work. Along the way, a lot of TV receivers and condominiums were consumed, too. The symbolism of all the government buildings in Mexico City collapsing during the earthquake is overpowering.

The world must spend the next five to ten years learning to live within its means. Budget deficits must be pared down, or your currency will be destroyed in a marketplace that now no longer sleeps. There is twenty-four-hour trading in just about every commodity and option known to man. Rejoice in paper assets, stocks and bonds. The image of 250,000-deadweight-ton super tankers steaming slowly toward Taiwan to be vivisected by the Chinese into scrap is all too powerful. Ships that cost $80 million designed for carrying $6 million in oil cargo from the Persian Gulf to our deep ports sold for $6 million in the scrap market. Ten percent of the world's big-tanker tonnage was scrapped last year. The oil companies just write it off the asset side of their balance sheets, and in corporatise the expression is "downsizing" or "restructuring." Everyone nods his head and agrees that it was impossible to project that the world would have learned how to conserve oil consumption.

You have to know how to be greedy to make a lot of money. Let me help you dream a little. Long-term interest rates in Germany and Japan today are hovering below 6 percent. It is difficult to measure any inflation there whatsoever. The history of the world's interest rates suggests that long-term rates track inflation with an average premium of 2 percentage points. It was true here in the pre-Vietnam sixties. Today, real interest rates in the Western world are 6 points above inflation because everybody believes that inflation is around the corner. If everybody's wrong, you make a lot of money. I could drive you crazy with academic models of stock-market valuation, but believe me, the valuation of the market is tied closely to interest rates, and if our rates drop from 8 percent to 6 percent, the stock market will zip along with many 30-point-up days.

When supermarket chain Pantry Pride outlasted Revlon in its takeover bout, the forty-two-year-old headman at P.P., Ronald Perelman, peeked into the Revlon corporate jet for the first time. He was a little surprised to find that the richly appointed Boeing 727 had gun racks. Do New York City boys know from gun racks? What was a fingernail-polish purveyor doing with gun racks? The gutsy house on Wall Street that bankrolled almost all of the hostile takeovers wasn't surprised at all. One of their corporate finance tigers got it right when he said, "Corporate America! They all look alike, dress alike, and talk alike. We're out to change all that."

Union Carbide and Phillips Petroleum—household names for perhaps a hundred years—escaped. They leveraged themselves more than the would-be predators who had lined up billions and billions of high-cost money: most of it from Drexel Burnham, but some from the money center banks who like to play when the fees are fat. Many didn't escape or learned to play the game. Over $150 billion in equity valuation was sucked out of the market by friendly and unfriendly takeovers, leveraged buyouts, and share-repurchase programs. That $150 billion is more than the total valuation of the stock market of Germany, the fourth largest exchange in the world. Most of this happened during 1985, and the buybacks and buyouts reduced the supply of Big Board stocks by 12 percent. It goes a long way toward explaining why everyone had a good year.

The newspapers don't tell you about asset-transfer values. There are two quotes for every stock on the board; the price it trades at, and the price someone is willing to pay to get control of the assets and cash flow of the enterprise. Maybe that someone wants gun racks, too. This is known as the "control" premium, and it is generally 50 percent above the market. When Kohlberg, Kravis, & Roberts reduced its price for Beatrice Foods, the arbs ran for the hills. Everyone suddenly realized that the control premiums had been built into too many stocks. Entire sectors and industries now trade in the marketplace as if they were going to be bought out tomorrow. Broadcasting, airlines, newspapers, food processors, chemicals, papers, drugs, oils, tires, conglomerates—the shopping list stretches longer and longer. Money managers believe in America almost 365 days of the year. Arbs don't. They measure everything by the "cost of carry," the implicit interest cost for owning something that doesn't change in value. Many of the arbitrageurs have decided to let the money managers own the pricy goods that might not be "in play" tomorrow.

One day in January 1986, the slippage of two-tenths of a percentage point to 6.8% in the unemployment rate signaled the bond crowd that the deflationary modality of surplus labor was coming to an end. But around the Western world, teenage unemployment ranges between 20 and 30 percent. How else do you explain youth riots in Liverpool? Why should the Federal Reserve Board make money more plentiful? In the short run, the bond crowd was right. By 2:30 P.M. Henry Kaufman, chief economist at Salomon Brothers, had rushed into print with a new forecast that the Fed would not cut its discount rate. This is the same Henry who a year earlier had projected a strong economy and interest rates in the low teens. The FRB is rightly anxious about our leveraged financial institutions. Why give the boys more Monopoly money to play with? But M&A operators (mergers and acquisitions) will figure out new paper to make deals with. Everyone learns to live with our flat-footed institutions.

The disenfranchisement of all shareholders by rapacious managements with kept boards of directors—some paid consultants to the very same corporations—has cost shareholders billions upon billions. Nobody protects the small investor. The New York Stock Exchange is interested solely in its trading share of the financial markets and in keeping members healthy and prosperous. Governor Cuomo sponsored an antitakeover bill at the behest of CBS, the perennially poorly managed media conglomerate. The administration rightly believes in the marketplace as the final arbiter of who should own what, but the SEC had refused publicly to take a stand against greenmail and golden parachutes. At one point, Michel Bergerac, chairman of Revlon, had $36 million in lump-sum compensation due him. The proxy statement denoted salary and bonus payable through 1992. The full package. Bergerac also sits on the CBS board.

For more than fifty years the New York Stock Exchange was considered the ultimate protector of shareholders' voting rights. No longer. It refuses to delist corporations that dilute the one share–one vote rule. Even the state courts have upheld the concept of common shareholders' being treated differently. A corporation can choose to pay a premium to some shareholders but not to others. This is a new kind of common law. The establishment is striking back.

My experience as a money manager suggests that the entrepreneurial instinct equates with sizable equity ownership. Force top management to take half their compensation in stock, and then maybe we'll see better results. Actually, the sub rosa practice of paying greenmail is part of this broader issue of the abject failure of most custodial managers to deliver any reasonable rate of return to shareholders while ferociously insulating their tenure, inclusive of $600,000 salaries and bonuses with the passive accord of stockholder proxies.

Barnett Newman, who reduced his art to the point of emptiness, said, "The big question was what to paint." He began as if painting were not only dead, but never existed. Newman's work took off in the fifties and spawned lively movements that are still with us. Color-field painting and the minimalists are derivatives of Newman's work. At a recent auction at Sotheby's, *Ulysses,* an elongated two-color-bar canvas, sold for over $1,595,000 to The Menil Foundation. In the investment world, unless you can be as reductive as Newman in terms of conceptuality, the chances are that you will lose money. Put another way, there are times to be all in cash, to think awhile, and then to start over with a fresh theme. If you can't summarize why you are "in the market" in twenty-five words or less, forget it. I put it slightly differently to my staff of security analysts and young money managers. "If you can't convince me to buy an idea in five minutes, it's too complex and therefore probably worthless."

I'm going to give it away: the most reductive theme for years to come in the Western world is *the need for low interest rates to grow out of our economic stagnation that dates back to the late seventies.* Twenty words. There is no other way to push down the unemployment rolls. All the central banks now understand this. Without low rates, the Third World reverts to the tribal-state conditions of the eighteenth century. Rejoice that our banks, for one point of vigorish, gave away $500 billion South of the Border. Their stupidity and the Latino corruption have birthed the bull

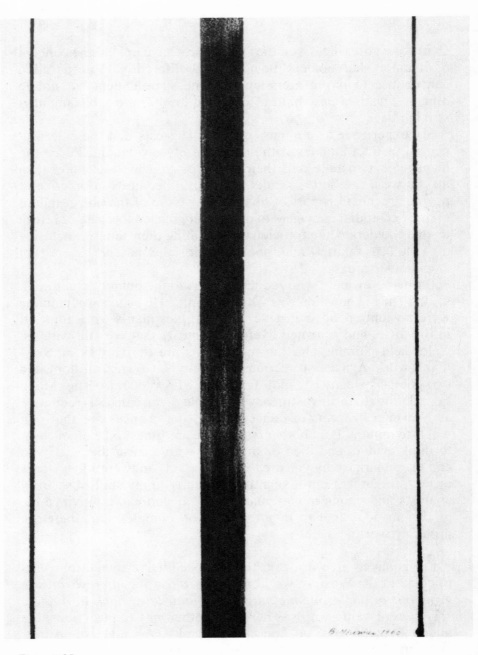

Barnett Newman
Untitled drawing. 1960
Ink on paper. 14″ × 10″
Collection of Estée Lauder Cosmetics.

market in paper assets. Irony and hubris exist in financial markets just as they did in ancient Greece.

Each morning's mail is a foot-high pile of analysts' reports, corporate press releases, prospectuses, and trade magazines that I devour in thirty to sixty minutes. Nothing helps me very much. Usually the economists' reports are useless. For every economist forecasting that interest rates are headed up 200 basis points, there are two projecting a 200-basis-point decline. The security analysts are no better. They missed the debacle in personal computers, ignored the precipitous decline in the quality of bank earnings, and now fear automobile stocks are overpriced at 4 times 1986 earnings.

How can a human being analyze information and shape politics and economics into an investment concept that makes sense? When someone asks me what I do, I tell them I'm a manipulator of stocks. When they press me further, I add that I am a manufacturer of money. My wife Toni will dig me with a sharp elbow, suggesting that I'm arrogant and not so funny. But I am serious. My buying power at the moment is several billion dollars. You can multiply me by a couple of hundred. There are equity pools of up to $40 billion: 1 percent of GNP. Money managers tend to talk to each other, go to the same dinner parties, and have comparable information-retrieval systems, staff analysts, computer-screening techniques. We all read the same trade publications, meet with the same politicians and their staffs, and interview the same corporate headmen. Sometimes we come to opposite conclusions after absorbing identical data.

About fifteen years ago, I decided to work a four-day week. I have never regretted it. It is now fashionable for money managers to take time off. Our excuse is that we are thinking all the time, and that the best conclusions occur in periods of tranquility. One Friday summer afternoon in Greenwich, six of us played some round-robin tennis. I counted up $60 billion in assets among us. This is 1½ percent of GNP. If we all decided that we wanted in or out of the market on the same day—or even the same week— the New York Stock Exchange couldn't open for at least a month. After all, even a hundred-million-share day is only a mere $4 billion in trading activity. So when I say that we are manipulators of stocks, it is true—at least in the short run. Over lunch that day, some of us decided that the big banks were disaster-prone, and others decided that the stocks had discounted everything but a declaration of bankruptcy.

None of us has perfect perception, nor even all the relevant data on which to back big decisions. Despite our many contacts, and information-retrieval capacity, we always remain on the outside looking in. No bank president is going to tell us how far underwater his loan portfolio is, nor is the president of General Motors going to reveal that his product line is less than world class in the upcoming model year, or that his plants will never match the Japanese in automation, robotics, and work-station productivity. Everything in America is new and improved—they still drill this message in to you from every billboard and television commercial. It's up to us to discover that perhaps it is not exactly new and improved.

Let me return to the four-day week. In the heady days of the sixties, when stocks sold at 20, 30, 40 times earnings, most money managers were not serious people. None of us talked about budget deficits, inflation, marginal productivity, or the probability of a negative yield curve. There was no inflation, no budget deficit, and no loss of productivity. Interest rates snaked along in a narrow channel between 4 and 4½ percent. When two money managers met for lunch, the opening question was always the same: "Have you heard any good stories lately?" We were like movie producers in gray flannel suits who purveyed fantasy as brazenly as Steven Spielberg, and for several years we got away with it. Then, one day early in 1973, the music died. Bye-Bye, Miss American Pie. Polaroid film stayed on the shelves. The Avon ladies sold fewer bottles of colored water. Airline RPMs crashed, and semiconductor booked-to-billed ratios fell off the page. A mild recession destroyed the valuation structure for growth stocks. Looking back, it is hard to believe that such companies sold at 5 to 10 times book value and 40 to 50 times earnings. Today they sell closer to book value and under 10 times earnings.

What does this have to do with the four-day week? Well, if your perceptions are far from reality, if you accept the investment framework without questioning, you might as well go back to sleep. All the ciphering in the world will get you nowhere. If you talk to the wrong people—98 percent of the analysts, economists, and yes, money managers, too—you will bury yourself. I always assume that the guy on the other end of the phone is dumber than I am. If he were brighter, he would be doing what I do. It follows logically that the most efficient work station for a money manager is the one that filters out the Wall Street mumbo-jumbo. This means that you end up talking to fewer and fewer people and concentrating on fewer and fewer decisions. Finally, you end up talking to yourself, especially on Friday, far from the roar of the crowd.

Talking to yourself is a very subjective way to make decisions. The data has been processed and it floats freely somewhere in your brain. This is known as a perceptive mass. The big decisions arrive viscerally after the brainwork is long over. When I go against my belly button and rely solely on the arithmetic of the situation, it usually costs me a lot of money. I refer to the easy analytical decisions that extrapolate numbers. They never make you money. It is only hard decisions for which there is no ready arithmetic that make the big money. One example will give you the idea. I hate banks and bankers, if only because there are more banks than bankers. They are the dull normals running banks with tens of billions in assets. Management owns no equity in these institutions. My staff analysts proved conclusively to me that the balance sheets and income statements of the 20 largest banks in the country were junk heaps. Reserves for losses were far too shallow, and adjusting the loans to Latin America for projected declines in interest income suggested to us that earnings were overstated by 40 to 60 percent, and that the net worth would vanish if precise accounting standards were applied to banks. The next time a bank asks you for references, ask them about Mexico.

One Friday afternoon I bought a block of Manufacturers Hanover at 3 times estimated 1985 earnings, yielding 12 percent. There were voices jabbering in my head, urging me on. "The pressure is coming off the banks. The dollar is too strong. Short-term interest rates are going to break and widen the earnings margin. Mexico is getting a little healthier, and the market is going to want interest-sensitive goods, not cyclicals, with the economy slowing down." Manny Hanny rose 20 percent in two weeks. How did I know? I used the same facts the analysts fed me, but I rearranged them in a different way and came to the opposite conclusion. Contrarian, perhaps, but definitely abstract.

I am an abstract illusionist. There is even an abstract illusionist group of contemporary artists. To make serious money, you have

A Lemon. Men's Review 1968...1969, 1969. Acrylic or canvas or canvas. 96" × 132". Collection of Toni and Martin Sosnoff.

to dream better than the marketplace, and you have to be in touch
with your feelings, sensing when pressure is about to come off
securities and when markets are psychotic and about to act out
their craziness.

Arakawa is the world's most abstract illusionist whose works
radiate layers of meaning. His art is not simply images, thoughts,
space, and symbolism but all given conditions brought together in
one place. Note how he deals with the ambiguity in this presentation
of lemons. Arakawa gets to the point faster. "Everything is
ambiguous as well as the judgment that something is ambiguous.
As soon as any fact is presented, ambiguity appears as the zone
of alternate possibilities." Yes! Note the interconnecting lines.
Each image radiates and is connected to the other images in a
spider's web of interrelationships. If I were to draw a picture of
the stock market, it would not be the stock tables, but the symbolism
of the distorting transmogrifications of a simple lemon into a pattern
of ambiguous concepts and facts—some false, some real—that
coexist and pull at each other with magnetic force.

For me, running money is the ultimate existential gesture: David
slinging stones at Goliath. My marginal utility is measured in
percentage points, and more than a little of the craziness in the
money-management business is generated by hyperactive greyhounds chasing a mechanical rabbit named Performance. I am
constantly saying yes or no. If I put a barrel on either side of my
desk, one labeled Right and the other Wrong, my decisions over
time would eventually fill up both barrels. As Arakawa suggests,
the lemon adumbrates ideas, forms, and relationships, but none of
us ever sees the true essence of lemon perfectly.

Silent Investor, Silent Loser deals with the disenfranchisement
of the investor. The public has not made any serious money since
the early sixties. Some of the blame goes to each successive
administration since the Kennedy days, and more is laid on the
heads of dense corporate managements. There is the unleveraged
capital structure of the typical American corporation that assures
a mediocre return on equity in our economy with trendline growth
of 3 percent. The sociology of token ownership of equity by both
officers and directors of almost all big businesses reinforces an
antientrepreneurial management style that is considered normal
behavior, even by the professional investor.

On the outskirts of Napoli, a black-uniformed highway policeman stopped our Mercedes, pointed to the gold earrings and necklace my wife Toni wore, and wagged his index finger. "Not in Napoli by the waterfront. You wear nothing or it will be gone," he said in Italian. We thanked him and drove on to see Herculaneum, the seaside village buried in lava 2,000 years ago. The iconography of Napoli is the sheets and underwear billowing from the windows of the oatmeal-colored tenements. In Herculaneum, as we parked on a side street, two eight-year-olds shook us down. *"Guardiamo la macchina?"* I gave them the universal hand and arm sign for "up yours" and was awarded slashed tires in return. Later, the garage gave us a phony incomplete receipt for the new tire purchases so we couldn't obtain the export-tax rebate, but I paid off two new *bambini* to guard our luggage while the tires were changed.

This is an object lesson of what happens in a country that has lived too long beyond its means. It is what America will look, be, and feel like in ten years if we just keep on doing what we keep on doing. Compound interest works. Keep the budget deficit at $200 billion, and before long the interest on the debt takes up half the annual budget. The food stamps have been confiscated from the Blacks and Hispanics by the guys in Washington who go jogging at dawn along the broad avenues of our capital. But it is the middle class that is bankrupting the country with cost-of-living increases on social security, government pensions, and a Medicare program that doesn't differentiate between financial need and the capacity to pay one's own bills.

There is a surrealistic quality that pervades all investment decisions. Everyone knows that in the long run we are all dead. But, how far out is the long run? Is it closing in on us fast? The long run may be the eighties or nineties, not some point in the next century. It is like China's scheduled takeover of Hong Kong in 1997 or the desert spreading through Tanzania. Only 3 percent of the families in our country earn over $75,000 a year. So why shouldn't the government tax the wealthy to death with inflation and allot the lion's share of the budget to the median-wage earners? Most of the world is operating on this unstated policy, and we are not very far behind. I can give you a hundred reasons why we should tax the privileged into oblivion and fifty reasons why we should think twice. The point is that we are on the eve of momentous policy decisions, and none of us knows how they will come out.

I cite the ultimate frustration: our government as the number-one odd-lotter, zigging when it should zag. When silver was $50 an ounce, the strategic stockpile stood pat, but when silver tumbled to $10 an ounce, the General Services Administration was thinking of lightening up. When gold was $750 an ounce and the Arabs soaked up their OPEC surplus with gold accumulations, we slept. Hundreds of billions of gold-denominated bonds could have been sold by the Treasury Department to domestic savers and foreigners who were paranoid about owning precious metals. The government could have saved tens of billions of dollars in interest payments on the national debt. But the gold still rests securely underground, just like in the fairy tales. Gold ticks at $325 an ounce.

Twenty-five years ago, the Dow Jones news tickers would ring a bell every time there was some good news. It was the custom for some junior analyst to race to the ticker and yell out the story to the research department: "IBM splits three for one," whatever. One day I heard the ticker sounding off every half hour like in a firehouse, and it was Joe Granville now hustling over, the first to devour the news. "General Motors declares regular dividend," the teleprinter jiggled out. "My God, they're ringing the bell for nothing," Joe whispered to me. "It's all over." This is how I'm beginning to feel. We are starting to ring bells just because Argentina hasn't changed its name and our banks open their doors at 9:00 A.M.

Don't worry too much. In France, when you eat in a bourgeois restaurant, they bring you a bottle of water with your wine, and everyone dilutes the wine by half. All the great vintages age in the New York wine-merchants' bins or in the three-star restaurants abroad. The middle class in France drinks cheap champagne, too, so it's still a long way to dog food for all of us in the Western world.

It is Mike Milken of Drexel on the phone.

"Lights are flashing all over my board from the M&A Group."

"So?" I say to Mike.

"You asked for the unaskable."

"I want a seat on Caesar's," I said.

"In the real world, you don't ask for a board seat. In the real world, you wait until they offer you one."

"What do you mean you don't ask for a seat? I own .13 percent of the company. Nobody on the board owns much more than a few thousand shares.''

"The lawyers see millions of dollars in fees. Flom, Skadden, Arps. They smell fee money, protecting the company's flanks.''

"But I'm friendly,'' I protest. "Henry's doing a great job. I just want to see what is going on from the inside.''

"You can do that without going on the board. Gluck will talk to you. Any chairman of the board would do the same thing. How does he know you're going to stay friendly? The first time he does something you don't like, it becomes unfriendly. Henry has to deal with 10,000 employees who aren't sure anymore who's supposed to be running the company. Two years from now you have a fight with your wife and decide you want to run the company. What does Henry do then? You've got to understand that no management in the country is going to sit by and let you buy more than 10 percent of their company without a standstill agreement or some written assurance that you won't control them. Why should they let you buy 15 percent, 25 percent and do nothing? It's not the way the country works.''

"I thought I was living in the free enterprise system, Mike. When a stock trades on the Big Board, you buy as much as you like, so long as you file timely SEC reports, whatever.''

"Marty, nobody files an SEC report where they ask for a board seat. You don't do that. It's not friendly.''

"I'm friendly.''

"If you're friendly, you amend your SEC report and say that you've thought about it and don't want a board seat. That's friendly.''

"I'm not going to do that.''

"Then you're not friendly.''

"I'm friendly, I'm friendly.''

"What am I supposed to tell my merger-and-acquisition people?''

"I'm the friendliest guy in the world.''

"I'm going to make believe we never had this conversation. You filed a 13D asking for a seat. Nobody does that. Icahn buys 40 percent of TWA and doesn't ask for a seat. Friendly people are *invited* on boards. You haven't been invited. It could take years and years.''

"Mike . . . Mike . . . Listen to me. Would Henry prefer somebody really unfriendly owning 4 million shares? Icahn, Steinberg, Lindner, whoever?''

"You don't understand, Marty. Management sees you all the same way. There is no difference between you and Icahn—or anyone else. No management in this country is going to stand by and let you gobble up their stock. One day it's 15 percent, then it's 25 percent, and after that you want it all."

"I'm not Hitler, and I don't have enough money to buy it all."

"Why should they assume you're not Hitler?"

"Mike, we'll have another conversation."

"It's heading in the wrong direction," Mike said. " The lawyers smell money." I heard some junk-bond quotes in the background and hung up.

Where is the real world? My world was the Big Board. Earnings, stock prices, computerized investment process data. I had made 100 million dollars in the pits. Alfred Sloan of General Motors once said that the men who control the money control all. Wrong, Alfred. I controlled nothing, a number on a broker's ledger sheet, signifying another silent Sam, a passive investor. Nothing. I checked the latest proxy statement and confirmed that I owned ten times more stock than the entire board of directors at Caesar's World. I might as well be resting in a nursing home, clipping coupons.

I felt like a number.

2 The Perception of *La Gioconda*

JUST BEFORE the Depression, my father bought a tarpaper shack on the Hudson 32 miles from New York City. He plunked down $250 in cash and got a $750 mortgage from the subdeveloper who had chopped a hill into quarter-acre lots and sold them to leftist intellectuals. We summered there for more years than I can remember. We left our apartment in the Bronx in June and returned in September, when school reopened. Rent was a big item during the thirties. Five of us lived in three rooms. My two older brothers and I shared an unfinished cubicle with three beds and three chests of drawers, covering every square inch of floor space. The raw two-by-fours turned honey brown over time, and the roof boards developed dark blots from rain leaks. My father spent his Sundays patching up the place: slapping the red asphalt roof with pitch, hacksawing water pipes for elbow fittings, and crowbarring stumps and rocks so my mother could at least plant a rock garden on the hilly slope that was ours. We called him Ben, the shoemaker, and it was usually dark before he got in his swim in the pond nearby.

In time, our neighbors improved their shacks. They packed insulation between the studs and finished off rooms in knotty pine. They installed furnaces and gas hot-water heaters, and some lived there year-round. We stuck with our summer shack. Our egalitarian neighbors gently but firmly suggested that our shack was an eyesore that was holding down land values. Our closest neighbor, an ardent Communist writer for the *Daily Worker,* built a spite fence to block us out of his line of sight. My mother never spoke to him again.

I learned in many ways what it was like to be poor. There were roly-poly 1939 cars in every driveway but ours. Ben hitched rides to the train station or walked the three miles. We had a fifty-gallon drum of kerosene outside. It fueled our two-burner stove and hot-water heater, but by early August I was chilled as soon as my feet hit the linoleum floor. I can still smell the kerosene permeating the house and the dampness and heavy veneer of dust. My mother hated housework and rarely lifted a broom. I swept out balls of dust under my bed and finally decided to sleep on our screened-in porch, away from my noisy and quarrelsome brothers. Our few warped doors and thin walls did little to screen out sound, even that of respiration. When you walked in the shack, floorboards creaked like a chorus of frogs. Only a curtain separated the boys' room from the living room where my parents slept on a double bed that in daytime, with a couple of bolsters, was transmogrified into a sofa.

My parents chose the middle of the night for expressing their sexuality. Somehow I was always awakened by their muffled groans and the insistent whisperings of my mother. When it was over, my father would always urinate very tactfully against the side of the bowl. If he flushed, there was an explosive hiss like the breaking of a vacuum and then an incessant gurgling awakened the house. The water closet took forever to refill, the bulb getting stuck halfway up. Then my father would bounce out of bed again and jiggle the handle, and the bulb would finally rest calmly on top of the filled water cabinet. The whole operation took at least fifteen minutes from start to conclusion. Thirty years later, as I watched Neil Armstrong bounding on the moon, I thought of the $40 billion America had spent to put a man on the moon, yet nobody can improve on that contraption behind all of our toilet bowls that tortured me so many years with its interminable trickling of water piercing my sleep. So I stayed out on the porch with the crickets chirping and a cool breeze that wafted over my puss each night. In the morning a family of squirrels would be leaping in the double oak tree's branches that brushed the roof, and I would hear the frenetic pattering of their toenails on the tarpaper. I must have been happy then, but didn't know it.

The porch had only one adornment on its weathered boards. My mother had tacked up on one of the wall studs an 8″ × 11″ two-toned print of a buxom young peasant woman in an open blouse and jumper with thick black hair cascading down her shoulders. With a winsome smile on her full but asymmetrical face and her eyes askance, as if she were watching someone on her flank, La Gioconda, as I would name her later, radiated everything a beautiful red-blooded wench is supposed to radiate. But she was as distant and inaccessible to my preadolescent explorations as the Taj Mahal.

The shack in Croton remained in our family long after I grew up, but I never went back. The memories were painful—the cluttered, damp rooms where Sunkist orange crates served as bookcases and dish cupboards, and where the daddy longlegs tiptoed across the cement shower-stall floor. I remembered the sounds of male and female urination, the dust balls under the beds, and the smell of kerosene on my hands after I filled a jug for the hot-water heater. My father had exhausted himself working twelve hours a day in his tailor shop, and he fell asleep buried under *The New York Times*. My mother sat at the white porcelain kitchen table, typing fiction that never saw publication. One step from the relief rolls, we had a summer shack in Westchester County for which I should have been thankful, but the image of pop flat on his back under the house, sawing away at a lead water pipe and grunting, "God damn it; God damn it; sonofabitch", bleached away the bucolic splendor of the honeysuckle creeping up the green crisscrossed wood slats that concealed the cellar foundation. It was a cantankerous family life that made me yearn for quiet, space, and La Gioconda. As a twelve-year-old, I had no way of knowing whether my chances in life were good.

More than thirty years later, La Gioconda and I met again. She was in the same chipped frame of brown wood, now mildewed into a pink crust. But the wench still smiled and bubbled with life's vitality. I had picked her out of one of my mother's footlockers, which are now stored in my garage, along with the flotsam of her personal effects, psychology books, and unfinished manuscripts that survived into her dotage. By that time mother was resting none too peacefully in a nursing home in Stamford, Connecticut, after eighty years on earth.

It took me no more than half an hour to go through mother's mildewed steamer trunk. Its hinges were nearly rusted off. There was little more than a heap of costume jewelry (it went to the Jamaican nanny) a pile of 3″ × 5″ family snapshots of her children and grandchildren—some Caucasian, some Eurasian. Mother's manuscripts ranged from short stories written in the thirties to her Ph.D. thesis on childrens' reading dysfunctions. Her prose was clean but without emotionality, and her people never fought or made love, but lived and played side-by-side like three-year-olds. Mother's characters were tunnel-vision zombies who saw everything and felt nothing. I discovered a 42-share stock certificate for

This oxidized stock table dated May 15, 1925, was the backing for *The Gypsy* print. It is historically interesting for the brevity of the alphabetical stock listings and for the high mortality of the cast of characters. Today there are over 6,000 securities listed on the exchanges. Call loan rates then were 3¾% in London. What happened to Chile Copper, Chicago Yellow Cab, and Consolidated Textile? Were they merged out or bankrupted in the crash? What about Dodge Bros., and who were Fidelity Phoenix, Fisk Rubber, and General Asphalt? Pierce-Arrow is gone, as is Cuban Cane Sugar. Note there are no technology enterprises—just basic industrials and commodity plays. No wonder the market operators needed pools to make the days fly. The prosaic content of the Big Board was souped up with low margin requirements. Today you can buy options on the stock-market indices or even on a segment of the market, a group of 30 technology issues. There are options on Treasury Bills, currencies, oil tanker rates—a smorgasbord of gambling tickets. The financial exchanges are the great murphy men of the eighties—yes, sir. We have black girls, yellow girls, white girls. Just leave us hold your wallet cause you can't trust my girls near money no way. . . .

Royal Dutch Petroleum, years old and mildewed. There had been several stock dividends since, and I later retrieved several thousand dollars from the registrar. Mother's and Ben's Mount Kisco burial-plot booklet I put away in my top bureau drawer. Cartons of dated textbooks filled our garbage barrels. I ruthlessly junked the core of her life's work. She was now humpbacked and dumpy, sharing a room in the nursing home she believed to be her girls' school in Russia. Molly, mother's roommate, thought I was her husband there to take her out for dinner and dancing on the Starlight Roof of the Waldorf-Astoria. So much for perception!

The stock market packages petty and vicarious dreams, each stock's symbol another story, and the man had some talent for envisioning tomorrow's stock tables. Don't ask how it is done. You are either a money maker or just another quantitatively oriented MBA, an overpriced cipher of yesterday's newspaper. There are a couple of dozen operators in the country with the capacity to think so abstractly that they know what the economic and political pressures of today's world will mean for tomorrow's financial markets. The Federal Reserve Board must deal with unemployment, so forget about high interest rates in a world where most countries are one step from bankruptcy. The Arab world's going from a surplus to a deficit means that funds come out of yen-denominated bonds. Currency parities riffle noisily into new relationships. A new car costs $10,000. It is deferrable. Instead, the spending goes for designer jeans and video games and so on. The president will not get all of his defense budget. There will be stretchouts on procurement and maybe even a deferring of the coming incremental tax reduction. Certainly this means something for interest rates, the momentum of the GNP, and it means that the consensus forecasts spit out by all the computer-driven economic models in Boston, Washington, and New York are in Stupidsville. Politics leads economics. Everyone knows this except economists.

I remember the last time I visited my mother. The nursing home reeked of a pungent disinfectant. As I moved through the hall, I glanced into the rooms, animated solely by wall-mounted television sets that baby-sat for the comatose bodies. My mother and her roommate, Molly, were sitting on their beds and I greeted them, raising my voice,

"Molly, how about dinner at 21 and then we go dancing?"

"Yah, sure. Can you get my wheelchair and put me out in the hall?"

I shifted her off the bed and threw a blanket over her lap.

"Are you her husband?"

"Come on, Molly, I'm her son."

"Nah. You're her brother. I'll bet you can eat apples off her head."

It was true. My mother who had been 5'4" in her prime had aged into a tiny butterball.

"Who am I, mother?"

She looked at me slyly, the dark eyes still sparkled.

"I've seen you before."

"One of your sons, mother. Which one?"

"Don't ask," she whimpered, and I grasped her arm and lifted her gently from the edge of the bed. I took a spring coat out of her locker and draped it over her shoulders. The coat reached to the floor.

"You have a great coat, just like Napoleon, mother. You could fight on the Russian front."

"I have to go to the bathroom." She sounded like a three-year-old. I felt her hand clutch my upper arm. So I took off her coat and guided her to the toilet. Then I hoisted her dress up over her haunches and tugged down on her bloomers. There was no waist. She was squirming, so I knew time was short. I guided her down on the seat just as there was a gush that resonated in the bowl. I noted the holes in her bloomers and the tired elastic of her waist band. The tops of her knee-high nylons were torn from where she had tugged them up maybe a thousand times. I was in good form with a four-year-old boy at home, and had no pangs wiping her. But it was not what I would recommend for an evening's entertainment.

The hardest part was leaving her. My mother still had extraordinary strength in her hands and would clutch at my sleeve, begging me not to leave. I should take her home. She had to walk to school soon and finish sewing her graduation dress.

"Where is Ben? I haven't seen daddy in a long time."

"Ben is gone, mother. He died ten years ago. You know that. Don't you remember when we put the headstone in the ground and the kids were playing touch football between the gravestones?" Suddenly I realized I had made a terrible *faux pas*. My mother could no longer handle the truth.

"No. What are you saying? Nobody told me Ben died. When did he die? Why didn't anybody tell me?"

"My God, mother, he's gone a long time ago. You're tired now. I must say goodnight."

"Nobody told me daddy died. You're kidding. The truth is he ran away with another woman and you don't want to tell me. You know daddy has a weak heart. Another woman could give him syphilis and kill him. They were all after him on the beach, you know. He made love to them in the water. I knew, but I never said anything."

"Mother, Ben had a massive coronary on the beach. The paramedics worked on him for two hours. He had a shot but couldn't make it. It was a good life, mother. Daddy lived to be eighty-three years old. You were together for fifty-one years." I tore myself loose and fled through the hall and down the fire stairs, holding my nose from the sickly-sweet stench of disinfectant. On the main floor I followed the yellow dots inlaid in the black striated linoleum that marked the exit. The air outside was delicious. I gunned the Mercedes out of the driveway, the gravelly pebbles rattling against the underbody.

Only in America could a son be so successful that his parents couldn't fathom the dimensions of his achievement. I remembered how my father would probe me for details when I visited the folks in their cottage in Miami.

"You're really doing good, Martin?"

"Yes, pop. I'm doing okay."

"You're not crazy and overextending yourself?"

"I'm pretty careful, pop."

"The sonofabitch stock market. It is too hard to figure. Your mother bought U.S. Steel, Royal Dutch, General Motors. Nothing crazy. None of them went up. I begged her to sell the steel, but she wouldn't take a loss."

"Pop, I keep telling you those are the wrong goods. You never buy the goods I tell you to buy. You listen to some dumb-bunny broker on Collins Avenue. I can't deal with it."

"He's honest and needs the business. Talk to your mother." My father never thought he'd make an easy dollar in his life, and he never did. He settled for his bowl of kasha, wolfing it down like the Russian peasant he was. If I were such a great success, where were the yacht and racehorses? *They* wouldn't let his son make serious money. The *They* knew everything and his son couldn't be in with the *They*.

He was wrong. There is no *They*. My four-year-old son packages and repackages presents for the entire family. He staples colored crepe paper and wraps his toy trucks with shoestring and Scotch tape and crayons over and over every square inch of paper. Each day the packages evolve in their awkward configurations, just as the 1925 stock tables backing La Gioconda adumbrated a graveyard of stale dreams. Theoretically, Freudians skilled at dream analysis should make great investors, stripping off the tinsel and fathoming the essence of a corporation's psyche and the sentiment that surrounds the company, its image and the preconceptions of "The Street," as to what the facts portend. In practice, there are few anywhere who isolate the pivotal variable, the reality.

When I was eight and nine, my job was to ride the C train down to Harlem, where my father had his tailor shop. Pop and his black presser sweated it out from eight in the morning until eight at night. My mother would cook him a hot supper and pack it in a pot-cheese tin. Pop would gulp down his summer dinner of borscht, bent over his rattling sewing machine, his summer union suit stripped off his shoulders and tied around the waist. There was a candy store next door run by a paraplegic who could only mouth a few moaning sounds from the back of his throat. Pop would take me next door after supper, and the three of us would down Pepsis together. I could hardly hold the 12 ounces, but the bloat felt good and we three—the mute paraplegic, the eight-year-old child, and the quiet, gentle father—would communicate silently in that dump of a store where the floors were black with dirt and smelled uriniferously from the back toilet. It was our campfire in the depths of the depression, when the poor huddled close to each other. As Mac the presser would say to me, "Kid, it's too hard to live but too expensive to die." Later, I subwayed back to the Bronx where all the rooms were painted baby pink and baby blue. Don't ask me why, but every apartment in the Bronx during the mid-thirties was done in those two shades. It's what the landlords ordered from their paint crews, and I think it did more for the economic growth of the world than the Marshall Plan. Getting out of the Bronx, away from the pink and blue walls, was a rallying call that

Frans Hals. *La Bohemienne*. (I called her La Gioconda). 1628–30. Oil on panel. 22¾″ × 20½″. The Louvre, Paris.

led to Nobel Prize winners, Pulitzer prizes, billionaires—everything except four-star generals and the presidency. So far.

I, too, have been stripping away the baby blue and pink from my life ever since. When I tell my children about the excitement and anxieties of growing up poor, they look at me with blank stares. So does my wife, the Hungarian countess who knows only postwar Long Island. If only I could ask my mother what La Gioconda was doing in her trunk. It is too late for that now. Yet I think I know. The picture was a fantasy of herself that never came true. It came to rest in the hands of her son, whose fantasy of love and riches became real.

La Gioconda, as I had misnamed her, rests comfortably in the Louvre. By 1870, the painting was called *La Bohemienne*. It was the work of Frans Hals, who finished it in 1630. The broad-shouldered, sensuous peasant girl challenges all comers. Her sketchily done clothes appear to have been an afterthought. What a fabulous nude she would have been. But the Haarlem Dutch were not ready for nudes, and Hals knew it. The blue sky at the right of her head, and her sunbathed countenance suggest a woman free as a bird. I was fifty years old when we reencountered each other in Paris. Where was she when I was thirteen? Nineteen? Any age? The real *La Gioconda*, of course, is the Mona Lisa, painted by Da Vinci about thirty years before. It took Leonardo four years, and even then he felt it was unfinished. King Francis I of France had it in his possession fifty years later at Fontainebleau, according to Vasari, and today it, too, resides at the Louvre and plays to the crowds of tourists behind bulletproof glass. If we are to believe Vasari:

Leonardo also made use of this device: While he was painting Mona Lisa, who was a very beautiful woman, he employed singers and musicians or jesters to keep her full of merriment and so chase away the melancholy that painters usually give to portraits. As a result, in this painting of Leonardo's there was a smile so pleasing that it seemed divine rather than human; and those who saw it were amazed to find that it was as alive as the original.

Forty years ago, we lived in three rooms in the Bronx. The rental was pegged at $40 a month and the bedrooms were 9' × 12', painted pink and blue. Standard ¾" gypsum wall board boxed in the rooms, and cheap hollow wood veneer doors slammed shut from the slightest of drafts.

Life's repetitious cyclicality gets even. Thirty-five years after "getting out," I was living in approximately the same square footage, but at a better address than 964 Sherman Avenue. The Trump Tower zips up from 57th Street and Fifth Avenue, an elongated glissando of glitz some 65 stories high. For $1 million you get 1,200 square feet there, probably the most expensive residential square footage in the world. The Beverly Hills crowd make up their pads here, seasoned with Gucci-wise Orientals, Latinos, and Arabs who buy these apartments because the boards of cooperative buildings prefer less peripatetic owners. My wife and I call it "the closet in the sky," and it was just about big enough to store all of Toni's clothes. For a while we considered making it one giant cedar closet, but the implicit cost—over $10,000 a month in interest lost on our $1 million—made the hurdle rate a bit steep.

The view from the 59th floor is instructive—you see practically nothing but the tops of other buildings, hardly any Hudson River, and just a tip of New York Harbor. New York is a real estate–dominated town, and the pols rarely get in the way of bigtime developers who would parcel out Central Park among themselves if given the chance and bid on the air rights over the Hudson River.

We were one of the first owners to move into our closet in the sky, and just so you know that the idle rich have their problems, too, let me tell you what it was like living alone in the Trump Tower. The air conditioner was a sometime thing, the toilet flushometers performed like asthmatics, and the hot water took forty minutes to reach our level. There was no intercom hooked up with the front desk, and elevator service frequently was cut off for several hours at a time. Somebody forgot to order the master TV antenna, and evidently the new IBM and American Telephone buildings were muscling us out of clear reception. It was obviously time for me to have a little talk with Donald Trump, so I wrote him about his coldwater flat in the sky and asked him to call me before I ran him over with a limo.

"Marty! I'm sooo sorry you had to write a letter like that. Marty, we are putting your apartment on Red Alert. Whatever we can do to make you happy, Marty."

"Donald, I wake up in the morning and I can't use the facilities. I can't take a hot bath unless I get up at 6:00 A.M., and then the air conditioning cuts off. The elevator is out of service. The counter on the microwave oven doesn't count, and the dishwasher doesn't wash with water. Donald, your building doesn't work.''

"Marty, I wish you wouldn't say that. We have a fabulous building. How do you like that gorgeous maroon and green decor in the elevators, Marty? And the lobby, Marty—isn't it fantastic, the marble and the art nouveau decor? How is the view from your apartment, Marty? I bet it's fantastic.''

"Donald, I look out at the tops of buildings. I am eye-to-eye with huge neon signs that say RCA and 666 and Newsweek and the time is 10:46 in 22-foot numerals.''

"Marty, how many people can look out their windows and see the tops of such fantastic buildings?''

"Donald, the air conditioning is too sophisticated. It cuts off because not enough people are living in the building.''

"Marty, we are going to simulate a fully inhabited building so you can have your air conditioning.''

"Donald, I thank you. But what do I do for an elevator? You are always checking them out, so they never run. My wife used the construction elevator, and I haven't seen her for three days. She is being passed around among two hundred construction workers, Donald. The last I heard, they made her into a runner peddling football pools between the thirtieth and sixty-fifth floors.''

"Marty, that's not funny. I will admit that a few nonunion workers sneak into the building from time to time, but the union boys would never do things like that, Marty.''

"Donald, forty minutes for hot water. Can you simulate a full load so the computer will be nice to me?''

"Marty, I already told you we have put you on Red Alert. And don't forget the party in the Atrium.''

The promoter's blitz was over, and I stared out at old 666. A police siren pierced the fifty-ninth-story aloofness. That was Tishman's place—by now, probably fully depreciated by three consecutive owners at higher resale values with little or no paid taxes to the city, state, and federal governments. In fact, the tax laws encourage accelerated depreciation on commercial real estate that never seems to depreciate at all. But my standard of living had depreciated greatly since the old Bronx days. I missed the smell of baked potatoes on every stair landing in the old walkup. From a working microwave oven there is only the electronic, odorless beep . . . beep . . . beep.

3 The Pathology of Representation

THE COAST of Normandy is a favorite of mine, a rocky, no-nonsense place, like Maine, with bluffs overlooking narrow strips of beach. My last visit turned out to be a pilgrimage that recalled to me America's finest hour, when we had all the momentum and a national purpose. The helpless giant had not been born. Coincidentally, the trip took place during the fall of 1982 when the market was stifled by high interest rates and the industrial might of the country seemed likely to float out to sea on a wave of bankruptcies. Normandy belongs to us. We Americans spilled our blood there, and the French know it. There are 30-foot-high marble obelisks honoring Patton and his hard-driving troops. (When our car broke down, the local Peugeot garage put a mechanic right on the job and had us on our way in an hour, our halting French endured patiently.) Traveling in our party was my best friend, a Park Avenue doctor, who twenty years ago as an army captain, was assigned to Zanuck's staff for the filming of *The Longest Day*. Because of his urge to revisit the landing beaches (the real ones, not the beaches used in the filming) we agreed, but with Mont-St.-Michel beckoning on the horizon, it was not our idea.

The enormity of the Allied invasion has been captured in painstaking detail in history books and vividly on film. But only in walking Omaha Beach and the bluffs above does this heroic undertaking reach epic stature. I had no idea that the British had as big a landing zone as we and that they created Mulberry harbors of floating piers at Arromanches, now a modest seaside resort. On D day we landed where we were unexpected. The Germans were comforted by the perpendicular bluffs.

Looking down from the bluff 400 feet above Omaha Beach is enough to take your breath away. This is not the dunes of Cape Cod, but a sheer cliff of rock and grassy hummocks. Imagine how the first waves of men streaming off those invasion barges felt. They had to be seasick after the rough crossing in those tiny landing craft bobbing across the Channel. Soaked from the ocean spray, they landed as the Germans lobbed prearranged artillery barrages on a strip of beach only 100 feet wide. And then to look up! They had to get off that deadly beach and take the high ground.

The American Cemetery that reaches to the edge of the bluff overlooking Omaha Beach was an unexpected pilgrimage for me. In a sea of cropped grass more than 9,000 crosses, punctuated with Stars of David, echelon out in lines of perfect symmetry. The white Carrara marble crosses have a simple elegance, their trailing edges beveled gently into graceful arches. A magnetism pulled us into the rows of crosses, the two couples, in their forties, edged into a field and radiated out at different vectors. Reading the simply chiseled inscriptions on the back of each cross touched a minor chord of patriotism we are seldom aware exists. Every small town in America is represented here. There are units and ranks that no longer exist in the U.S. Army's table of organization. It is another age.

The four browsers reunited, each with tears streaming down his face. "My God! They were babies." My wife's exclamation echoed our feelings. The two men traded thoughts—how we wished we could have been there and waded ashore with these men. This coming from two natural revolutionaries. The doctor had followed the country's protesting youth out into the streets during the sixties and bandaged their clubbed heads. Walking in the American Cemetery steeled my nerve to wade back into the totally demoralized securities markets during the summer of '82. After all, there was great resiliency left in the country. The Federal Reserve Board, I hoped, was not about to bankrupt everyone with 18 percent interest rates for much longer. It is only when you can stand alone with a fresh but unshaky hypothesis, for which there is as yet very little statistical confirmation, that you can push big blocks of money into the right sectors and find no competition because no one dares to share the insight with you.

The way we act in the world must change in the mid-eighties or, like Venice, the country sinks gently into the mud for the next four centuries. Long-term records for countries, like corporations, money managers, and athletes, are made up of many short-term decisions that in total are right or wrong. If our diplomacy and economic policy stretching back thirty years have been imperfect, we will have paid dearly.

REAL S&P 500

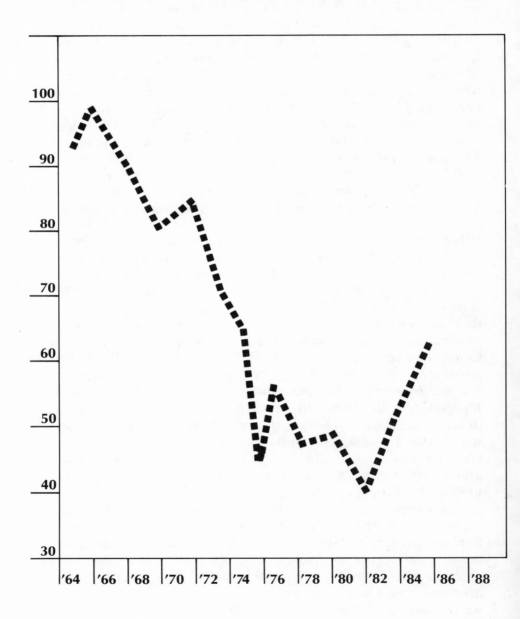

Standard & Poor's Index reveals decades of lost momentum. Adjusted for inflation it proves the rich have gotten progressively poorer in the market during each of the last several economic cycles. It explains the retreat into the refuge of collectibles and gold, and why real-estate geniuses have proliferated. From 1968 to 1983 the astute investor should have been accumulating houses, not equities. My 1983 purchase of 1,200 square feet of apartment space from Donald Trump for $1 million surely represents the topping out of the collectibles index relative to equities for the next fifteen years. Keep in mind that the gold bug's equity since 1980 has been halved. Collectibles outpaced equities over fifteen years for only one reason: the fear of galloping inflation. By the summer of 1982 the Federal Reserve Board had broken the spiral with 18 percent interest rates, and paper assets have since outperformed everything in sight.

E.F. Gombrich notes in *Art and Illusion,* a study in the psychology of pictorial representations, that a pathology of representation runs throughout art history from the Egyptians through the Renaissance. There are representations of lions that look more like dogs, locusts that appear as flying horses, sperm whales that have ears for dorsal fins, and rhinos that look like dragons. The study of pictures in artistic representation suggests that the familiar always represents the likely starting point for the rendering of the unfamiliar. An existing representation always exerts its spell over the artist even while he strives to record the truth. Even Leonardo made mistakes in his anatomical drawings. (He lacked the relevant schema for the heart.) Style holds the artist rigid in what he sees. Archaic art started from the schema of the symmetrical frontal figure, and the conquest of naturalism by the Greeks over a few centuries was remarkable considering the schema of Egyptian art hardly changed over 10,000 years. What was rigid is called early, and what is lifelike is dated later. The gradual accumulation of corrections came from the observation of reality and the discarding of outmoded ways of seeing things. It is no different down on The Street.

In his book on the Kennedy years, Arthur Schlesinger wrote how serving in the administration made it difficult to go back to reading *The New York Times* because of the manner in which it presented what was happening in the world. The way the financial press reports the affairs of Wall Street and the country's economic

STOCK PRICES vs. TANGIBLE PRICES

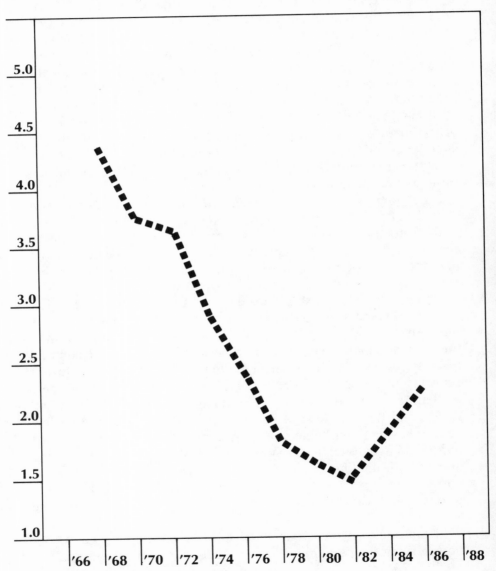

Source: AIG Global Investors, Inc.

condition is equally insufficient because they are always on the outside, trying to look in on the people on the inside (corporations, managers, deal makers, economic strategists) who want them to see only that which is cosmetically politic. One of the most gracious aspects of investment management is that you can call any or all of your peers and they will tell you everything they are doing and thinking—except, perhaps, some unfinished buying or selling. The reason for this good communication is that we all realized long ago how hard it is to comprehend what is happening that is important, even though we are usually on the inside looking in.

The neurotic pursuit of perfection is the motive that drives many men. I have learned to take enormous risks and do all right. To stand alone, David against Goliath, and slug it out with the unruly forces of speculation is stimulating and rewarding for me. But there is only perfection in the cemetery above Omaha Beach. There no crabgrass grows among the bright green blades cropped three inches above the earth. It is truly as Walt Whitman has said, "the hair of the Lord." And the crosses stretch out in that echelon of perfect longitude. The only perfection is in death.

I once asked Jerry Goodman (Adam Smith) why the economic doomsday books written by flaky characters with no credentials in the investment community sold millions of copies: the gold bugs, the stock-your-bomb-shelter-now hacks, and the Joe Granville bears who have staked out the 400 to 600 range of the Dow Jones as their private preserve. They all have been discredited cycle after cycle, yet they sell. Jerry explained patiently that you have to know your constituency. Each book has a limited audience, and unless you get yourself on the talk-show circuit in the twenty-four major markets, you won't even reach your public niche. The beauty of the scare-'em books is their vast public. Everyone over sixty-five living on social security and retirement annuities dreads the next inflationary epidemic when they envision themselves living off canned dog food and a 25-pound sack of potatoes. A book on how to prepare for the impending financial holocaust is just what sells in the mangrove flats jutting out from U.S. 95 north of Miami, where the trailer camps coexist with junked cars and rusting washing machines.

But there is only one way for a passive investor to try to make serious money on Wall Street. It is the highbrow route, and you must have a schema. It may begin with extrapolating financial ratios based on recent years' statistics dealing with the growth of specific industries, reinvestment rates of corporations, and horseback estimates of product demand whether it be toothpaste, beer, or desktop computers. Despite all the ciphering that goes on, and the reports published by thousands of analysts, money managers, and savvy businessmen, very few make it work. There are some good quants, and they know who they are. Unhappily, extrapolation near the consensus without an unshakable perception gets you nowhere. The mid–1982 deduction that inflation is dead may be all you have to know for the next ten years.

The other approach is the Low Road, and this is the route almost everyone else takes. It is much more uninhibited, and fun, because you don't need a discipline. All you do is peer into the back window of a parked car and hope to spot who is tumbling whom in the back seat. Dan Dorfman feeds this crowd, and to his credit, he tries to be the equalizer between the "they" and you. If you want to know what the lawyer for *The New York Times* said to Saul Steinberg over lunch, or find out early why Larry Tisch bought 5 percent of XYZ, Dan gets there first with the mostest. His column is what it should be. Like bellydancing, you enjoy it on one level but don't probe for cosmic significance. *Fortune* magazine would love to be earthy, too, and draw some serious conclusions, but their staff is too straitlaced, and it comes out bland. Whenever I find myself drifting into a mindless reading state, I know trouble is ahead.

Twenty-five years ago, I read thirty trade magazines a day, looking for nuggets of industrial and corporate insight. Today I read reflective journals like *Foreign Affairs Quarterly* and the Federal Reserve Board monthly bulletin. It is enough. If you are spending more than $100 a year for financial publications you are wasting money. Long ago, I stopped reading glorified joke books like *Fortune, Barron's,* and *Business Week,* which hardly do more than rehash financial news that has already been discounted in stock prices. Anyone who believes the inside back page of the *Wall Street Journal* is close to a moron. Therein is a summary of the previous day's stock market, giving you six or seven reasons why stocks rose or fell that day. They are almost always nonsensical rationalizations of Wall Street hacks who somehow get on reporters' telephone lists—the reporter being a high-school dropout who is paid less than your secretary. In our country all the bright newspapermen cover wars or Capitol Hill; unlike France, where you are surfeited with intellectual and urbane newspapers like *Le Monde* and *Le Figaro,* or London, where the *Financial Times* makes the *Wall Street Journal* look like a surburban sheet published in Grand Rapids. American newspaper chains like Gannett learned long ago that if you published garden-club news and Little League scores, you kept your readership without having to spend money on foreign correspondents. Gannett's operating profit margins are 10 points higher than those of *The New York Times.*

Bob Lenzner, one of my old buddies from the Goldman, Sachs arbitrage department, now bureau chief for *The Boston Globe,* was offered a major financial columnist's spot by *The New York Times.* It paid about $57,000 with a two-week vacation. Junior securities analysts and lawyers fresh out of Harvard do better. A.J. Liebling had it right when he said in *The Press:* "The publisher out of force of habit and because he does not wish to be called a piker, usually provides for the customer a smattering of press association scraps and syndicated features. The saloonkeeper, in the same moral position, puts out a few stale pretzels and moldy salted peanuts." Foster Winans, the *Wall Street Journal* reporter convicted of conspiracy and securities fraud for providing advanced information to brokers from his "Heard on the Street" column, was paid $530 a week by Dow Jones & Co., his employer. Dow Jones makes a 25 percent return on its equity and has the highest profit margins in the business.

Down on Broad Street, Alan Abelson writes the longest column known to mankind. Its format is a political cackle starting with jabs at the administration's fallibility, moves into stock market punditry, and ends with corporate tidbits of limited investment significance. I can see Abelson smirking all the way up in my midtown office. When does Steinberg get another karate chop from the dynamic duo, Briloff and Abelson? "Hey! We made millions on Steinberg's paper—what are you guys worth?"

Shortly before and right after we went public in the summer of 1986, two Dow Jones publications, the *Wall Street Journal* and *Barron's,* attacked the offering of Atalanta/Sosnoff as pricey. Alan Abelson, on the front page of *Barron's,* suggested we had capitalized ourselves at 80 times earnings. On the inside back page of the *Wall Street Journal,* Linda Sandler used dated numbers to reach a comparable conclusion. Abelson never even gave us a chance to talk to him and did not refer to our reported mid-1986 earnings. The numbers, if extrapolated for 1986, put us at 14 times earnings, less than the August valuation multiplier of the stock market. What kind of financial journalism is this? The policy of most powerful and well-heeled Dow Jones & Company allows its columnists to say whatever they want without affording their subjects a courtesy phone call to discuss the pertinency of the facts or the validity of their conclusions. Columnists like Abelson seem happier titillating themselves and their readership. Information is a secondary characteristic. I leave untouched a bigger question. Why did Dow Jones give so much press prominance to little us?

The only question about financial writing is whether it is supposed to be entertainment or shed some perspective on events. It seems as though the media cannot make up their minds. The press's treatment of Joe Granville's patter, for example, divided into two camps: both on the wrong level. *The New York Times* once slapped a picture of Joe on its front page and treated him like a frocked Wizard of Oz. The other approach—the *Wall Street Journal*'s—portrayed Granville as Frank Morgan and had Dorothy scolding him for emitting so much smoke. (Joe had caused a 30-point drop one day.) Interestingly, nobody dealt with what Granville uses as his technician's input: the ratio of stocks advancing to those declining, the quality of leadership, declining new highs, and the nonconfirmation of broader-based indices than Dow Jones. Granville uses this data, as do all of us who work in the pits. He just packages it better. Whether his subscribers bet with him or against him is their affair. Joe is a piece of Americana whom brokers may use to improve the circulation of their jaded clientele.

In the late fifties, my office and Granville's were back-to-back at E. F. Hutton. I was a struggling junior analyst and Granville was the house technician. We both began our day at 7:30. My opening gambit was a newsletter that went out over the wire system. On the reverse side of the page was Granville's market letter. This sheet hit the R.R.s' desks by 9:00 A.M. around the country and was digested with coffee and donuts. Don't ask me if anyone ever made any money with it.

My friend Larry Zieberg reminds me how he isolated the Confidence Index in *Barron's* for Joe Granville. I think the Confidence Index is a yield ratio of high-grade bonds to low-grade bonds and is supposed to suggest when investors are turning bullish or bearish by their predilection for either the high- or low-grade spread. Granville snapped up this catchy index and would quote it daily. Perhaps he still does. The only problem with the index, according to Zeiberg, is that there is no statistical correlation between a rising or falling market and the index. It simply doesn't work.

My God! Think if it *did* work. It would be a barometer that never lied. You could wake up every morning, read the index, call your broker to buy or sell, and then fall back to sleep. Isn't this what's wrong? We all want someone to give us courage, a heart, and a brain. It took a fourteen-year-old Judy Garland to show us that courage, a brain, and a heart don't come from the Wizard, but from within. The only serious money I have made came when I have stood alone with a unique perception as to what was happening to a company, an industry, a country, or even the Western world. (The solar system I leave to other adventurers.) If what I had considered doing was easy, I knew intuitively that the idea was worthless. Bob Wilson, a great short seller, puts it another way: "If I have to think for more than fifteen minutes whether a stock is a good short idea, I know it's too complicated and therefore no good."

Granville had 11,000 subscribers: cowardly lions waiting to be told how to act. This is made to order for a Wizard. If you are wrong all you have to do is contradict yourself and fall into line. What I remember best about Joe was his ultimate flexibility. If he called the market wrong on Monday morning, by midday he found six reasons for changing. The Confidence Index gave off a false signal. It was really the consumption of shellac in the Northeast Corridor that had not been weighted. For a time, Joe was big on shellac. The acceleration of shellac consumption for making grinding wheels was an early-warning indicator of the Industrial Production Index. You couldn't have more grinding wheels on order without the acceleration of factory production.

A friend of mine in Las Vegas is hooked on football. He subscribes to all the betting sheets and reads all the columnists and reporters who are in the swim. To keep his losses down to a bearable level, I bank all his bets. He has never averaged more than a 35 percent win ratio week after week. On Rose Bowl day, he called me excitingly reporting a "Lock of the Year" pick from

one of his services costing $150 per subscription. Needless to say,
I banked his bet on Michigan minus 10 points and lost. Which just
goes to prove that anyone can be right some of the time.

We look for wise men who will make us rich. Some do it by
proxy through the world of the Granvilles, and some of us play
our music riffling computer readout sheets. Who is right or wrong?
I wish I could make more money looking into back seats of cars.
It's a hell of a lot more exciting than computer sheets. But the
facts are that I never made money looking into car windows, taking
the temperature of a Confidence Index, or just scanning computer
printouts of corporate statistics. All my money has been made
through a medium in Hartford, Connecticut, and if you think I'm
going to reveal her phone number, you're crazy. The statistical
validity of my medium correlates with the sparsity of her pigeons.
Even Joe Granville knows that an overexposed index loses forecasting power exponentially.

Despite its pretense of giving a few liberals some column space,
the *Wall Street Journal* is pure establishment. It must be watched
for its pro-corporate-management biases, typified by Paul Blustein,
a staff writer ("Let us Now Consider Carl Icahn"), and Peter
Drucker ("Curbing Unfriendly Takeovers"), who have worried
about the sharks with pearly teeth menacing corporate America.
Mr. Drucker, who is Corporate America's resident egghead, thinks
that prosperous medium-sized companies spend their waking hours
fending off predators like Carl. This is bad. Meanwhile, Mr.
Blustein has forecasted job losses as the Icahns of this world
liquidate their way through America like Sherman marching through
Georgia. Blustein pleads for the small investor, whose long-term
investment horizon must be nourished, and both advocate direct
or indirect regulation at the federal and state levels—possibly bank
loan restrictions on unfriendly takeovers.

All of us in the investment world know that the unfriendly
takeover game may end shortly because the poor innocents have
learned how to fight such bullies as Icahn, Steinberg, Posner, and
Boone Pickens using their own muscle men—those specialist
antitakeover law firms that are as tough and pugnacious as the
young Muhammad Ali. You can drop $5 million in legal fees to
essay an unfriendly takeover, and Mr. Icahn is to be compli-
mented—if only for his iron pants, sitting through weeks of legal
depositions and personalized attacks by teams of corporate lawyers.

I feel no need for government protection from those who would eat, but from those who would be eaten. Considering who the big banks loan their money to—Mexico, Argentina, Brazil, and Poland—they, too, should not be considered the final arbiters of who gets to buy whom. Our government's vigilance already protects the individual investor sufficiently. There are reasonable standards of accounting and financial reporting—but, more important, none of your budding robber barons can cause an *en baisse* by short selling on downticks. This is probably the greatest piece of securities regulation ever conceived in the twentieth century, in its simplicity and far-ranging protection of all investors from narrowly contrived market manipulation. As for protecting smaller shareholders with long-term investment horizons, I leave this one where it belongs: somewhere on the horizon. Small shareholders don't necessarily have horizons, they just want to make a little money. It is the large investors who need protection, but let me first dispose of a few more arguments.

Mr. Drucker suggests that our high-technology sector is about to lose its manhood to the predators, and that this is bad for America. Another dead horse! The list of high-tech companies is so scoured over by the professional investor that price-earnings multiples have moved from about 1.2 times the valuation of the market to approximately double. At two times the market, no company needs more than an ounce of protection because nobody can afford to take them over and make any money. Try liquidating a high-tech operator selling at 5 times book value and see what you get: 20 cents on the dollar. Strong, prosperous companies don't need protection. What Messrs. Drucker and Blustein are advocating is protection for the weak lambs. These companies sell at discounts to the market, discounts to book value, employ millions of workers, and have millions of loyal small shareholders who love managements who haven't made them money in decades. Yes? It is no secret that Mr. Icahn must look to companies that are underperformers, like textile operators who go through all the motions of being in business for generations but have feeble returns on equity, never grow, and provide few new employment opportunities. The parking lots are full in Silicon Valley, and Icahn can't go there.

Each decade generates its own investment silliness, which is usually taken care of by the market mechanism. In the late sixties and early seventies, there was conglomeration, and the marketplace took care of that. The sellers proved smarter than the buyers. They always are. Harold Geneen failed with all his eighteen-hour-a-day dedication and comprehensive management-reporting systems, proving conclusively that it is humanly impossible to manage a loose-jointed company with a hundred-odd profit centers. The press considered Geneen the genius of geniuses. Anyone want to buy his Rayonier? Ironically, IT&T now sells for a below-average valuation and had better watch its flanks. Somebody may be crouched in the bushes.

The SEC is more concerned about putting an apprentice printer in jail for peeking at a tender offer than about disciplining corporate managements who feather their nests and make mindless acquisitions only so that they can reward themselves with higher salaries and longer-range Gulfstream jets. The *Wall Street Journal* gives prominent space to every poor proofreader or broker who breaks the rules and is caught. Is this supposed to be a public-service deterrent to wrongdoing, or is it just the *Daily News* format for pages 3 and 4—titillate 'em with blood and sex?

Who has protected shareholders from poorly conceived acquisitions and capital-spending programs of entire industries these past several years? We have witnessed bankruptcies or near-bankruptcies of major corporations in the airlines, farm equipment, steel, automobile, natural-resource, and even the utility and banking sectors. Where was the watchdog press? Looking for corporate success stories to showcase? There is a catch-all buzzword covering these mistakes: whole sectors of our industrial complex have been forced to "down size"—sell assets, reduce debt, pare the employment rolls. Actually, few corporations have made their discounted cash-flow projections on the past five-years' expenditures. If they did, the "controversial" Mr. Icahn would be back in arbitrage or walking the beach. The managements of all those tired blue chips own little or no stock, except what they get from option programs. The extent of shortchanging investors is dramatized in this chart showing the thirty-year erosion in dividends as a percentage of GNP. It is just starting to turn up.

I remember walking through the Egyptian Wing of the Metropolitan Museum with Saul Steinberg, who liked to hold his annual meetings in the cozy Grace Rainey Rogers Auditorium. Saul was coming off a very successful year for the insurance business of

DIVIDEND/GNP RATIO

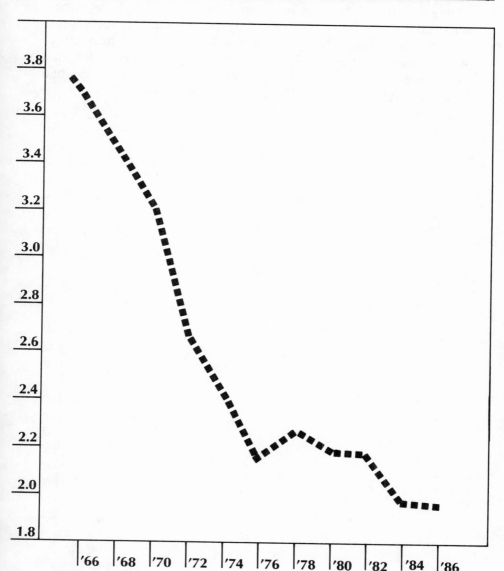

Source: AIG Global Investors, Inc.

Reliance, and he had just sold his sea-container subsidiary to a budding young financial conglomerate for a profit of a couple of hundred million. "Look at those poor mummies," Saul said. "They are my old shareholders from the sixties and early seventies, when all I knew how to do was buy in French. I'm forty years old, and I have finally learned how to sell in French." The acquirer of his subsidiary, Gelco, almost choked to death a year later on a worldwide surplus of containers. Slippage in world trade had destroyed the industry's rate structure and utilization.

4   The Search for Reductiveness

ROBERT PERLESS lives in a house that looks like a gallon paint can minus its label. Aside from a bed, dining table, chairs, plus a chaise, there is just an expanse of space. The cupboards are flush with the walls, and a color scheme of charcoal black, white, and silver gray prevails, down to placemats and doormats. One of Bob's suspended wind sculptures of tiered horizontal struts, lacquered white, turns independently, and, viewed from below resembles a three-dimensional snowflake. The only other ornament in a living space that suggests an airplane hangar in terms of its cubic air capacity is a highly burnished bronze sculpture: a gigantic corkscrew revolving silently on its motorized base. When I tell Ellen, Bob's wife, that they have reduced their living quarters to the equivalent of a Plains Indian couple in a teepee of buffalo skins, at first she rejects the concept. After all, there were years of agony from conception to execution and much money. Three teams of contractors were dispatched when they couldn't properly weld the steel railing for the staircase that suggests the connecting ladders of the upper and lower decks of an elegant sports-fishing boat. Bob's art requires sure and true welding that can be polished to the point of invisibility. Twenty years ago, as a farmhand, he toyed with a welding gun, and he hasn't put it down. Bob's New York gallery sold so many of his elegantly wrought geometric sculptures that he and Ellen took off a few years and sailed the Bahamas. I have watched Bob cut through a two-ton sheet of steel with a blowtorch that reaches up to 70,000 degrees. It is like a pizza cutter dividing a pie—you don't get your fingers near the flame, or they will go up in smoke.

For two years, each day of sailing was a new decision based on a compass reading. Nothing was planned. When their library of paperbacks was dog-eared, they traded with the other windblown boats. For fresh bread, they baked their own. Unlike William Least Heat Moon, who circumnavigated the country in his homemade

Interior of the Robert and Ellen Perless House.

camper stowed with Whitman's *Leaves of Grass,* and talked with everyone on the back roads (*blue highways on the road maps*), theirs was a more elemental and primeval interlude. It is no accident that many of Bob's sculptures are windblown pieces that swivel on ball bearings.

The German Neo-Expressionist painter, A. R. Penck, writes:

Since I came to the West I waver between this economical use of methods and their waste. Still I hold fast to the discipline of the economy. This means above all, activity and control. Furthermore it is clear to me that it is unavoidable to take into the picture of control more and more aggression. This could lead to a new convention after the old convention has been destroyed directly through the economy. . . . A picture is an essential criterion for determining the condition of the system and that every proceeding involved with paintings represents exactly such criterion.

Penck's *Standart West II* typifies the economy of statement in this three-figure piece. Note the blue male penetrating the female symbolized by the funnel (ovum) in her middle and what looks like a fetus in her tummy. The white and brown background suggest a field of male spermatozoa. Is the little red fellow on the right witnessing a primal scene, or is this just an innocent family grouping? The absence of such painterly conceit as flesh tones and body detailing challenges the history or art and is the greatest source of strength for the piece. Worked over, I understand, in bright sunlight, the canvas has a kinetic, almost psychedelic quality that gives it tension. It is a good example of the almost brutally reductive qualities that make German-Neo Expressionism come alive.

Rather than reductiveness or frank originality, the weathervanes on Wall Street point not infrequently in the wrong direction. It works like this: If everyone knows IBM is going to earn exactly $3.25 a share in the fourth quarter and IBM does earn $3.25 a share, the stock does not budge. If IBM earns 2 pennies less, it may collapse; and if it earns a few pennies more, it may rise fractionally or collapse. The earnings shortfall causes anxiety. If IBM shortchanges the Street, it may mean that its growth rate will decelerate, and the sellers want to unload before such a slowdown is obvious to all. On the other hand, if earnings rise a few pennies,

A.R. Penck. *Standart West II*. 1983. Acrylic on canvas. 111″ × 107″.
Collection of Toni and Martin Sosnoff.

it could be construed bearishly, too. This would happen if a generalized forecast of an economic slowdown was the consensus. For example, if General Motors were to earn $25 a share, but everyone believed it was the last time in many a year that GM would hit those numbers, the stock would collapse. The patient was cancerous and on his way to the charnelhouse.

For the man who can stand alone in the theater when everyone is panicking for the fire exits, the theater is his. If he goes down in flames, at least he dies alone. And, if there is some smoke and no fire, our hero has traded on everyone else's anxiety and commands the theater. The capacity to stand alone comes in many shapes and forms. Each has its own schema, which may be shrouded in fog. The fog is a function of the man behind his schema. After all, why should he tell you how to survive? He is standing there with a bushel basket to catch all the goods you are about to jettison because of your anxious state communicated to you by the consensus. Lest you discount these fellows with cast-iron stomachs as oddballs of no significance, I cite a few schemata of more than modest scope and dimension.

The I/B/E/S* Consensus on IBM as of February 1986

| Company | Actual | | | | |
	Fiscal Year	EPS	5 Year Growth Rate	Stability	Year
INTL BUS MACH	12/85	10.67	16.3	6.4	86
					87

| | | | | Estimates | | | | |
Mean	1 Mo. Percent Chg.	Median	1 Mo. Percent Chg.	High	Low	Coeff of Variation	Number of Total	Up
12.56	−0.8	12.56	−1.1	13.50	11.75	3.1	40	2
14.43	−3.2	14.40	−4.0	15.50	13.50	4.8	7	0

*IBES: The Institutional Brokers Estimate System published monthly.

Note the IBES earnings concensus on IBM early in 1986 was $12.56 a share. By mid-1986 IBM management started to tell analysts that earnings looked flat for the year. The consensus estimate immediately dropped to $10.50 a share. A train-load of analysts had missed the leading growth company's earnings by almost 20 percent. They did it again in the third quarter. IBM probably will not earn $9 a share for 1986.

The Antiestablishment Establishment

Batterymarch Financial Management handles a big barrel of money—over $11 billion in assets—with a handful of people. There are no secret holdings on Wall Street any longer. The SEC requires all investment advisers to file quarterly form 13F, which lists the inventory of invested positions for all the assets under management. This is public information available for the asking. The last Batterymarch inventory report I studied at yearend 1985 was 28 pages long with approximately 800 stocks. You would think that the organization had gone crazy and bought everything in sight. After all, the Standard & Poor's Index—the heart of the market in terms of asset value—contains only 500 stocks. The Dow Jones Industrial Average, of course, is 30 large companies.

Nothing could be farther from the point. A scan of Batterymarch's 13F reveals enormous investment concentration in depressed cyclicals and relatively low-multiple stock groups like automobiles and oils. Simply, what Batterymarch has said to Wall Street is, "Okay, guys. You are worried about the quality of earnings of banks, lower oil prices, and nuclear power plants bankrupting the electric utilities. We will take these goods off your hands at our price. Incidentally, we will only pay you a commission of a penny or two. If you don't want to play with us, don't. By the way, if you have any crappy steels, motors, aluminums, and coppers, we will buy those, too, at the prices we specify."

The iron-willed capacity of Batterymarch to implement its schema during 1985–1986 was unsuccessful in the cyclicals, partially successful in oils and banks. Batterymarch's money managers couldn't have analyzed an inventory of 800 stocks individually. Theirs is a top-down strategy that forecasts the dominant investment theme for each phase of the economic cycle. They conceptualized that the market would turn around and bought the cyclicals that had been discarded during the stagnant economic setting. With the fortitude to accumulate hundreds of issues that fit their schema, Batterymarch could manage tens of billions, perhaps 1 or 2 percent of GNP.

BATTERYMARCH'S 20 MAJOR HOLDINGS
YEAREND 1985

	Market Value (in millions)
Allied Signal	153
Aluminum Co. of America	101
Amoco	102
Atlantic Richfield	116
Boeing	181
Caterpillar Tractor	166
Celanese	94
Chevron	112
Corning Glass Works	100
Deere	121
DuPont	127
Eaton	105
Ford Motor	151
General Motors	135
Halliburton	101
Honeywell	113
Mobil	123
NCR	115
Smithkline Beckman	125
Texaco	97
U.S. Steel	106

There are some questions—the "what if" kind. What if Battery-march's scenario proves dead wrong? The economy zigs when it should zag. Batterymarch underperformed during 1984–1985 and the first half of 1986. Cyclicals ran out of early foot and finished last. Part of this "being wrong" possibility is taken care of by buying right: you buy stocks only when they are selling far below some standard of valuation, either absolute valuation or historic relative valuation to other sectors of the market such as growth stocks or even to themselves. If banks historically sell at 70 percent to 90 percent of the Standard & Poor's Index and you buy them for 60 percent because the market is worried about all those loans to Brazil and Argentina, hopefully you have a cushion going in. If Argentina and Brazil change their names and float away, of course the cushion turns to lead. And there is no cushion if things keep going to hell, as they did during the Great Depression. Even during the thirties, Roosevelt kept the establishment banks and insurance companies in business although they were truly insolvent. It was good for the country to do so. Once you get very big, it is difficult to go out of business. There are too many issues that impinge on national policy. When Chrysler got in trouble, the state and federal governments figured out that it would be cheaper to bankroll the company for a few years rather than pay all those unemployment benefits. Despite twenty-five years of mismanagement, International Harvester was kept alive by its suppliers and banks. Under new management, the company was downsized but did come back in its core business of farm equipment during the economic recovery of 1983–1984. A few years later, Chrysler earns a couple of billion dollars a year and has the lowest breakeven point in Detroit.

And so it goes. The doomsday scenario rarely occurs, except in the minds of panicky investors. If you buy 'em right, like when Batterymarch's computers riffle out intrinsic values and favorable anomalies in relative price-earnings ratios, the game is half won. Then you have only to call the turn in the economic cycle better than the consensus. If you are wrong, you are not going out of business because you didn't overpay for your goods. At worst, you will have dead paper for a while that may underperform the market. Nobody is going to sue you for flat performance. Maybe your asset base stops growing for a while, but if you already manage 1 percent of GNP why lose any sleep?

The reverse of the Batterymarch schema was the Morgan Guaranty Trust game plan of the early seventies. Considering that the Morgan was then the crème de la crème of investment management for much of the sixties and early seventies, it took the bear market of 1973–1974 to uncover the hubris of the organization's senior investment managers. Although they wore dark suits and white shirts and believed in America 365 days out of the year, the establishment corporations that they were invested in came close to destroying this temple of investments. Of the $28 billion in assets under management in the early seventies, $22 billion was in equities, and half the assets were concentrated in 30 stocks. These goods sold at enormous premiums to the market, many ranging from 30 to 40 times earnings. The investment game plan for the Morgan in those years can be summed up easily: Buy and hold the best noncyclical growthies and keep your fingers crossed that they don't stop growing or that you overpaid.

The intellectual crux of money management today is the image of minimalist art. There has been a downgrading of talent, facility, virtuosity, and technique. Conceptual power is everything. What matters is not a money manager's will to discover facts, but his orientation. Too few of us are willing to admit this. We remained stubbornly as participants in the game of musical chairs when we should have been thinking about whether it was worth our while to play at all. As Warren Buffett of Berkshire Hathaway says: "Wait for your pitch." The market in 1973 and 1974 was saying that it was too difficult to perform. If you need some proof of this, let me show what happened to the Morgan's 1972 year-end list of 25 largest holdings during the first ten days of January 1974. It dropped a fast 10 percent—10 percent in ten days! My God!

Only the art market is as capricious as the stock market. In *The Economics of Taste,* Gerald Reitlinger chronicled the rise and fall of picture prices since 1760. "Sometimes fantasy prices were paid by princes and cardinals, like Arab khalifs who filled the mouths of poets with gold. But quite often high prices were reached because two or three magnates wanted the same picture." The best of Rubens and Van Dyke failed to exceed the prices of the Napoleonic Wars until the Duke of Marlborough's sales of 1884–1886. Rembrandt and Titian fell miserably during this seventy-year span. Reitlinger notes that the causes of flatness and decline were within the market itself What told against the Old Masters was the loss of the mood of overconfident optimism in which so many works had been bid up beyond their merits. A hundred years ago, perhaps one or two Old Masters sold at Christie's in any year for over 1,000 guineas. Genius was not an easily marketable commodity in early and mid-Victorian times. Until the 1860s, Rembrandt's paintings could be had at auction for less than £700.

In May 1974 I attended an evening auction of postwar and contemporary art that was held at Sotheby's in New York. The press of dealers and serious collectors spilled over into several rooms, and I was to be discomfited and disappointed when I was outbid for the few things I coveted. Many pieces went for twice their estimated value, and afterward, when I chatted with my dealer friends, they told me why. There were syndicates of several European dealers who were flush with other people's money, and they were open to buy everything they fancied. The conceptual pieces were the most popular. Christo's *Wrapped Vespa* motorcycle done in 1963 went for $50,000 and drew a round of applause when it was knocked down to the bidder. Ten years later, I was to

The Morgan is Schmeissed

HOLDINGS WITH MARKET VALUE EXCEEDING $150 MILLION ON
DECEMBER 31, 1972

Stock	Market Value	Stocks off 10% or More
AMP	$ 192	
American Express	306	17%
American Home Products	330	11
Avon Products	651	19
Coca-Cola	320	11
Disney (Walt) Productions	473	23
Eastman Kodak	1,138	11
Exxon	309	
First National City	210	18
Ford Motor	180	
General Motors	344	
Halliburton	179	11
International Business Machines	2,094	
Johnson & Johnson	206	14
Kresge (S.S.)	285	14
Louisiana Land & Exploration	153	
MGIC Investment	203	
McDonalds	262	14
Merck	274	10
Mobil Oil	286	10
Philip Morris	272	12
Penney (J.C.)	279	
Polaroid	423	
Proctor & Gamble	396	
Schering-Plough	207	11
Schlumberger	390	18
Sears, Roebuck	605	
Squibb	188	
Texaco	212	
Westinghouse Electric	182	
Xerox	596	12
Average Loss		10

experience these pieces in many outlying museums in Germany
like Mönchengladbach.

There is nothing wrong with paying $50,000 for a wrapped Vespa.
After all, you are paying for the conception and daring of the
creator to be provocative and to challenge your ideas on art and

possibly even offend your bourgeois sensibilities. The problem may arrive if your Vespa goes out of style. You run the risk of looking a little foolish. The reason for the applause in the auction room was for a gutsy play. The Morgan list was similarly a beautiful collection of wrapped motorcycles bought with other people's money. It should be viewed with respect, and then it's time to leave the museum and go out into the real world. The two-dollar bill, probably the handsomest of our paper currency denomination, with the founding fathers signing the Declaration of Independence, is shunned by merchants because 2 looks too much like a 5.

What has changed in the past decade? Well, the Morgan still has more than $30 billion in assets under management, but the investment schemata is unrecognizable compared with the go-go years of the early seventies. J. P. Morgan & Company had changed its spots. By 1986, on a $16 billion equity portfolio, the only outsized position was still IBM, approximating 9 percent of assets under management. The 20 largest positions no longer showed the extreme bias toward growth at any price. Aside from IBM, there was scarcely a position greater than 1 percent of assets, except for General Electric. The process had changed markedly toward a valuation bias denoted by the many positions in the energy sector, banks, utilities, and basic industry. The average price-earnings ratio for the Morgan looked a little less than that of the market. The hubris was gone, now, but no doubt still a fond memory.

Sanford C. Bernstein & Company outperformed the market during 1983–1984 with a very disciplined dividend-discount-model schemata. Briefly, a dividend-discount model works on the premise that stock groups bear close historical relationships to each other and to the market, and that these relationships from year to year can widen or narrow because of temporary circumstances or misplaced changes in investor sentiment. According to this model, the overreaction of money-center bank stocks because of their foreign-loan problems made them buys during 1983. This is another form of contrarian investment philosophy. You take stocks off the hands of worried or panic-stricken investors who pay you to relieve them of the anxiety generated by their holdings. To the extent that valuation relationships come back into phase (it can take a year or more for this to happen), the buyer is the winner.

J.P. MORGAN'S 20 LARGEST HOLDINGS
MARCH 31, 1986

	(In millions)
Allied Signal	175
Atlantic Richfield	152
Capital Cities/ABC	153
Chase Manhattan	140
Citicorp	193
Dun & Bradstreet	123
Exxon	250
General Electric	358
General Motors	207
IBM	1,427
Marion Laboratories	163
Marriott	145
Pacific Telesis	202
Ralston Purina	156
Royal Dutch Petroleum	134
Toys R Us	129
U S West	130
United Technologies	160
Wal-Mart Stores	125
Washington Post	149

Conversely, when stock groups reach overvaluation compared with other groups, the contrarian sells them no matter how favorable the near-term outlook. Everything is for sale—at a price. To the extent that the valuation structure of the market is not destroyed by a financial panic or by a Great Depression, the dividend-discount model works. It does require enormous discipline and a cast-iron stomach. The discipline centers on implementing everything your model says you must do, even if you have misgivings intellectually or viscerally. When everyone was selling IBM in the opening weeks of 1984, you had to step in and buy after the stock dropped from 134 to 107.

The Bernstein list is a model of discipline and fortitude. Half its invested assets of $7 billion rests in 15 positions. All its investments are related to the call for exceptional recovery in the industrial sector in an environment of rising commodity prices and a declining dollar. The banks and Philip Morris are there because they are considered inefficiently priced within the Bernstein dividend discount model universe.

15 LARGEST HOLDINGS OF S.C. BERNSTEIN & CO.
MARCH 31, 1986

	Market Value (in millions)
Alcan	202
Aluminum Company of America	151
Caterpillar Tractor	220
Chrysler	456
Deere	217
Digital Equipment	324
Ford Motor Company	487
General Motors	333
IBM	624
Royal Dutch Petroleum	283
Texas Instruments	181
Philip Morris	195
Wang Laboratories	169
Manufacturers Hanover	167
Chemical New York	137

The Bernstein portfolio was the exact reciprocal of the Morgan portfolio of 1972–1974. Bernstein buys the industry groups that sell at the lowest relative valuation to the market. It works a helluva lot better than paying a premium for growth or trying to find the next ten technology operators who have bottled lightning and are going to the moon. It is one of the more rational ways of running big money just so long as the inefficiencies in the market are meaningful and the ultimate financial risk of long-lasting recession doesn't surface. Patience is important, too, for the anomalies in the marketplace can last for a year or two. After all, the Morgan got into trouble because its growthmanship worked so well from 1962 until 1973. The recession of 1973 proved that their gods had feet of clay and valuations then crumbled. Nothing is forever. The economy zig-zagged most of 1986, and the Bernstein portfolio underperformed up to mid-1986.

Twentieth Century Ultra Investors mutual fund typifies the racier aspects of money management. Actually, what Ultra does is not money management at all: it is institutionalized speculation. Many of the mutual funds didn't get away with this mufti-pufti in the late sixties and early seventies when they were flushed out into the river with their noxious effluvients: Minnie Pearl Chicken, Four

Seasons Nursing Homes, King Resources, and National Student Marketing. Each generation has to learn its own lesson about overspeculation. Sooner or later, your fingers get singed, and the goods you bought don't come back. General Motors, even Xerox and U.S. Steel came back, albeit scaled down. There is nothing wrong with this brand of one-upmanship if you know when to get off the bus. Very few manage to get out whole. From April 1983 to February 1984, this fund declined over 25 percent. To its credit, by mid-1986, the fund manager was dealing in more defined, broader capitalization merchandise.

It is one thing to find the guys who make the better mousetraps. Digital Switch did it in telecommunications, but Elscint missed in parts of the medical electronics sector, and Cordis never held its primacy in cardiac pacemakers. Over 40 percent of the 98 percent of invested assets was concentrated in computer products and software, medical electronics, and biochemistry operators. If you know what half these companies do, you are ahead of me: Cipher Data Products, SofTech, Inc., ASK Computer Systems. Who are you? My guess is that all these stocks sold at 3 times the market valuation and at least 5 times book value. If anything goes wrong, forget it. Would Ultra's money managers put their own assets into Ultra Investors? Unlikely. During 1982, 1984, and 1985 Ultra underperformed the market significantly.

Do investors in this fund understand the risks? Probably not. Catch its president, James E. Stowers, writing in June 1983 just as the market was topping out: "We believe there are many indications that the recent stock-price upswing is not the end—but only the beginning of a very long-term market advance in coming years, even though there might be adjustments in the market from time to time. The future could hold disappointment for those who still remain 'in cash' or for those who sell out believing the rally is over." Not content with his own bullishness, Stowers's rocky salesmanship whips those investors who dare to withhold some cash from the maws of the Twentieth Century Investors. For all of 1984 and most of 1985, technology stocks underperformed the market.

Our mid–1985 portfolio, which outperformed the market, combined the dual theme of moderate consumer-driven economic recovery within an environment of low interest rates and minimal inflation. Overweighted positions in retailing, nondurables, growth

TWENTIETH CENTURY ULTRA INVESTORS PORTFOLIO AS OF APRIL 30, 1983

		Market Value (In millions)
Computer Products—19.1%		
50,000	Apollo Computer	2
100,000	Cipher Data Products	4
127,000	Commodore International	11
189,500	Convergent Technologies	6
52,000	Emulex	2
52,500	SCI Systems	2
173,000	Seagate Technology	6
593,000	Tandon	15
349,000	Telex	8
Computer Software & Systems—9.3%		
82,000	ASK Computer Systems	3
227,500	Cullinet Software	9
48,000	Evans & Sutherland Computer	2
150,000	HBO & Co.	5
130,000	Intergraph	5
28,000	Policy Management Systems	2
35,000	SofTech	1
64,000	Systems & Computer Technology	2
Medical Equipment & Products—13.2%		
50,000	ADAC Laboratories	1
77,800	Bolar Pharmaceuticals	2
105,000	Collagen	2
82,000	Cordis	6
82,000	Dynatech	3
154,000	Elscint	4
64,000	Enzo Biochem	2
80,500	International Clinical Labs	2
150,000	Nuclear Pharmacy	2
68,000	Spectro Industries	2
25,500	Stryker	.9
61,000	Thompson Medical	2
293,000	U.S. Surgical	9

companies, airlines, automobiles, and media implemented this thesis, along with interest-sensitive issues like the banks and insurance companies. Note the absence of cyclical issues. The only industrial security held was IBM, which has underperformed. The complete absence of energy-related securities was consistent with our conviction of disinflation for raw materials, and thus eliminated 20 percent of the market's valuation from portfolio

TWENTY LARGEST HOLDINGS
ATALANTA/SOSNOFF CAPITAL MID–1985

Description	Percent of Total
Loews	6.6
IBM	5.6
New York Times	5.0
J.P. Morgan	4.6
Boeing	4.5
Chrysler	4.3
Pepsico	4.3
CBS	4.2
American Express	4.0
American Cyanamid	3.3
American Broadcasting	3.3
AMR	3.0
Chubb	3.0
Citicorp	3.0
Salomon	2.9
Capital Cities Communications	2.5
General Reinsurance	2.5
R.H. Macy	2.4
Borden	2.3
Pillsbury	2.2

consideration. It was a good call. Note that there were no small-capitalization positions. Big money does well if the portfolio is properly boiled down to the essence of the economic realities for the investment cycle.

In today's art world, the obtuseness of any consensus of which contemporary artists possess greatness contrasts markedly with the almost universal admiration of the French academic painters in the Nineteenth Century. Today, to win critical acceptance, an artist must be revolutionary in subject matter, technique, and materials, with a challenging aesthetic base.

Present day money managers not only revolt against the consensus, but periodically challenge their own hypotheses.

In Nineteenth-Century French salon painting, the conventions on male and female modesty had to be observed strictly. There was never more than a hint of pubic hair, and the females routinely were made love to by some young Adonis with wings. Bourgeois sensitivities prevailed until Impressionists like Renoir broke out of this box with his Rubenesque *baigneuses*. Note the spent

F.E. Picot. *L'Amour et Psyché*. 1817. Oil on canvas. The Louvre, Paris.

William Bouguereau.
Le Ravissement de Psyché. 1895 Oil on canvas. 209 × 120 centimeters.
Private collection.

condition of the female sprawled on her double bed as L'Amour, with an abbreviated penis, slips away. A salon painting by F. E. Picot, *L'Amour et Psyche,* done in 1817, was acquired by Louis Philippe, Duke of Orleans.

Similarly, William Bouguereau, in his rendition of *Psyché,* has his female, obviously on the way up to her orgasm, transported into the heavens by a winged young male. Eroticism masked in mythology was okay in nineteenth-century Europe. Richard Wagner pulled the same trick for Isolde, who sips the magic love potion and then openly expresses her sexuality for Tristan.

It took the American naturalist painter Thomas Eakins, who studied with the French academicians for years, to restore the human body to its natural condition. For most of this life, Eakins could scarcely sell a canvas. Chastised by the critics for ignoring the conventions of American painting of the late nineteenth century, when every canvas had to be uplifting, pretty, and suitable for a girl's boarding school, Eakins then turned to portraiture. And because he wouldn't idealize his subjects, many commissions were rejected by his sitters and later by the public. Eakins's monumental canvas, *The Agnew Clinic,* came close to equaling Rembrandt's *Anatomy Lesson* technically, and can be faulted only for some derivativeness. Eakins had a tough time gaining its acceptance for exhibition.

One of the great paintings of the nineteenth century, *The Agnew Clinic* was initially commissioned for $750 as a portrait by the undergraduate classes of the School of Medicine, University of Pennsylvania. Eakins chose to make it the largest work of his middle years. A horizontal canvas with an asymmetric design that focused on Dr. Agnew's erect carriage and finely chiseled head, it utilized the counterpoint of his stooping assistants. The painting created a scandal in art circles for depicting an operation on a woman's breast. Eakins's response, with tears in his eyes, was, "They call me a butcher, and all I was trying to do was to picture the soul of a great surgeon." During Eakins's lifetime, *The Agnew Clinic* hung in the School of Medicine where it was seen by medical students but not by the art public. For a 1970 exhibition, this piece was insured for $500,000 and its companion canvas, *The Gross Clinic,* for $1 million. In 1951 The Philadelphia Museum of Art held its Diamond Jubilee exhibition of masterpieces of the world and included *The Gross Clinic.* Museumgoers were asked to vote

Thomas Eakins. *The Agnew Clinic*. 1889. Oil. 74½" × 130½". University of Pennsylvania.

for their favorite picture. Of 20,000 votes, the top three were a Rubens with 3,500 votes, an El Greco with 2,700, and *The Gross Clinic* with 2,200 votes. Eakins had been dead only thirty-five years.

In the investment sector, experience suggests that the decisions that are agonizingly difficult to implement invariably reward you the most. Eventually. Our investment portfolio took off in the opening months of 1986, but it was essentially the same as mid–1985. Nearly every stock challenged the prevailing analytical opinions. Tobacco stocks were bad because lawsuits were mounting. The companies prevailed in court. Almost to a man, the analysts believed that banks and insurance stocks had had their run. The reported 1985 underwriting losses for fire and casualty underwriters were horrendous. We bought more because we understood that the up cycle would stretch for many years and recapture losses incurred. As spot oil hit $15 a barrel, the bank stocks wavered, but we figured out that even if you reduced interest payments from Mexico by half, the stocks remained historically undervalued. Morgan led the market. The automobile stocks were supposed to have a terrible time with the growing influx of foreign cars and a consumer surfeited with installment debt. But the dollar fell 35 percent relative to the yen, and the car makers reduced rates on car loans. Nobody saw these cards before they were turned face-up. The surface-noise level of Wall Street research repeatedly misled investors with concerns that were momentary rather than momentous.

Just as good art in every succeeding generation challenges the establishment's conception of what art is and should be, the smart money in each economic cycle is the grave dancer over the moribund consensus which never sees change until it is reported in the next day's newspaper. Stupidity in the art market can last for generations if the critical consensus is deeply ingrained in the consciousness of the buyers of art: the rich and powerful. On Wall Street, the rich and powerful pay for their mistakes overnight. A new consensus re-forms immediately after the facts unfold. The same people who believed that oil would hang in at the mid-twenties a barrel now have no problem believing that the new price is $15 a barrel. Reciprocally, those who foresaw $15 a barrel are challenging their own hypothesis and are looking ahead to a scenario where prices will move back up.

5 The Anatomy Lesson

DOCTOR NICOLAAS Tulp Demonstrating the Anatomy of the Arm was painted in 1632 by Rembrandt, a young, recent arrival in Amsterdam. The work made his name. This painting hangs in the Mauritshuis in The Hague, where it glows with uncanny iridescence and tension. It is an establishment work which utilizes the body of an executed criminal by the surgeons' guild in Amsterdam to commemorate their annual anatomy lesson. Just as art mirrors its cultural milieu, this piece is heavy with historical associations and many layers of symbolic meaning. It is a painting of great theater—presenting ultimate truths in a formal, yet charismatic setting which adumbrates a pseudo-religious rite comparable to a requiem mass. The doctors are acolytes of Dr. Tulp, who demonstrates his virtuosity as an anatomist.

The decade of the 1630s in Amsterdam was a period of great professional and intellectual aspiration and of aggressive social ambition. [In Rembrandt's early self-portraits, he dressed himself like an elegant dandy.] In Amsterdam, an anatomy lesson was a social event of cachet comparable with an opening night at the Metropolitan Opera. The dissection took place the day after an execution and was followed on the third day with a torchlight parade and feast. The criminal's punishment ended not with his execution, but in a cathartic theatrical spectacle. The intellectual level of the painting suggests the ultimate triumph of science over evil. Dr. Tulp, the foremost anatomist in Holland, is demonstrating the functioning of the muscles of the left arm. Tulp has dissected the brachial musculature and is demonstrating the delicate adductive mechanism of the extremity with his own left hand.

Rembrandt's tour de force is the dramatic disposition of figures in three-dimensional space. You are shocked by the intensity of the figures and the contrapuntal ivory coolness of the cadaver. Dr. Tulp radiates self-confidence and overshadows his colleagues. The deep message seems to me: Know thyself and atone for your sins.

Rembrandt Van Rijn. *Dr. Tulp Demonstrating the Anatomy of the Arm.* 1632. Oil. 67" × 85". The Hague, Mauritshuis.

The melding of the two major strains of symbolic meaning—the apotheosis of the scientific spirit and man's triumph over death—done in such an undidactical way by Rembrandt gives this piece its motive power. The forceful realism of the canvas, the interweaving of glances, and the chiaroscuro shadow (of death) on the face of the cadaver suggest the painter's technical virtuosity. The painting was considered a full realization from the beginning and was appreciated as such by all. Young Rembrandt had painted the perfect picture.

Unfortunately, in the world of investments there is no perfection, only change. The money manager is condemned to an endless labor of building his mosaic of stones that are always changing their color, shape, and durability. The closest one comes to perfection is making one big call right. In the opening months of 1986, we had this certain feeling about financial assets. All the central banks wanted lower interest rates as oil sank to $12 a barrel. Inflation disappeared in Germany and Japan. Unemployment remained high and economic activity recovered slowly. Long-term Treasury yields fell to 7 percent, a level nobody even had dreamed about a few months before.

Perfection can be slighted just as easily. Giorgio Vasari in his *Lives of the Artists,* which was published in Florence in 1568, notes the peculiar collecting habits of the *cognoscenti* in the fifteenth century. Instead of collecting early paintings of the Italian Renaissance like Giotto, Uccello, and Masaccio, the popes, cardinals, and Medici were fighting over Greek and Roman gems and coins, which they thought had the greatest aesthetic merit. Many were counterfeit. The young Michelangelo was busy faking classical sculpture, for which he was paid more in commissions than for his creative work.

In *The Rare Art Traditions,* Joseph Alsop notes that, as art collectors, the fifteenth-century Medici sought classical works—the products of antiquity—exclusively. No works by any of the great Italian masters they patronized were ever truly collected by them. Petrarch was given his Giotto *Madonna* by a friend in Florence long after Giotto was in his grave. Even before his death in 1337 and until early in the fifteenth century, Giotto was considered to be the preeminent Italian painter. Meanwhile, the Venetian nobility were bidding vast sums for badly mutilated stone horses by Phidias and Praxiteles, and fake coins of Alexander the Great. In the mid-fifteenth century, classical antiquities preoccupied Cosimo de' Medici far more than the art of his generation. His inventory of Italian masters was very small, and the commissions handed out by this ruthless politician and cold-blooded banker were earmarked for public buildings: libraries, churches, convents, and for his palazzo. The great flowering of Renaissance painting in Florence was largely relegated to public patronage for political power and prestige. Botticelli's *Madonna* for the *sola grande* of the palazzo cost the Medici 35 florins. Frameworkers got 24 florins, and the gilding fee was 38 florins. In comparison, a featherbed and two pillows were valued at 15 florins and a classical carved urn went for 200 florins.

When the Medici were expelled from Florence in 1494, an inventory of their palazzo showed Renaissance artworks valued at 968 florins, whereas household clothing added up to 3,700 florins. The Masaccios, Giottos, Donatellos, Fra Angelicos, Uccellos, and Van Eycks, the sum of collecting over three generations of Medicis during the entire fifteenth century, were valued at little more than the family's spoons and forks.

A few hundred years later, in the eighteenth century, street urchins handed out woodblock prints in the Yoshiwara, or red-light district, of Yedo, now downtown Tokyo. These were come-ons for the many houses advertising their licensed girls to the johns strolling in the streets. In the late nineteenth century, collectors showed some interest in these prints, called *ukioye*. Today, they would be comparable to a copy of the Marilyn Monroe calendar. Original editions of Batman and Superman comic books fifty years after publication are selling for $10,000. Who can tell what is ephemeral and what to squirrel away?

Every generation has its great insights as well as its color blindness. In the economic sector, the establishment's prognostications are almost always wide of the market. The government is invariably inaccurate in its forecasts of GNP growth, interest rates, and the budget deficit. The myth of economic forecastability is kept alive in the financial press that gives these stories spacial prominence, if for no other reason than it has nothing better to fill its columns. Keep a suspense file for six months and you will see what I mean. But do not be taken in or amused. The government, as the ultimate odd-lotter, is a working hypothesis rich in meaning. A close reading of the notes of the Federal Reserve Board's Open Market Committee, particularly in its quarterly meetings during 1982, suggests that these wise men saw recovery around every corner while the economy was slipping deeper into recession. As my old buddy, Joe Rosenberg, of Loews says, "What do you expect? The Federal Reserve Board is a committee, and when have you heard of a committee forecasting anything close to the mark?"

For the individual investor, playing David to the establishment's Goliath is the perfect role. Never assume that the establishment knows what it's doing. Forecasts of interest rates are made by economists with shiny pants and top-heavy home mortgages, and they are always wrong. The bond traders at Salomon Brothers never listened to their senior partner, Sidney Homer, a charming man and the greatest student of interest rates the world has yet produced. Sidney studied interest rates over thousands of years, but he still missed the inflationary destructiveness of the Johnson administration's guns-and-butter policy in the early sixties. A twenty-year bear market in bonds thereafter gripped the country.

Tensions in the 1982 financial markets came close to bankrupting major sectors of the country's industrial might. Farm-equipment producers, auto makers, and steel companies floundered to stay out of bankruptcy court by downsizing their capacity and sweeping out their administrative headquarters personnel. Wall Street dubbed the Midwest the Rust Belt. Capacity utilization for the country touched a postwar low. Wall Street analysts were projecting the exhaustion of the net worth of the strategic heartland of the country: aluminum, steel, farm equipment. At least two auto makers were no more than four quarters from bankruptcy unless the economy turned.

In Washington, the Federal Reserve Board, with the greatest economic information retrieval system in the country, slept soundly. The Federal funds rate during the first half of 1982 was maintained at 14½ percent, while conventional mortgage rates moved above 17 percent and 20-year U.S. Treasury bonds averaged over 14 percent. The prime rate for banks oscillated between 16½ percent and 17 percent. By summer, the stock market had declined 20 percent from the yearend 1981 level. The American Stock Exchange had dropped 30 percent. Meanwhile, unemployment rose sharply to 10.8 percent. The industrial production index slipped a point a month from 143 in February to 135 in the fourth quarter of 1982. By year-end the index was 11½ percent below its latest high of July 1981. Housing starts sank to 888,000 units during August. Meanwhile, consumer and producer price inflation declined to a 4 percent rate.

The minutes of the Federal Open Market Committee during 1982 read like the fable of the Blind Men and the Elephant. At the March meeting: "Real activity is expected to accelerate with most of the growth coming in the second half of the year (it was flat) with inflation continuing to be substantial." (It wasn't.)

At midyear, and in July, the staff projections of moderate growth were endorsed by the board:

> Consumption seemed likely to rise in response to the 10 percent reduction in federal income taxes at midyear. . . . The risks of exacerbating inflationary expectations remained serious. In any case, the underlying rate of inflation was not so low as might be inferred from the recent behavior of major indices of prices and the rise in the indices was generally expected to pickup somewhat from the substantially reduced pace of 1982 to date.

As late as September the committee felt forced to reiterate its standing goal of restraining the growth of money and credit in order to contribute to a further reduction in the rate of inflation. By now they were blind.

With the country practically at a standstill in early summer, the Federal Reserve Board at last allowed the federal funds rate to decline from the 14½ percent level. The discount rate was reduced in three steps from 12 percent to 10½ percent. The board had finally seen reality, but it couldn't resist a parting slap at inflationary expectations which they thought would intensify in coming months. (Prices rose more slowly than in 1981.)

By the fall of 1982, the staff appeared to be a captive of the moderate growth scenario that they had been forecasting throughout 1982. They made a similar forecast for the new year. At the October meeting, the board finally saw the light on inflation: "progress in reducing the rate of inflation had been substantial, exceeding expectations of many. . . ." Actually, in 1983, the economy burst out of the recession with a recovery in the GNP of close to a 10 percent rate by the second quarter. The Federal

Reserve Board had finally decided on a moderate money-supply growth above the targeted range. The intermeeting range for the federal funds rate dropped to a range of 7 to 10½ percent. Now, at last, the boys had realized the damage they had done throughout most of the year. The inflation index at 3½ percent was now half the rate of 1981 for producer prices. Consumer prices also were half the 1981 experience. Many members during the November meeting still held that any recovery during 1983 was likely to be anemic. (It wasn't.)

For almost the entire year, a majority of Federal Reserve Board members misread the vital signs of the economy. High interest rates stalled the economy and almost sent a good portion of smokestack America to the junk heap. But an understanding of FRB policy is crucial to the investment outlook. Interest rates influence the valuation multiplier of corporate earnings. More incisive is the perception of where policy will take interest rates and whether that policy is right or misguided. Stock-market practitioners who religiously followed their dividend discount models signaling enormous investment opportunities, had to develop cast-iron stomachs during the first half of 1982. Perhaps the only lesson to be learned is that misguided monetary policy can last nearly a year and cause a severe heartburn before it's rectified.

The following chart suggests that the bond market in aggregate is much smarter than the Federal Reserve Board's wise men. The discount rate followed rather than led the decline in both short- and intermediate-term interest rates. Falling from the interim peak of 14 percent, five-year Treasuries reached an 11 percent yield from May 1984 to year-end. During these eight months, there was no change in the discount rate.

The course of the long-term bond market has nothing to do with FRB policy emphasis, but rather the singular condition of disinflation in the country since 1982. The rest of the world witnessed much slower declines in prices. Real interest rates rose here relative to the rest of the world and attracted hundreds of billions of dollars in bond investments. The gap closed during 1985–1986, but notice the disparity between us and Japan. It remains two percentage points.

The next table shows the enormous variances in quarterly GNP economic forecasts compared with the actual growth rates, even during expansions—any year of the economic cycle. Such swings

SELECTED INTEREST RATES

Averages of Daily Rates
1984-May, 1985

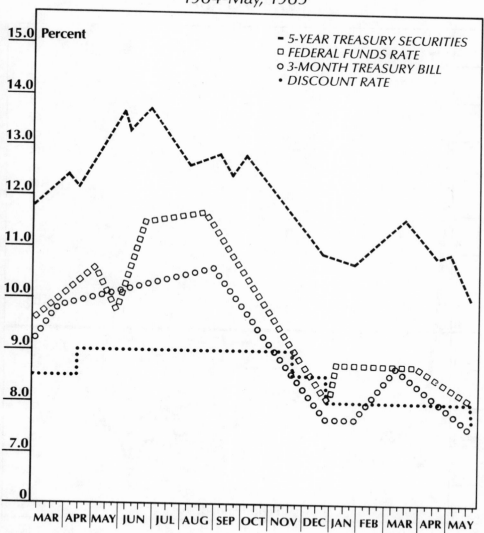

15.0 **Percent**

- ▬ *5-YEAR TREASURY SECURITIES*
- □ *FEDERAL FUNDS RATE*
- ○ *3-MONTH TREASURY BILL*
- • *DISCOUNT RATE*

14.0

13.0

12.0

11.0

10.0

9.0

8.0

7.0

0

MAR APR MAY JUN JUL AUG SEP OCT NOV DEC JAN FEB MAR APR MAY

Source: Federal Reserve Bank of St. Louis

REAL FOREIGN INTEREST RATES

(Percentage Point Difference vs. U.S.)
1979-3/1986

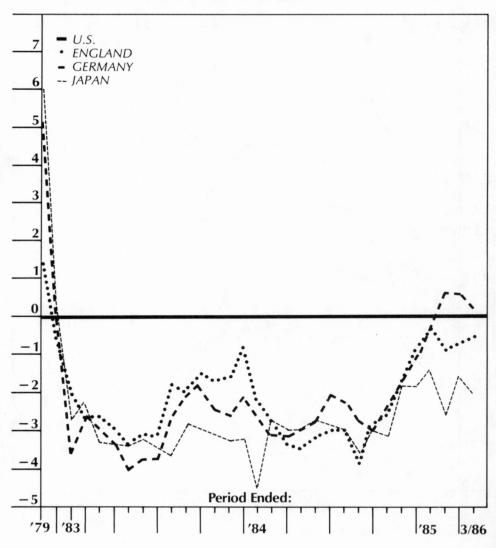

suggest that interim reports are misleading and that they can distort annualized growth rates. Forecasts always underestimate the probability of both extremes. As David Levine of S. C. Bernstein notes: "Although GNP has declined in 17 percent of the past 123 quarters, negative GNP appears in only 5 percent of the forecasts of the Blue Chip survey. More startling, GNP growth has equaled or exceeded 7 percent more than 20 percent of the time since 1954. None of the forecasts contain any such megaquarters." The consensus is always within 1 to 1.5 percent of the 3.4 percent trendline for GNP, thereby suggesting its uselessness.

Understanding and anticipating how the Federal Reserve Board will react to changes in economic phenomenon help in forecasting monetary policy. At year-end 1983, despite a 4 percent inflation rate, real interest rates were historically high, with Treasury bills at 9 percent and long-term governments at 11.75 percent. Henry Kaufman continued to murmur about long governments yielding between 12 and 13 percent and the federal funds rate trading between 10 and 11 percent. Before the Boston Economic Club on November 16, Henry ended his speech on an ominous note: "For those of us who must focus on narrower aspects of economic life— the direction of interest rates—I conclude with a modest warning: Long government bond yields, at their peak in this cycle, will exceed 13 percent."

Not to be outdone by Dr. Doom was Al Wojnilower, the feisty chief economist of The First Boston Corporation, Dr. Death. His prognostications paralleled Henry's throughout the cycles of 1980–81 and 1982–84 and into 1985. Both missed the turn in interest rates during the summer of 1982 by several months. From the summer of 1983, Al had the federal funds rate rising inexorably, reaching 11 percent by year-end (wrong) and extending into 1984. Long-term government bond yields were due to reach 13 percent by year-end. (They didn't.) "Eventually, inflation will accelerate as the dollar declines. (It hasn't by summer of '86.) Then the public and the Federal Reserve will become alarmed and interest rates will rise faster. Whether this will happen in six months, or thirty months or even later, I'm not prepared to guess." Both Henry and Al missed the big call on inflation. There wasn't any.

The impact of Dr. Doom and Dr. Death on the consensus of interest rates is enormous. Both men write frequently and at some length, explaining the rationale for their forecasts. Kaufman and

FREQUENCY DISTRIBUTION OF GNP GROWTH
FORECAST VERSUS ACTUAL—1954–1984

GNP Growth	% of Quarters	
	Forecast	Actual
7.0% or Higher	0.0%	20.3%
6.0–6.9	1.3	5.7
5.0–5.9	5.3	8.1
	6.6%	34.1%
4.0%–4.9%	16.2%	8.9%
3.0–3.9	32.9	16.3
2.0–2.9	25.4	8.1
1.0–1.9	10.5	6.5
	85.1%	39.8%
0.0%–0.9%	3.1%	8.9
(2.0)–(0.1)	3.5	6.5
(2.1)–or lower	1.8	10.6
	8.3%	26.0%

Source: Blue Chip Financial Forecasts and Department of Commerce.

Wojnilower book speaking engagements all over the Western world, appearing before the most prestigious and economically sophisticated professionals and businessmen. Everyone takes these men very seriously. That Henry Kaufman is a frail man with a very weak chin and Al is downright short perhaps explains the somewhat pugnacious stand these two take on the podium. There have been times when they are called down to Washington to explain themselves, and for a while much of Wall Street believed that the Federal Reserve Board, if not a captive of Henry's and Al's chastisements, winced every time they forecast chaos for the financial world.

By now it is obvious that there is no North Star for economists to steer by because the economy never behaves rationally in the short run. It is only over fifty years that the secular growth rate evens out at 3 percent per annum. In the interim cycles, there are crazy patterns of inventory accumulation, labor hoarding and dishoarding, and wild securities markets that can destroy the net-worth statements of individuals and households or enhance them by as much as 50 percent within a matter of 18 months, thereby unleashing major swings in savings or consumption.

Actually, my favorite economist is David Levine, who makes few speeches but does a thorough job of fluoroscoping the vital signs of the economy and projecting the dialectics of each cycle. Every quarter we have an encounter session where we shout each other down—I claiming that he is totally insane while he screams that I have a million misconceptions about what the Federal Reserve Board is really focusing on.

"David, we both agree for a change that there is no inflation in the country, so why is the Board keeping real interest rates so high?"

"The Board isn't focusing on the current rate of inflation. They are more concerned with the possibility of a rapidly accelerating economy. As soon as we have a couple of quarters of low growth, the board will allow rates to go down."

"You already are two quarters overdue in projecting galloping momentum for the economy," I said.

"I am three quarters off, but it is going to happen as of yesterday" (June 15, 1986) he said.

"David, you projected the unemployment rate wouldn't decline to 8.8 percent until the end of 1984, and we reached it in September of 1983. Now you're telling me the inventory accumulation phase is starting. The Industrial Production Index just fell sharply and unemployment rose back above 7 percent."

"The recovery is right around the corner," he said. "The leveraged effect of inventory accumulation will add one and one-half percent to GNP from mid '86 to mid '87."

"David, retail sales just flattened out in May."

"Another fluke," he said.

"Do you own Treasury-bill futures in your own account?" I asked.

"Now it's copper futures. They stink."

"Levine, they are going to carry you out feet first."

"Maybe."

I include David's forecast on unemployment because it goes far beyond the consensus, and if correct, suggests an extended period of low inflation and low interest rates. There will be no reason for corporate America to give away the store as they did during the seventies, thereby creating the cost-push inflation that came close to destroying the currency. The 4 percent GNP growth line is the most probable scenario, and for David it suggested that we would not be approaching the yellow warning level of 7 percent unem-

THREE SCENARIOS FOR UNEMPLOYMENT

The Reality By Mid-'86

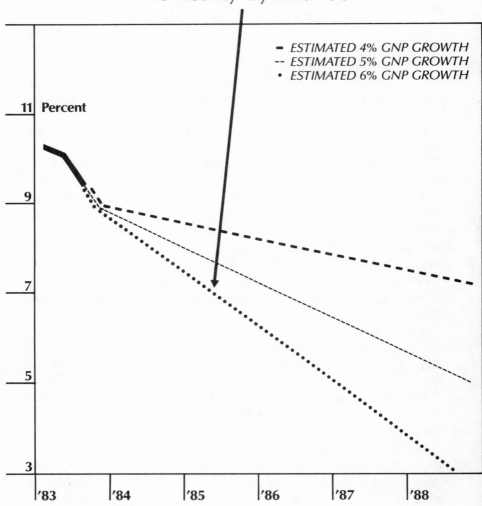

Source: Sanford C. Bernstein & Co.

ployment until sometime past 1988. In reality, the economy hit close to the 7 percent level of joblessness early in 1985 while the economy was hardly growing at all!

If I dwell on Federal Reserve Board policy, it is only because I felt it was the pivotable variable in the investment outlook for 1985–86. Unfortunately, it is never only one variable. There are sixty or more to consider, and the chart enumerates an investment-outlook blueprint that never stays in focus for more than a short time. The art of investing serious money consists of pushing big blocks of assets into the right repository: cash, bonds, or equities.

Before we get too excited about the prospect of compounding at 50 percent a year, think of all the slippage in this flow chart (see inside cover). Among the sixty variables, the probability of isolating the telltale ones each year is not very high. If the Federal Reserve Board can misguide the economy for an extended period, and if the brightest and most articulate economists can't even agree on what's ahead for the next six months, who can get it right? Nobody can do it right for very long. But you can try. After all is said and done, I've learned to act viscerally. When the headman at Eagle Computer totaled his roadster and himself two hours after going public in the spring of 1983, it marked the end of the new-issue market. The accident suggested that the state of mind in Silicon Valley was rather psychedelic, and it was obviously getting too easy to make money in the computer industry. This sector topped out a year later, with many, many casualties. By mid-1986, Eagle Computer had filed a Chapter 11 bankruptcy petition.

A very simple insight late in 1980 was the fact that the dwindling OPEC surplus had latent, cosmic significance. Consider the linkage: The Hunt family—rich in oil, overspeculated in silver, up to $60 an ounce, and lost billions. The complacent, coffee-sipping Arabs had parked surplus capital in gold, and there was a sympathetic decline as Indian matrons sold their silver bracelets, and London dowagers turned in their silver services for meltdown. This incremental supply broke the silver futures market. Wall Street houses like Bache were badly shaken by the Hunts' skimpy collateral. Phibro had to take back $300 million in unproven oil acreage in northern Alaska. It was written down in 1984. Meanwhile the OPEC countries had committed for enormous infrastructure projects: fertilizer plants, roads, hospitals, airports, the F16 warplanes.

Budgets were based on extrapolations of $50 oil, for that is what the oil economists had predicted for 1985—not the $25 reality. But Japan, Europe, even the States learned to conserve fuel. The statistically bound oil analysts on Wall Street had extrapolated huge increases in oil-industry earnings based on worldwide economic growth maintaining its trendline of 3 percent and the coefficient of consumption holding its .6 linkage. It never happened.

The dwindling OPEC surplus led to less excess capital to recycle, and the London Interbank Deposit Rate soared. This created enormous debt-service problems for Mexico and South America, which were the direct recipients of the OPEC surplus. The money had been force-fed to them by worldwide consortiums of the biggest banks who lusted for higher-yielding paper that increased earnings per share. At home, the oil patch was deeper in hock to the money-center and regional banks—they, too, believed in $50 oil. The banks, the drilling-rig boys, and the wildcatters in the Anadarko Basin saw a natural-gas price of $6 to $7 per 1,000 cubic feet just around the corner, right? Wrong.

So the whole world believed in oil at $50 a barrel, but it never happened. The world stopped growing for a while, and the coefficient of consumption disappeared off the page—there wasn't any. The consumer learned to conserve fuel. More efficient cars, new boilers, lower thermostats did the trick. Lowering the thermostats a few degrees has bankrupted most of Latin America, plunged the ten largest banks in the country into a technically bankrupt capital and surplus condition, and destroyed the investment performance of many money managers overweighted in energy and natural resources—as most were.

The dwindling OPEC surplus has created a credible disinflation thesis for the first time since the early sixties. The corollary to a disinflation thesis, if developed by the investor in early 1981, led to a completely new hypothesis for investing serious money. Buy the beneficiaries of declining commodity prices, lower interest rates, and less inflation as well as countercyclical companies—a big recession had to lurk around the corner, and it did. From that inflection point, bonds even outperformed the stock market. By year-end 1983, the OPEC surplus had turned into a galloping deficit, with serious implications for lower oil prices in 1984–85. During the summer of 1985, Saudi Arabia threatened to double its production because no OPEC consensus on price was reachable at its

July meetings. This threat became a reality at year-end. Spot oil collapsed to $14 barrel, practically overnight. This was the one big unmarked door everyone passed by.

I remember meeting with the chairman of the board of a major oil company in London. I asked him what his staff economists were telling him now. "They are telling me that oil is going to $10 a barrel by year-end 1986," he said.

"You mean the same group that extrapolated $50 a barrel last year?" I asked.

"Yes, the same people."

"Do you believe them?" I said.

At this point, my impeccably tailored silver fox dragged reflectively on his Romeo y Julieta. "If I believed my people," he whispered, "I would blow my brains out."

We both laughed at the frailty of the human condition and ordered double espresso.

By the summer of 1986, spot oil prices touched down at ten bucks a barrel. Nobody dreamed it was possible.

6 The Unmarked-Door Phenomenon

THE BERKSHIRE Hathaway annual report contains 19 pages of prose by Warren Buffett, its chairman. There is no glossy cover, and there are no photographs. How many annuals have you read that start this way: "Our gain in net worth during 1984 was $152.6 million or $133 per share. This sounds pretty good but actually it's mediocre. . . . To earn even 15 percent annually over the next decade . . . will require a few big ideas—small ones just won't do. . . . I do not have any such ideas at present, but our experience has been that they pop up occasionally." Warren can afford to be candid. He is worth a billion dollars and still works.

What kind of reading should the silent investor pursue? The list can be so long that many of its items cancel each other out. Financial journalism is a form of entertainment. The reporters concentrate on day-to-day stuff without any attempt at interpretive analysis. When I reported owning 9 percent of The New York Times Company to the SEC, I was beseiged with calls. The reporters all wanted to know whether I had the money to buy more. Nobody asked me why I thought the stock was cheap or how it fit into our total investment strategy. (We had put over 30 percent of $2 billion in media and broadcasting securities.)

Wall Street's analysts are no better than journalists, but they do make five times as much money. Late in June 1985, IBM management met with hundreds of Wall Street securities analysts who covered the data-processing industry. The economy was sloshy and IBM was between product cycles. New orders were slow and management had to scale back its optimistic spring forecast on earnings. It was as if our president had proposed that we merge the United States share-for-share with the Soviet Union. Trainloads of analysts stumbled over each other in scaling down their earnings projections and changing opinions from "strong buy" to "weak hold," as it's worded in wire-house brokeragese. What this actually means is, "We screwed up and you should dump your stock posthaste." Again, in mid–1986, the comedy of errors prevailed.

Why weren't the analysts out there analyzing? The semiconductor suppliers to the industry had no new orders and were firing thousands of production workers. Anecdotal evidence in the computer industry suggested that, without exception, every major mainframe producer had fear in his eyes. No new business was being written by the salesmen, and production backlogs had dwindled. The government's statistical series clearly depicted a peaking in new orders for capital goods for several months, so the final nail was easy to extrapolate. Within the statistical series, data-processing equipment was far above trend for the past eighteen months in terms of dollar shipments as a percent of total capital expenditures. The industry simply was due for a cyclical contraction, but everyone missed it. Even we, without the misplaced optimism, owned the stock on the rationale of its reasonable price. IBM sold at the same earnings valuation as the market, and, after all, it is the best of the world-class corporations this country has fielded in the past thirty years.

So we owned IBM because it was easy to do. Even my partner, who projected the cyclical decline for the industry correctly and had developed an impressive case against the company based upon product saturation levels and impending Japanese competition encroaching on IBM world trade, did not advocate the sale of our holdings early on. It was, after all, a tough call to make on a valuation-case basis. IBM had performed poorly since late 1983. We decided to ignore the surface noise of the analysts and hold on. IBM was just too cheap, and six months later was 40 percent higher than when the analysts ran for the exits.

The Big Board is the great humbler, but it is possible to learn by doing. You learn nothing from your mistakes except the recognition of your stupidity and lack of perception. It follows that, to gain perception, you should start out knowing what everyone else thinks he knows. The Blue Chip Economic Indicators cover the economists who dare publish their forecasts. It costs $332 a year to keep track of the forecasting errors made from month to month. But it is not necessary for you to subscribe because the forecast is reproduced widely in the financial press. The projection of 2.8 percent GNP growth for 1986 is totally worthless as an investment tool. You either have to project zero or 6 percent GNP momentum to have any chance of catching the turn in the economy.

BLUE CHIP ECONOMIC INDICATORS
'86 Real GNP Consensus Steady At +2.8%

MAY 1986 FORECAST FOR 1986 SOURCE:	Percent Change 1986 from 1985 (Year over Year)								Average for Year—1986			Total Units—1986		
	1 Real GNP (Con. $) (Output)	2 GNP Deflator (Prices)	3 Total GNP (Cur. $)	4 Consumer Price Index[1]	5 Indust. Prod. Total[2]	6 Dis. Pers. Income (Con. $)[3]	7 Non-Res. Fix. Inv. (Con. $)[4]	8 Profits Pretax (Cur. $)[5]	9 Treas. Bills 3-Mo.[6]	10 Corp. Aaa Bonds[8]	11 Unempl. % Labor Force[7]	12 Housing Starts (Mil.)[9]	13 Auto Sales Domestic (Mil.)[10]	14 Auto Sales Import (Mil.)[11]
TOP TEN														
Bostian Research Assoc.	4.3H	2.6	7.1H	2.8	5.5H	3.9	7.9	16.0	6.8	9.2	6.6	1.95	8.2	3.0
Wayne Hummer & Co.	3.8	2.4	6.3	2.2	3.6	3.5	4.8	12.0	6.4	9.0	6.9	2.10	7.8	3.1
Econoviews International Inc.	3.5	3.3	6.9	1.5	3.1	3.4	8.0H	6.2	6.6	9.4	6.7	1.90	7.3L	3.4H
Chamber of Commerce of USA	3.5	2.3	5.8	1.6	4.8	2.4	2.8	20.8H	5.4L	8.2	6.8	1.98	8.3	3.0
Econoclast	3.5	2.0	5.5	0.5	2.0	3.2	2.0	11.7	6.1	8.8	6.8	2.01	8.0	3.3
E.I. Du Pont Co.	3.4	2.5	5.9	3.1	2.8	3.1	1.7	6.0	5.8	8.5	6.8	1.94	7.8	3.0
Morris Cohen & Associates	3.2	2.9	6.2	2.8	3.2	3.5	2.0	9.0	6.5	8.0L	6.5	2.00	8.2	3.0
Polyconomics Inc.	3.2	2.0	5.4	2.1	3.1	5.3H	4.2	11.0	6.2	9.1	6.9	1.90	7.9	2.9
UCLA Business Forecast	3.2	2.6	5.9	2.2	2.3	3.4	0.2	13.2	6.2	9.2	6.4L	2.07	8.1	3.1
Fairmodel-Economica Inc.	3.1	2.9	6.0	2.4	4.1	2.4	-0.4	5.5	7.2	9.5H	6.8	2.10	8.6H	3.3
BOTTOM TEN														
Morgan Guaranty	2.5	2.7	5.3	1.9	1.6	2.9	-7.2L	9.7	—	—	7.0	2.00	8.1	3.1
Prudential Insurance	2.4	2.8	5.3	2.3	2.1	3.0	1.4	2.9	6.2	8.9	7.0	1.90	8.1	3.1
Arnold & S. Bleichroeder	2.4	3.0	5.5	2.1	2.2	2.8	-0.3	6.5	7.7H	9.5H	7.1	2.08	8.0	2.9
Chase Manhattan Bank	2.4	2.7	5.2	2.6	2.5	3.2	-1.3	4.0	—	—	7.1	1.85	7.4	3.1
Morgan Stanley & Co.	2.4	2.7	5.1	2.1	1.3	3.1	-0.3	3.5	—	—	7.0	2.00	7.8	2.8
Metropolitan Insurance	2.4	2.9	5.4	1.4	1.4	2.8	-1.3	8.3	6.2	9.1	6.9	1.86	7.6	2.8
Prudential Bache	2.3	2.0	4.5	0.0L	3.0	2.8	-0.3	4.0	6.1	9.4	6.9	2.10	8.3	3.1
U.S. Trust Co.	2.3	2.7	4.6	2.3	1.6	3.0	3.1	10.0	6.5	8.9	7.0	2.00	7.9	2.9
Univ. Of Michigan M.Q.E.M.	2.2	2.0	4.2L	1.4	2.2	3.3	0.1	2.0	6.3	9.0	7.1	2.01	7.7	2.9
Business Economics, Inc.	1.9L	2.3	4.2L	2.5	1.0	2.3L	2.0	5.0	6.2	8.5	7.3H	1.95	7.7	3.0
Siff, Oakley, Marks, Inc.	1.9L	2.6	4.5	2.1	1.1	2.9	-0.2	2.8	6.6	9.1	7.1	1.90	7.6	3.0
1986 CONSENSUS: JUNE Avg.	2.8	2.7	5.5	2.1	2.3	3.1	1.0	7.4	6.4	9.0	6.9	1.97	7.9	3.0
TOP 10	3.5	3.1	6.3	2.8	3.8	4.0	5.0	12.8	6.9	9.4	7.1	2.10	8.3	3.2
BOTTOM 10	2.3	2.1	4.7	1.3	1.1	2.5	-2.1	2.5	6.0	8.4	6.7	1.88	7.5	2.8
MAY Avg.	2.8	2.7	5.6	2.3	2.6	3.0	1.8	8.1	6.4	9.0	6.9	1.95	7.8	3.0
ACTUAL 1983	3.5	3.8	7.4	3.2	5.9	3.2	-1.8	42.5	8.6	12.0	9.6	1.70	6.8	2.4
1984	6.5	4.1	11.0	4.3	11.5	5.7	11.5	27.8	9.6	12.7	7.5	1.75	8.0	2.4
1985	2.2r	3.3	5.7	3.6	2.2	1.6	9.7	8.1r	7.5	11.4	7.1r	1.74	8.2	2.8
DIFFUSION INDEX	46%	44%	44%	33%	22%	69%	29%	43%	57%	59%	60%	66%	61%	58%

The only other usable seminal document is IBES, the Institutional Brokerage Estimate System. This monthly report chronicles all the estimates of individual company earnings made by serious analyst specialists, giving the high, low, and median on a per-share basis. It is axiomatic that a company that hits its IBES can do nothing but go down or remain unchanged—all the news is already discounted in the stock's price. If the IBES estimate is under-achieved, the stock reacts adversely to the bad news. If the analysts' estimates are lowballs, the stock rises to discount the unexpected good news. We are now moving into the hunting grounds of the contrarian. Unless you can go against the collective wisdom of the Street, you will make money only when the consensus makes money, which is hardly ever. If you are a few quarters behind the facts, consistently, you are not entitled to more than a salary, and even that is debatable.

I almost forgot the one other thing you need to know: *what's going on in the world*. Interestingly, it is easier to find out "what's on" there than here because you can paint with a much broader brush. It is also much cheaper. The $12 "World Economic Outlook" is published in April by the International Monetary Fund in Washington, D.C. It gives you all the baseline scenarios you need for the next five years, as prepared by a busload of economists who can afford to be pretty unbiased. All you have to do is pick the scenario you think has the highest probability of occurring and extrapolate the charts and graphs accordingly. Note the unem-ployment trends for Europe during the eighties, a very sick chart, and you decide what this means.

Keep in mind that if the Socialist-oriented politicians did every-thing right, they could not boost Gross National Product more than ½ percent per annum, and if they continued to do everything wrong, they would not reduce GNP more than ½ percent annually. Countries survive, and the beer tastes just as good when you're poor as when you're rich.

For a domestic overview, you can subscribe to *The Federal Reserve Bulletin* for $20 a year. Published monthly, it details the minutes of the Open Market Committee and shows how it interprets the vital signs of the economy. Changes in policy emphasis on the money supply are recorded, but lag the implementation by a month or two. The Fed may zig when it should be zagging, but at least you know how they are reading the entrails; so if you think they

UNEMPLOYMENT RATES

In Major OECD Countries

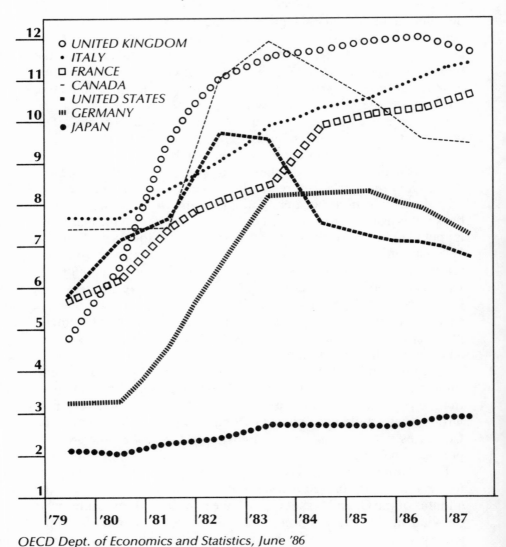

OECD Dept. of Economics and Statistics, June '86

are wrong, you assume they will rectify their errors, and you act in advance of their change in course. The Federal Reserve Bank of St. Louis publishes weekly cumulative data on the monetary base, bank deposits, business loans, and borrowings from the Federal Reserve Banks. There are some interpretive paragraphs on interest rates cogently expressed by this monetarist arm of the FRB. Their views do not necessarily reflect the official position of the Federal Reserve System. This unbiased document can be absorbed in five minutes and costs practically nothing.

There are only two kinds of books on the stock market that book publishers like to promote. One shows you how to take a C-note and turn it into a million in six months. Why only a million? This is a fantasy few people in the world have experienced, and there are a lot of charred bodies along the side of the road. The other, a Granville kind of book, reveals an esoteric formula for "reading" the market. It is a daily strategy for maximizing stock-market profits while minimizing risks. At least, it recognizes that markets do fluctuate and even go down, but you must exit before the fan spreads the manure. In the book trade, this is known as a "prescriptive" work that has enough structure to satisfy the reader's need for order and security. It is supposed to make the market understandable and is usually written by a journalist or market technician whose tax return might suggest that the country has not been able to build too many missile silos utilizing this person's tax payments. When Larry Zeiberg was at Hutton with me and Joe Granville, he used to have a standing daily dollar bet with Granville. Joe would call the market with a thumbs up or down at the opening bell. At the end of the year, Joe owed Larry for a lot of bad calls.

If all of Wall Street spends its time trying to figure out interest rates and corporate earnings power, maybe there is someplace else to look for the magic formula. You call it the X Factor, I call it the Unmarked-door Variable. There is always somebody operating behind the unmarked door who can affect stock prices. During 1984–86, Carl Icahn and Boone Pickens, whom the newspapers dubbed "controversial takeover artists," were not behind unmarked doors. But one was: He is Mike Milken of Drexel Burnham, operating out of Beverly Hills with a staff of hundreds. Michael raised the money for Pickens and Icahn by constructing many-tiered debt packages of high-yielding debentures with skimpy

BROKERS FAVORITES
TWENTY MOST HEAVILY FOLLOWED STOCKS
BY BROKERS: 1985

	Number of Analysts	Last Actual EPS	IBES Mean		Est. 5 yr. Growth Rate		Price	FY1 P/E	Yield	Mkt. Cap. $ Mil.	Sector
			FY1	FY2	Median	S.D.					
AMERICAN TEL & T	42	1.25	1.75	2.10	10	4	24	14	5.0	24531	TECHNOL
INTL BUS MACH	39	10.77	11.35	*13.49	15	2	119	11	3.7	73139	TECHNOL
NATL MED ENT	39	1.74	2.05	2.46	18	3	30	14	1.8	2243	HEALTH
ATLANTIC RCHFLD	38	2.21	6.47	8.07	8	5	58	9	7.0	12587	ENERGY
BELL ATLANTIC CO	38	9.94	10.62	11.29	6	1	91	9	7.5	9090	UTILITY
BELLSOUTH CORP	38	4.28	4.63	5.04	7	1	41	9	6.9	12261	UTILITY
EXXON	38	6.77	6.93	7.31	7	3	52	7	6.6	39880	ENERGY
HOSP CP AM	38	3.35	4.00	4.68	18	2	47	12	1.3	4154	HEALTH
STERLING DRUG	38	2.39	2.56	2.80	10	1	31	12	3.9	1860	HEALTH
U S WEST INC	38	9.24	9.71	10.44	7	1	80	8	7.2	7694	UTILITY
AMERITECH	37	10.17	10.98	11.68	6	1	93	8	7.1	9054	UTILITY
DIGITAL EQUIP	37	5.73	6.85	8.73	18	2	89	13	0.0	5207	TECHNOL
HUMANA INC	37	1.96	2.23	2.64	17	3	33	15	2.1	3172	HEALTH
INTEL CORP	37	1.70	0.67	1.53	24	7	24	35	0.0	2675	TECHNOL
TEXACO	37	4.45	4.44	4.88	7	3	37	8	8.1	8861	ENERGY
ABBOTT LABS	36	3.34	3.82	4.39	15	2	57	15	2.5	6833	HEALTH
AM MED INTL	36	1.64	2.22	2.58	17	3	25	11	2.9	2010	HEALTH
BANKAMERICA	36	1.96	2.15	2.87	11	6	19	9	8.1	2869	FINANCE
CHEVRON CORP	36	4.48	4.55	5.02	7	3	36	8	6.7	12273	ENERGY
MERCK & CO	36	6.71	7.47	8.47	13	2	112	15	2.8	8176	HEALTH

*Overestimated by 35 percent!

coverage of the interest payments due the bondholders. Mike controls all the players by his distribution capacity to raise money for their deals. It is he who has single-handedly shifted the balance of power from the corporate boardroom to the level playing field of the stock-market operators. It is he who has changed the valuation structure for a sizable part of the market. Oil stocks no longer sell on the basis of earnings and dividends, but rather what a barrel of reserves is worth today. It is cheaper to buy a barrel of oil from Milken than looking for it in Texas or Oklahoma. (As of this writing, Global Marine, a drilling-rig operation offshore, has just defaulted on $1 billion of debt.)

And the boardroom fights back. Ted Turner wants CBS for $175 a share. CBS stock ticks on the NYSE at par. Management offers to buy back 21 percent of its capitalization at $150 a share. The stock then ticks at $118, despite an earnings projection 20 percent lower. Nobody cares about earnings anymore, but rather what a company is worth in the real world. The stock market is no longer the financial world. The media companies sell on the basis of what entrepreneurial individuals are willing to pay for control. John Kluge takes out his Metromedia shareholders 50 percent above the last sale on the Big Board. A year later, Rupert Murdoch takes out Kluge and assumes the debt, packaged initially by Mike Milken and then repackaged by Milken for Murdoch.

What's the fuss all about? During the mid-sixties stocks sold on the Big Board at enormous earnings valuations and at huge premiums over book value. Today most equities sell at modest valuations and at little more than book. You had to be crazy to acquire companies in the sixties at 2 times book and 20 times earnings. Today the same companies sell at 10 times earnings and book value. You can structure a deal with high-yielding debentures and come out well—maybe five to ten times on your money in five years if your financial projections ring true.

Much of the time, the market is not about earnings at all, but rather what a few guys in the back room are willing to pay for control. Then why did IBM stock go down when earnings fell short? Well, nobody is about to structure a deal for IBM. It is just too big and too expensive, and maybe the Federal Reserve Board can manage it, but not even Milken has the buying power for this one. Maybe $5 billion, $10 billion, yes, but $100 billion, no. IBM is 5 percent of the Big Board's total value. You might as well try to buy the Pacific Basin from Red China, Hong Kong, and Singapore.

Give Wall Street credit for never lagging too far behind the realities. The computer quants now crank out data sheets called asset transfer values. The emphasis is on cash flow rather than earnings. This is how a businessman looks at a company. Not how high can I report earnings and pay taxes, but how much money can I control without paying any taxes. While the Treasury Reform Act proposals of 1986 deal with some of the inequities between the martini lunch crowd and the guys in the work boots, nobody has touched the deductibility of interest payments on acquisitions but the writing up of assets and real estate, thereby creating more depreciation and less tax revenues for the government is gone. It is forever easier to make a billion dollars in this country than to make your first million. Believe me, growing hashish in the Bronx is a much more difficult cash crop than oil-patch drilling. There are corporate biggies like General Electric that generate huge investment credits. Masters of financial leasing like GE don't pay any federal income tax. None.

Finally, Prentice-Hall take note. Here is the secret prescriptive formula for investing billions without risking a penny. First, find yourself a world-class company whose product you like. It could be anything: soda water, beer, cigarettes, a jet aircraft, or a newspaper. Maybe a Japanese car. Send for the company's annual report and proxy statement. Throw away the annual report and read the proxy statement. Look at the compensation schedule for management and how much stock they own. Look at the makeup of the board of directors. If it reads like a Who's Who, be careful. It's probably a passive board friendly to management. If management and the board have no meaningful stake in the company—at least 10 to 20 percent of the stock—throw away the proxy and look elsewhere or determine that you are going to force them to act in the shareholders' best interest. This is impossible unless you are prepared to acquire arithmetic control or get the majority of shares voted for you in the proxy balloting. Management usually wins a proxy fight because shareholders rarely read the proxy statement and don't vote, thereby effectively voting for management. Actually, it's impossible for a shareholder to get anything substantive on a proxy card short of a full-fledged proxy fight which could cost you $10 million to pursue.

THE UNMARKED-DOOR PHENOMENON

When I invested in The New York Times Company several years ago, I had no idea that an asset-transfer value thesis was brewing behind closed doors. I liked the paper. Management was on the stodgy side, but frugal. The Sulzbergers had worked for a century to make *The Times* a paper of record, and it was a great franchise. *The Times* throws off tens of millions in net free cash flow. But interestingly, the family was a net seller of stock when earnings took off. They hadn't heard of asset transfer values, either. While John Kluge was leveraging Metromedia, the Sulzbergers were paying down debt. Metromedia went around the clock 25 times in the early eighties, *The Times* four. If you're wrong, you file a Chapter 11 bankruptcy and ask the debenture holders to forego interest and take back longer-maturity paper and common stock. Milken will restructure the exchange offer for $5 million.

What can you learn about the profile of a successful investor? Warren Buffett, headman at Berkshire Hathaway, does it out of a frame house in Omaha, Nebraska. A passive investor with most of his capital, he votes his proxies dutifully for management, but picks them carefully. Our early 1985 count showed a $2 billion spread over only 10 investments. By early 1986 many of them were sold out to buy Capital Cities/ABC.

BERKSHIRE HATHAWAY'S MAJOR STOCK HOLDINGS
(EARLY 1986)

	Cost	Market
	(000s omitted)	
Affiliated Publications	$ 3,526	$ 55,710
Beatrice Companies, Inc.	106,811	108,142
Capital Cities/ABC	517,500	690,000
GEICO Corporation	45,713	595,950
Handy & Harman	27,318	43,718
Time, Inc.	20,385	52,669
The Washington Post Company	9,731	205,172
	$730,958	$1,751,361

Source: 1985 Annual Report

Almost all of the assets were concentrated in media and insurance, more than 75 percent in Geico and Capital Cities Broadcasting. Buffett likes the managements, likes their businesses. This thematic treatment runs throughout the portfolio. Positions like Geico have been in the portfolio for ten years, since Geico almost destroyed itself, cutting insurance-premium pricing, going for a greater share of the market. During 1985 representative holdings like ABC, Geico, *The Washington Post,* and General Foods repurchased sizable percentages of their stock—management was working for you. Later ABC and General Foods sold out at big premiums. Buffett doesn't care about next month's IBES earnings consensus report on IBM or anything else.

There is, finally, the symbolism of Buffett's portfolio. If a .400 hitter found only a handful of stocks that tickled his valuation standards—beware. And why media operators? *The Washington Post,* like *The New York Times,* is a paper of record. This means you have to read it. When Chrissie plays Martina in the finals at Wimbledon, the world stops what it's doing at 3:00 P.M. and watches television. Wall Street missed the franchise concept of media stocks. Advertising rates, circulation prices ratchet up annually. The presses print profits. They are inflation hedges, deflation hedges, everything. If you can't figure out the holes in investment research screens, you should not play. Better get yourself a McDonald's franchise. The rate of return is still exceptional for pushing french fries and Big Macs across the counter.

There are several thousand Certified Financial Analysts and hundreds upon hundreds of money managers out there playing the game of finding hidden values. Almost all of these practitioners think and act alike. When I put a photomontage by John Baldessari on our office wall, a delegation of my people told me I had to take it down, that it would offend many of our clients coming through New York. I threw my head marketing man out of the office, pleased that a work of art had triggered such a negative response. The piece had to be good. A year later, the subway vigilante, Goetz, shot four young blacks at close range and the grand jury refused to indict him, even though one or two had been shot in the back, running away. My marketing genius crawled back into my office on hands and knees and told me what a work of genius *Kiss/Panic* was. It was years ahead of the news.

This is what it's all about. You don't hit .400 unless the next pitch they're going to serve up is already processed in your head. When you swing, you hope you know.

One of the most complete realizations of an inflation scenario by a mutual-fund manager is the schemata created by John Neff for the Windsor Fund for 1985–1986. What it shows is that you

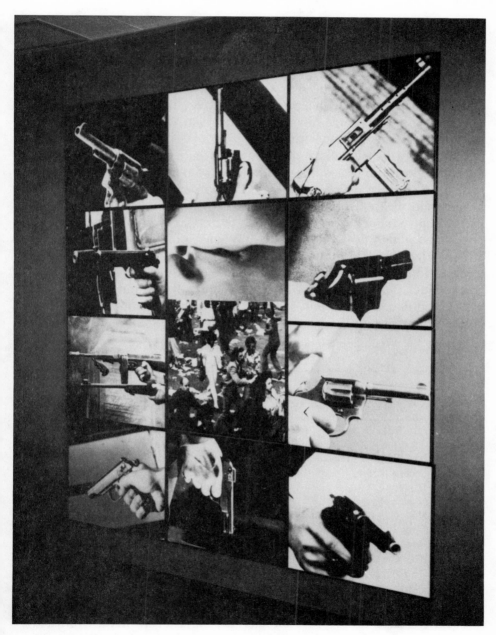

John Baldessari. *Kiss/Panic*. 1984. A photographic montage. 80″ × 72″.
Collection of Toni and Martin Sosnoff.

can take a lot of money, $4 billion, and concentrate on one concept: rising prices in a moderately growing economy. Neff had practically half his assets in 10 stocks with low volatility but he underperformed the market during the first half of 1986. Half the assets rested in cash, oils, and automobiles, and it hurt him. Actually, if your portfolio is not so conceptually reductive, the chances for even average performance dissipate. Contrast the reductiveness of successful professional investors like Neff and Buffett with the average professional or the public at large, overdiversified, or whose portfolio is a random collection of ragamuffins.

Years ago, a psychiatrist friend of a friend came to me with a portfolio written on the back of a brown paper bag. There were about fifty names, some of the stocks bought twenty years ago for reasons which no longer existed. When I pointed out that stocks like Alcoa and Mohawk Data Processing might not be the best thing today, this old practitioner with eyes darting off the walls like black pearls, snatched his list from my hands and stormed out of my office. I yelled out, "You are an incurable collector. Better go see somebody."

WINDSOR FUND'S 10 LARGEST EQUITY INVESTMENTS
(APRIL 30, 1986)

	Value in Millions of Dollars
Ford Motor	308
Citicorp	267
Royal Dutch Petroleum	244
General Motors	243
Tenneco	242
Atlantic Richfield	219
Shell Transport & Trading	173
Texas Utilities	165
First Interstate Bancorp	129
International Business Machines	123

Although I would quarrel with Neff's investments in the oils today, he is a valuation player who loves low-price-earnings securities that other professionals have learned to hate. Contrast this portfolio with Buffett's equity investments early in 1986.

Buffett's portfolio was largely an inflation hedge for the intermediate term. Most of his money is in the media sector, where we know you can raise rates if you have semimonopoly status. To an extent, today Buffett is a captive of previous successes. He bought media properties cheap, at valuations below the market. Today almost all media properties sell at 1.5 times the Standard & Poor's Index of 500 stocks. Capital Cities may be selling at 10 times 1990s earnings but it is pricy at almost 20 times the estimate for 1986. The tendency to rationalize the holding of one's successful plays can be disasterous. Witness the Morgan Guaranty Trust portfolio in mid–1972, which contained all the so-called great growth stocks at 30 to 40 times earnings. The schemata was equally simplistic: the best companies with positions on the board—Avon, Polaroid, Xerox, IBM, et al.—would do well in a worldwide environment of orderly growth. Early in 1973 the world moved into a recessionary mode. The earnings of the best and brightest did not hold up, and the stocks were drawn and quartered. Nothing is forever. No investment schemata I know has lasted out a decade, but a few like Warren's have played the cycle with Rostropovich virtuosity.

Outside my office window on Park Avenue, the striking hotel workers are marching towards the Waldorf-Astoria chanting to rhythmic blasts on their whistles. Whew——Whew. Whew—— Whew——Whew! The lowliest-paid help in the workforce is asking for 6 percent more, and the owners have offered 4 percent. Not exactly the stuff inflation is made of. There must always be conforming data stuffed into the meat processor. Look around.

Behind the unmarked door is no "they" crowd, but the guy who has made the right call and holds onto his working hypothesis until it stops working.

7 The Efficeint Mart Stocket

Once a money manager loses his nerve, fire him.
                    ——The author, in a moment of frustration.

THERE ARE lean years and fat years, just as the Good Book says. The art of money management is staying out when the returns are too skinny to make the game worthwhile. It works out that during the past thirteen years there were bunched rates of return for bonds, stocks, and cash equivalents. You could have earmarked all your money for Treasury bills since 1973 and done about as well as stocks and bonds without risking a single sleepless night.

The highest rate of return yielded a respectable 19.9 percent compounded annually. If you had successfully predicted each year that stocks, bonds, or cash would excel, you would have doubled the average return. The investment problem is not whether IBM or General Motors are any good. Is the market any good? Are bonds better, or is cash best? If you had stayed out of stocks during the down years, your annual rate of return averaged 15 percent. Few professionals have done better. The far right column is the great humbler. If you were good enough to own the top ten industries every year, your money would have compounded at 51 percent. Nobody is that good. The handful of professional money managers with outstanding records for this time span show returns between 14 and 20 percent. The average manager hovers around the return for bonds and Treasury bills. For all his spun wheels, he has provided no value added.

The thirteen-year table also belies the precept that, over time, prudent asset allocation will reward its practitioners. It didn't matter much whether you were 50 percent, 80 percent, or 100 percent in stocks or bonds, or whether you kept ample cash reserves. What mattered was a bedrock decision you made each year pinpointing the sector with the best return. All over the country corporate financial officers, endowment and foundation

IMPACT OF ASSET ALLOCATION ON POTENTIAL RETURNS
HISTORICAL RATES OF RETURN
13–YEAR PERFORMANCE OF STOCKS, BONDS AND CASH

Year Ended December	Highest Return Category	100% Stocks	100% Cash Equivalents	100% Long-Term Corp. Bonds	50% L-T Bonds/ 50% Cash Equiv.	Avg. Return of Top 10 Industries
1973	6.9	−14.8	6.9	1.1	4.0	36.0
1974	7.9	−26.4	7.9	−3.0	2.5	23.5
1975	37.2	37.2	5.8	14.6	10.2	121.0
1976	23.6	23.6	5.1	18.6	11.9	62.6
1977	5.2	−7.4	5.2	1.7	3.5	13.5
1978	7.1	6.4	7.1	−0.1	3.5	33.2
1979	18.2	18.2	10.0	−4.2	2.9	75.9
1980	32.3	32.3	11.4	−2.6	4.4	89.8
1981	14.2	−5.0	14.2	−1.0	6.6	26.8
1982	43.7	21.4	10.9	43.7	27.3	78.9
1983	22.4	22.4	8.9	4.7	6.8	49.3
1984	16.4	6.1	9.9	16.4	13.2	23.0
1985	31.7	31.7	7.3	30.1	18.7	65.1
Over last 13 years	19.9%	9.4%	8.5%	8.4%	8.7%	50.8%

Step I   Capture minimum zero return in down equity years. This brings 13–year equity return average to 15.3%.

Step II   Capture some percentage of top 10 industry returns.

Step III   Capture some percentage of the specific equities with the highest returns.

trustees wrestle with policy directives to their money managers, laying down maximum risk tolerances for equities of anywhere from 25 percent to 100 percent. Almost all are firm in the conviction that they are dealing squarely with the question of securing at least a minimum rate of return consistent with the long-term needs of their institution. In fact, all they have done is hamstrung their investment professionals from putting all the assets to work in the category with the highest return.

Trustees unwittingly expose their funds to mediocre results. This is how investment committees invest, some knowingly and others unknowingly. The smart, but very conservative, establishment committees put limits on equity percentages for their money managers because they retain harrowing memories of 1973 and 1974, when Morgan and its ilk failed to get out of the market.

Foundation and pension-fund money in this country sat for haircuts of 40 to 50 percent. It is very difficult for a university to pay good wages to professors or build new dormitories when its endowment fund collapses. It is even more difficult to convince the alumni to fork over additional sums if your university is a consistent loser.

The other "they" who invest megabillions in securities markets play other kinds of games for different reasons—all destined to produce indifferent investment results. Aside from the money-market funds that invest $200 billion in short-term paper averaging no more than 120 days in maturity, there is the mutual-fund industry, which almost always remains fully invested. They sell their funds to the uninitiated on the basis of a professed belief in growth in America 365 days out of the year. The thirteen-year table shatters that belief. The public pension funds totaling hundreds of billions are discovering the stock market. Until recently, state and municipal laws had restricted equity investments to a small percentage of assets. The stock market was viewed as a den of thieves, and these pension dollars languished in long-maturity bonds, and even municipals. The results were dismal.

The corporate pension funds play a more subtle game. The pension fund is viewed as a profit center. If investment results are good, you don't have to add annually to the pot. All you do is periodically increase the actuarial assumptions for the plan so that from time to time the corporation can pull millions out of these funds and add them to earned surplus.

In recent years, the corporate sector has boosted rate-of-return assumptions for pension plans from the 4–6 percent level to 7–9 percent. Many large corporations are at 9 percent, and I know a few that have convinced their actuaries to agree that a 10 percent assumption is reasonable. They do this by steadily increasing the asset allocation of their funds into long-maturity bonds with yields to maturity averaging over 10 percent. Corporations are doing just what state and municipal plans did thirty years ago, with the exception that they are operating in a period of high bond yields rather than the 4 percent paper bought by many public funds. Thus, more and more the corporate sector is going to want to increase actuarial assumptions and thereby move more money into bonds. The implications for the demand side of equities is less cash flow and perhaps lower price-earnings ratios five to ten years out if equities become less serviceable investments for the big pension funds. Some way, there is always enough money around for a good story, so I tend to discount long-term money-flow analysis as it impinges on stock-market prices.

The agenda for all the billion-dollar-and-up money pools is not what it appears to be on the surface. The name of the game is not making money, but doing what is considered prudent and socially acceptable within one's peer group. If the name of the game truly is making money, there would be no restrictions on how to invest. The thirteen-year table suggests that your head must be freed to go for it—the *it* being an above-average rate of return.

Barr Rosenberg, writing on modern portfolio theory, notes that a good investor is a good storyteller in the sense that the stories are true more often than not and that the money manager as a storyteller of assets must exceed the skill of his competition. An investment methodology available to anyone is useless unless it is supplemented by unique insight and implementation. It is the unusually wise and creative arrangement of the elements of the story that leads to success. If the prescient money manager can be compared to an artist, how then can it be meaningful to subject him to a rigorous statistical cathechism? Unlike a work of fiction or a painting that is more than the sum of its parts in terms of aesthetic impact and symbolism, an investment portfolio is never more than the sum of its parts. If the money manager is a storyteller of asset allocation, his portfolio should be 100 percent consistent with his artistic insight. The finished product should reflect a construction whose risk/reward trade-off is optimal. Once we have fixed the schemata for the investment setting as to where the highest rate of return will be attained—stocks, bonds, or Treasury bills—the computer button is pushed to find the best recipe for the feast. Consistency and discipline throughout the process is as critical as implementation. If the money manager doesn't have the courage to implement both his insights and what his methodology work dictates, he should be fired. Obviously, if he is proven wrong time after time, he should be pushing spaghetti in Hoboken.

In *Group Think,* author Irving Janis notes that experts trained in statistics make mistakes in drawing inferences from the information available to them when they are making vital decisions. Analysts overloaded with complicated information to be processed in order to arrive at an optional choice often resort to oversimplification and thus fail to weigh the complexity of the issues at hand. "Then, too, there are ego-defensive tendencies and all sorts of self-serving biases that incline a person to lapse into wishful thinking rather than expending the effort to obtain the best available realistic information and to evaluate it critically." Look what happened to the space shuttle *Challenger*.

The futility of even the Federal Reserve Board's attempts to temper its federal funds rate to the decelerating or accelerating rate of change in the Industrial Production Index is suggested in the following graph. Except at extremes such as mid–1980 and the summer of 1982, the change in the funds rate relative to the production index is random. It suggests that the funds rate, a proxy of Federal Reserve Board policy, as applied to smoothing out economic activity, is impossibly difficult to apply constructively despite all the computer power available to the board. It raises the question of whether the money manager should waste his time examining weekly, monthly, or even quarterly changes in Federal Reserve Board actions except at crisis points. Too much information can often kill an insight, which perhaps should be on another level. The board's misplaced perceptions on inflation governed policy in the early 1980s. Until economic activity plummeted in mid–1982, it refused to take any action. It couldn't even think straight. By the end of 1984 the Fed had finally synchronized the funds rate with the decelerating industrial production index. The zigs and zags were in the right direction.

The difficulty lies in being right most of the time. It is endemic to the business. Since the peak in 1968, we spent fifteen years paying for the sins of an unruly Wholesale Price Index. Induced initially by Lyndon Johnson's escalation in Vietnam, it was perpetuated by the budgetary profligacy of succeeding politicians. The net interest payments on the national debt are heading off the page. The interest burden is the Trojan horse. We have opened our gates to it, and it will destabilize the country if it is permitted to continue. Unfortunately, politicians and voters respond only to gut issues like unemployment, high interest rates, and bringing the boys home. When Martin Feldstein, chairman of the Council of Economic Advisers, pointed to the debt albatross, he was told by Treasury Secretary Regan to shut up or be right somewhere else. It proved unhappily, once more, that politicians lead economics and securities markets wherever they wish them to go.

FEDERAL FUNDS RATE vs. INDUSTRIAL PRODUCTION INDEX

1975-1986/3

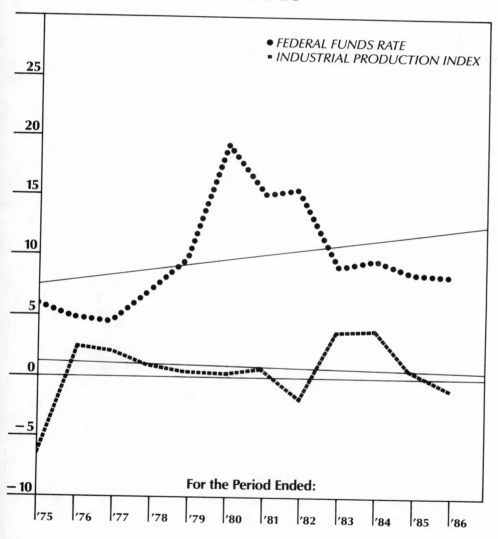

INTEREST PAYMENTS ON THE NATIONAL DEBT/GNP

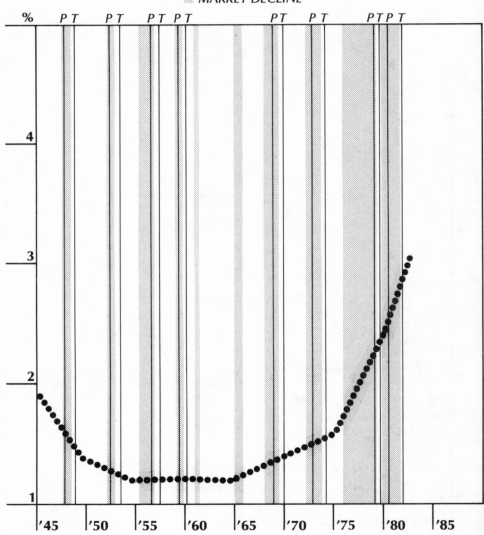

P PEAK OF ECONOMIC CYCLE   T TROUGH OF ECONOMIC CYCLE
MARKET DECLINE

INDUSTRY PERFORMANCE RELATIVE TO THE S&P
TOP TEN

6 Months June		12/31/85	
S&P 400	20	S&P 400	16
Tobacco	37	Tobacco	29
Household Appliances	30	Household Appliances	26
Building Matls Comp	23	Building Matls Comp	23
General Merch.	19	General Merch.	18
Hospital Supplies	18	Entertainment	18
Entertainment	18	Beverage-Soft Drink	16
Chemicals	17	Chemicals	15
Gaming Cos.	17	Hospital Supplies	15
Publishing-Newsp	16	Gaming Cos.	14
Beverages-Soft Drink	14	Hotel-Motel	14

BOTTOM TEN

Electronics-Semi.	(10)	Copper	(8)
Coal	(10)	Metals-Miscellaneous	(11)
Metals-Miscellaneous	(11)	Comp & Bus Equip	(12)
Copper	(12)	Tire & Rubber	(12)
Air Freight	(13)	Railroad	(12)
Railroad	(14)	Air Freight	(15)
Natural Gas	(17)	Natural Gas	(17)
Commun-Equip/Mfrs	(18)	Commun-Equip/Mfrs	(20)
Oil Well Eq & Svcs	(26)	Oil-Domestic Integ.	(23)
Oil-Domestic Integ.	(28)	Oil Well Eq & Svcs	(26)

Industry Ranking Based on Relative Percentage Change Thru 6/4/86

The big intuitive call in the spring of 1984, when the stock market wobbled and bond markets looked demoralized, was whether President Reagan would get his way or be forced by his own party to stretch out his military shopping list. The short-lived utility of the major calls on the direction of the economy and political drift is highlighted by looking at the establishment economists' forecasts for 1984. By as early as March, the calls on unemployment, interest rates, and the presidential election were outdated. The unemployment rate already had dropped to 7.7 percent. Long-term Treasury bonds rushed up to the 12.5 percent level, and Mondale was fading before the Kennedy-like charm of Gary Hart. Note the political tone to the AFL-CIO economist's reading. Oswald put long-term

FORECASTERS PREDICT 1984'S ECONOMIC AND POLITICAL LANDSCAPE

Name	Affiliation	Real Economic Growth	Inflation	Jobless Rate	Long-Term Treasury Bonds	Three-Month Treasury Bills	President Elect
Lawrence Chimerino	Chase Econometrics	4 %	5.5%	8 %	11.7%	9.2%	Reagan
Otto Eckstein	Data Resources	4.5%	4.8%	7.8%	11.5%	8.2%	Reagan
Robert Eggert	Blue Chip Forecast	4.4%	5.3%	8 %	11.5%	9.2%	Reagan
A. Nicholas Filippello	Monsanto	4 %	6 %	7.7%	12.5%	10 %	Reagan
Avery Haak	Dayton Hudson	4.5%	5.5%	7.5%	12.5%	9.5%	—
Walter Heller	University of Minnesota	4 %	4.5%	7.8%	13 %	9.2%	Reagan
Arthur Laffer	A. B. Laffer Associates	6 %	5 %	7.4%	11 %	7.7%	Reagan
Tor Meloe	Texaco	4.3%	5.5%	7.5%	12 %	9 %	Reagan
Richard O'Brien	Hewlett-Packard	4 %	5.3%	7.8%	12 %	9 %	Reagan
Leif Olsen	Citibank	3.9%	6.2%	7.7%	12.5%	10 %	—
Rudolph A. Oswald	A.F.L.-C.I.O.	3 %	6.1%	8.1%	13.5%	12 %	Mondale
Albert T. Sommers	Conference Board	3.9%	6.1%	7.7%	10.8%	8.3%	Reagan
Donald H. Straszheim	Wharton Econometrics	4.9%	5 %	7.4%	11 %	7.7%	—
Marina Whitman	General Motors	4.3%	5.5%	7.6%	12 %	9.5%	—
John O. Wilson	Bank of America	4.2%	5.6%	7.8%	11.8%	10 %	Reagan

Notes: Real economic growth and inflation are the fourth-quarter 1983 to fourth-quarter 1984 change in real gross national product and in the Consumer Price Index; unemployment rate and interest rates are those prevailing at year-end 1984, and the President-elect category reflects a disinterested appraisal of current environment, not an endorsement. Where no name appears, the forecaster made no prediction.

Treasuries at 13.5 percent and the jobless rate at 8.1 percent, a non sequitur considering his choice of 3 percent GNP growth.

Going back to the table on rates of return, note the conformity in the first half of 1986 of the top ten and bottom ten industry performers to a clear-cut schema. The best performing groups were the non-cyclical, consumer-related companies and beneficiaries of low interest rates. Just what you would expect in a slow growing economy with an overlay of declining interest rates. The worst sectors clustered around the industrials and oils, sectors hurt by declining unit production and commodity price weakness. The consensus expected the economy to gather momentum along with inflationary pricing and sharply higher interest rates. It didn't happen.

Every six months, Callan Associates, a pension-fund consultant, surveys a cross section of money managers, including us. They solicit our economic and market projections for the following six to twelve months. For 1986, the consensus projected a decline in bonds and a 4 percent gain in stock prices. It was the smallest increase in stock prices ever projected since inception of the survey in 1973. This forecast turned out to be dead wrong almost from the start. By mid-June the market had soared 18 percent, one of the strongest showings in recent history. Bonds weren't too far behind—up 13 percent. It is axiomatic with us that as our projections approach the consensus, we know there is quicksand ahead.

One conclusion we reached in mid-1986 was that interest rates had more room to move on the upside than on the downside. A computer simulation showed what would happen to rates-of-return for intermediate-term Treasury notes. If rates moved up or down 75 basis points from the 8 percent level, we bracketed the return between 5 percent and 10 percent. If we guessed wrong and rates declined, we would still make 5 percent on our money, compared with a 14 percent return for Salomon Brothers Bond Index, with much longer duration. If interest rates headed toward 9 percent, our 5 percent return would still look respectable compared with Treasury bills and the nominal 1.75 percent return for the Salomon Brothers Index. The big decision we made was to keep our money in the stock market where the rate-of-return expectation was higher than bonds. This strategy flowed easily from the simplistic rate-of-return analysis that called for an upward bias to interest rates stopping at the 9 percent level. If interest rates rushed past 9 percent, we would burn our fingers more severely than if we took the easy road of intermediate-term bonds. The pressure to perform at least a few percentage points better than securities markets never stops.

How many economists make money in securities markets? Well, there was Keynes. There are thousands of hard-working securities analysts and hundreds of portfolio managers responsible for money pools ranging from $1 billion to $30 billion. Few are money makers for their clients and themselves. By now you know why. It is tough to have the right feel for what is going to happen next and then implement your investment strategy courageously.

The comparison of money management to the minimalist art movement of the late sixties and early seventies is downright irresistible. Minimalism, with its roots in the geometric traditions of constructivism, was later to reflect the restrictiveness of geometry (postminimalism) but in its essence was nothing more or less than the crux of money management today, an abstract reductivist enterprise. Typically, Sol LeWitt's work incorporates this generalized sphere of geometric structure. Shown on page 110 are his hollow metal boxes ornamented in striped pattern sequences. The work suggests a compulsiveness toward pattern making. And the art is in the thinking, not the doing. Anyone following this artist's directions can execute such a piece. The originator literally paints himself out of the picture. The only thing left is the originality of the idea. Not coincidentally, minimalism flourished during Vietnam, when anyone under thirty was invested in "dropping out." Artists rejected painting and sculpture as too establishment. And they chose to deal in junk, rags, rope, nails, and cheap vinyl. The preferred look was geometric, and complexity was generated through the utilization of a grid or a serial structure. Finally, preoccupation with exactness, measurability, and dependability led to its own demise. Several minimalists later surfaced as conceptual art and earthworks practitioners.

In money management, the sequence is inverted. The conceptualists surfaced in the late sixties. Nobody looked at balance sheets then. The next recession carried growthmanship out to sea, including that member of the fiscal establishment, Morgan Guaranty Trust. The revulsion felt from losing the game has led to a more disciplined approach to investing. Everyone now talks to his computer, seeking specific answers to narrowly defined questions. The computer spits out multicolored charts, graphs, and scatter diagrams just as the minimalists did in the sixties. This urge toward seriality and reductiveness is exemplified in our scenario spectrum analysis that follows.

Another mournful dirge burst from Henry Kaufman's mouth early in 1985. If the government continued in its profligacy, if capacity utilization climbed past 80 percent, if unemployment declined further, if GNP highballed along at 5 percent a quarter . . . If! If! "Long-term treasuries could exceed the 1982 highs of 15.4 percent." The stock market shrugged off this pronouncement. After all, many stock groups had already suffered 10 to 30 percent shrinkage. By mid–1985 the bond market was outperforming the stock market, and thirty-year government bonds were approaching 10 percent yields, a new low for the eighties. Al Wojnilower was equally off the mark in his year-end forecast for 1985. "Economic growth will quicken and short—as well as long—interest rates will be higher than now, sometimes by a little and sometimes by a lot."

In January 1985 Henry seconded Al. "The Federal Funds rate may reach 10½–11%, and yields on long governments will probably rise to 13–13½% by the summer."

At our morning investment meeting the four money managers raised their hands, one by one, voting to sell our 60 percent position in equities down to zero. Yet they left the exact timing of the implementation to me. The monthly economic readings were too tough to call. Retail sales had started to weaken, but automobiles showed late strength. Consumer credit and durable-goods orders dipped, but not enough to worry about, and housing starts had jumped above 2 million units. The GNP reading might range as high as 7 percent for the first quarter. If autos sold briskly into the spring, Detroit would not cut back production seriously, thereby deferring any meaningful slowing in the economy to the second half. Henry might be right! I pointed out that the market was ripe for a political event.

The internal pressures on Reagan from his party could lead to a stretchout pronouncement on defense spending. The question was when. If action came soon, credit markets would be assuaged. If tabled until the fall campaign, fiscal policy would be relegated

ATALANTA/SOSNOFF CAPITAL CORPORATION
CAPITAL MARKET SCENARIOS
1984/1985

Scenario	Description	Yield to Maturity		Total Return	Scenario Spectrum
		Current	Expected		
A	SAL. BONDS	12.53	10.26	34.2%	VERY POSITIVE
	4.0 DURATION	11.91	9.76	19.9%	Falling Rates
	CASH	10.00	9.00	9.0%	GNP Growth = 2.5%
B	SAL. BONDS	12.53	12.52	12.9%	POSITIVE
	4.0 DURATION	11.91	11.70	13.0%	Flat Rates
	CASH	10.00	10.00	10.0%	GNP Growth = 3.5%
C	SAL. BONDS	12.53	12.52	12.9%	POSITIVE
	4.0 DURATION	11.91	11.70	13.0%	Flat Rates/Rising P/E's
	CASH	10.00	10.00	10.0%	GNP Growth = 3.5%
D	SAL. BONDS	12.53	13.00	9.1%	NEGATIVE
	4.0 DURATION	11.91	12.20	11.2%	Rising Rates
	CASH	10.00	10.50	10.5%	GNP Growth = 3.5%
E	SAL. BONDS	12.53	14.00	2.3%	VERY NEGATIVE
	4.0 DURATION	11.91	13.22	7.9%	Rising Rates
	CASH	10.00	11.50	11.5%	GNP Growth = 4.75%

1983 Yearend Call

New Call in Mid-January

B O N D S

D S

Scenario	Period	S & P Earnings Per Share	Price/ Earnings	S & P Yield	Total Return	Scenario Spectrum	
CURRENT	12 Mo. 3/31 (E)	$15.40	10.2	4.5%	N/A		
A	1984 1985	$17.00 $18.00	11.5 11.5	4.0% 4.0%	28.8% 36.1%	VERY POSITIVE Falling Rates GNP Growth = 2.5%	
B	1984 1985	$17.50 $19.50	10.3 10.3	4.0% 4.0%	19.0% 32.2%	POSITIVE Flat Rates GNP Growth = 3.5%	1983 Yearend Call
C	1984 1985	$17.50 $19.50	11.0 11.0	4.0% 4.0%	26.9% 40.9%	POSITIVE Flat Rates/Rising P/E's GNP Growth = 3.5%	
D	1984 1985	$17.50 $19.50	9.0 9.0	4.5% 4.5%	5.0% 16.5%	NEGATIVE Rising Rates GNP Growth = 3.5%	New Call in Mid-January
E	1984 1985	$18.50 $16.00	8.0 8.0	4.5% 4.5%	− 1.0% −13.8%	VERY NEGATIVE Rising Rates GNP Growth = 4.75%	

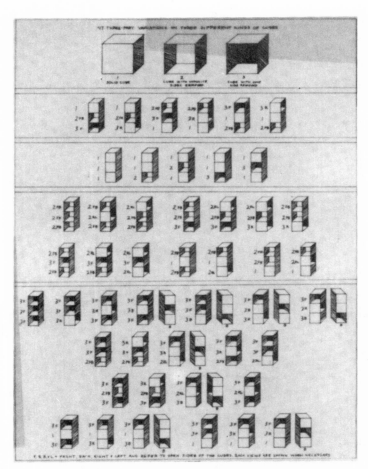

Sol LeWitt. *Three Part Variation on 3 Different Trends*. 1968 Photograph and construction. Private collection.

to just another campaign plan. At the close of markets early in March, Reagan made his first shift toward an arms budget stretch-out, and pressure came off securities markets at the opening bell the next day. It forced us to review our scenario construction that ranged from very positive to very negative. Early in January we had shifted from a positive scenario of flat interest rates to rates climbing to 13 percent. The expected returns on stocks and bonds changed markedly. We had projected bonds to earn at least their coupon during 1984, but under the rising-rate scenario, this return would diminish below Treasury bills. Early on, stocks looked as if they could put together another good performance back-to-back with 1983, but now the valuation multiplier for earnings would decline and stocks, too, showed just a nominal return. We had shifted almost half our assets into the bond sector with two years' duration, hardly more venturesome than T-bills.

More is less. The strength in the Industrial Production Index was eating up factory capacity. By now utilization had recovered from 69 percent to 81 percent. By definition, anything close to 85 percent reads too hot. Inflation plays like Phibro-Salomon, and Alcoa glowed brightly. Any change in Federal Reserve Board policy emphasis toward easement was pushed out farther. The year's performance hung in the balance. If the buoyant economy lasted several more quarters, we were caught without much money in commodity cyclicals. If Volcker worried about a feverish country with enormous credit demands in the system, our call for interest rates stopping at 13 percent was out the window. The easy call would have been to go with the flow. High interest rates would not inhibit housing and autos. Inventory accumulation was expensive only when final demand faltered. The decline in the dollar suggested that our trade deficit would subside and exports rise to meet accelerating demand from European and Japanese economies.

There were other straws to catch. The Japanese had cut interest rates after the yen appreciated 5 percent in a matter of days. The dollar could not decline much more if the disparity in our rates and the rest of the world widened. The Wall Street pundits on investment policy had shifted to a capital-goods orientation, over-weighting basic industrials and commodity plays. Merrill Lynch's analyst was projecting earnings of Cummins Engine, a maker of heavy duty diesel motive power, at $20 a share in 1985 after a deficit-ridden 1983. By mid–1985 Cummins was laying off thousands of factory workers in its Columbus, Indiana, facilities. What is obvious never makes money. If Merrill Lynch believes that Cummins Engine will earn $20 a share, so does all the world and it was in the price of the stock ($79).By late 1986 Cummins was reporting quarterly deficits.

Taking the other side was more enticing. Interest-sensitive securities like money-center banks and savings and loans already were selling as if 15 percent interest rates lurked around the corner. The nondurables growth stocks like Budweiser and McDonald's, both with rising shares of their markets, languished at low valuations. And so on. We decided to stay put with our invested position structured on scenario D. Economic momentum would slow to a 3.5 percent rate in the second half. If interest rates held in the 13 percent channel, a period of orderly trendline growth might prevail. (This was the right call.) Less would be more. The Federal Reserve Board might not be forced to tighten the credit supply. After all, there were still Argentina and Brazil out there as debtors to the tune of almost $200 billion. If dollar-denominated debt carried higher rates, those countries just might change their names and default. From mid-1984 through 1986 there was no reason to change from the slow growth scenario.

The processing of data has no meaning until it leads to a conclusion that ponders the dialectics of all the changes. If interest rates are going to 15 percent—what next? A recession or a rapid increase in money supply? How long will interest rates go up? How long will earnings of corporate America rise? Is the $19.50-per-share projection for the market in 1987 the last good year or is there more? Nobody knows. But you must have a point of view. Then parse that into a scenario and see where you come out. If your insight is less than perfect, you still may have the broad configurations on rates of return correct. If not, you must move the scenario to its next shade in the spectrum of positive-to-negative that seems to fit. The least rewarding scenario is always the consensus, and the most profitable the one that moves farthest off center, not because there is more data put on the table—nobody can match an econometric model—but because the insights are on a more abstract level.

This is a computerized chart in which the readout is pure, unadulterated garbage. We were looking for a relationship between

RATE OF CHANGE IN AGGREGATE DEBT vs. INTEREST RATES

1973-1985

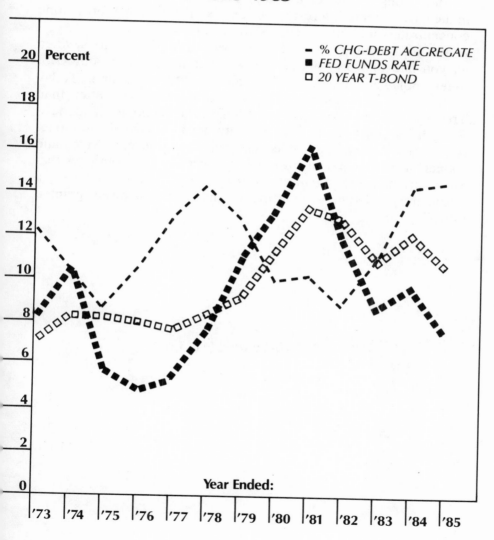

short-term and long-term interest rates in terms of changes in the total demand for credit. You would think that interest rates would rise when the demand for money swells. The chart proves just the opposite. Interest rates can rise for years while the demand for credit declines, and decline for years while the demand for credit increases. Furthermore, the focus on GNP momentum as it relates to forecasting credit demand may be a totally irrelevant variable in the movement of interest rates. Yet that is what most forecasting concentrates on, with no consistent accuracy.

And so, I thought, if only I were operating in the twenties, when all you had to worry about was whether the guys in your U.S. Steel pool were double-crossers and might unload first. Today there is so much money chasing a rate of return better than Treasury bills that you have to out-think the econometric models. Sometimes you have to add and subtract in a surrealistic mode. Arakawa's *Lemons*. More is less because it is excessive, and sooner or later less leads to more. I never found a computer that knew anything but standard arithmetic. Like perfect pitch for a musician, good timing for a money manager is a rarely granted gift.

8 The Art of Packaging

I LOVE to read a finely crafted prospectus. Its symbolism can be as abstract as a Grimm fairy tale. In the spring of 1983 red herrings littered my desk at the rate of a dozen a day, ranging from personal computer manufacturers in business about twelve months to genetic laboratories that wouldn't have any product to sell for three years. The common denominator in these deals was the enormous dilution suffered by the last-in investor and the reciprocal benefits to the promoters and underwriters who put up virtually nothing. Actually, that summer you could sell anything to the public, and everything was sold. The underwriting calendar moved from a normal monthly rate of $0.5 billion to $4 billion. Almost all new issues were successfully placed, and often expanded to meet demand. The public speculation in trash coexisted with the Big Board's shuffling of its stodgy merchandise; the multinationals of the late sixties and early seventies had tired blood. Stocks like Procter & Gamble, Avon, Pepsico, and Philip Morris sold under 10 times earnings despite returns on equity averaging consistently over 20 percent. Nobody cared because they didn't have a story, and the market wanted stories.

An operator like Steve Wynn of The Golden Nugget split his stock 5-to-1 to get it back down into the teens, so when the public went to his casinos and saw the crowds bumping up against the crap tables, they would go home and buy a hundred shares. Almost all the money managers grossly underestimated the public's need to get back in the game. After washing out in 1974 near the bottom, during the next nine years the small investor moved out of mutual funds and the stock market and into money-market funds. Short-term funds bulged to $200 billion by year-end 1982, and have stayed there. The Standard & Poor's Index of 500 Stocks became the domain of professional money managers. Yet by early 1983 gambling stocks and nearly defunct airlines like Pan Am and Western doubled in price and were able to raise hundreds of millions of dollars, underwriting bonds, stock, convertibles, and warrants. When Merrill Lynch's stock hit par and sold at 3 times book value, Merrill sold 2 million shares publicly. Even the WASP-y companies couldn't stand being upstaged by the Hoboken securities houses peddling their wares to the Seventh Avenue garmentos across the river. The players bought anything, sight unseen, assured by hundreds of streetwise brokers that they could bang out the goods at an overnight premium and promptly move on to the next issue coming out of the box.

There is always an outstanding prospectus that sums up the cycle. It is a herring that adumbrates greed, packages a plausible concept, and has a cast of characters well known to all for promotional flair and business acumen. Integrated Barter International got my vote. Packaged by Southeast Securities of Florida, Inc., located in Hoboken, New Jersey. Sixty million units were floated at 10 cents consisting of equal amounts of stock and warrants. The Hoboken underwriter took down 10 percent of the value of the underwriting as his commission—about double the normal underwriting discount for respectable merchandise. You should know that the total capitalization of Integrated Barter was 180 million shares and 60 million warrants. Keep in mind that the company was just in the planning stage and had not yet engaged in operations. There was actually just $4 million in cash available for acquisition of barter businesses and an inventory of barterable goods and services. Oh, yes. Our Hoboken underwriter had been subjected to years of SEC surveillance and sanctions.

There appeared not to be any haste to start operations, either. The next twelve months were needed to investigate its chosen vocation. In the meantime, the company set up headquarters in a midtown-New York suite with a temporary telephone number. The management stated boldly that it knew hardly anything about the barter business:

> The company has not engaged any independent organization to conduct a study of the barter industry. Accordingly, it is management's view of the opportunity to develop a viable business within the barter industry that alone forms the basis for this corporate undertaking. . . . No member of management has previously been involved in either the management of a business engaged in barter or in the acquisition of such a business.

(The SEC will allow you to underwrite anything as long as there is full disclosure.)

The offering price of 10 cents bore some scrutiny. My prospectus proclaimed blandly: "The public offering price of the units offered hereby bears no relationship to any recognized criterion of value." In fact, the prospectus draws attention in capital letters to the immediate dilution of public shareholders of approximately 8 cents of their 10-cent cost. Moreover, again in capital letters, the prospectus warned all takers that these securities should be purchased only by persons who can afford to absorb a total loss on their investment. Widows, stay away! As of August 1982 there was a net deficit in book value for the company's stock. Evidently, the promoters put in hardly anything for their 180 million shares. Their book value would be increased by almost $3.5 million if the underwriting were successful. It was.

The dimensions of this underwriting began to take shape. We were looking at a total capitalization of 240 million shares—not a lot less than IBM's. The promoters knew little or nothing about the business they were embarking upon. [And the public's 10-cent stock was diluted down to 2 cents from go.] There was $4 million available to do business. Temporary headquarters were set up in the corporation's counsel's space, but some 2,500 square feet will be leased upon consummation of the offering. Twenty-five hundred square feet is 50' × 50', or something less than a regulation volleyball court. One more fact: by early June the stock had moved up tenfold to approximately a buck a share. Soooo . . . hold on to your hat.

A couple of guys with a grabby idea found an underwriter who placed $5 million worth of stock that was now selling for a total market capitalization of approximately $240 million, despite the fact that nobody knew much about the barter business and there was just $4 million in cash to start operations with. If Integrated Barter were to make 100 percent on its capital base during the first two years—assuming that it took the initial twelve months to survey its field—the $4 million income spread over 240 million shares counts out to little less than 2 cents a share spread over two years. Excepting the hawking of marijuana sticks, nobody in business makes 100 percent on his capital base repetitively. Phibro, perhaps the preeminent trading company in the world, during the oil shortage of 1980, when prices escalated to $40 dollars a barrel, made over $600 million in operating profits but no more than a 30-percent return on its capital base. Phibro has been in business fifty or a hundred years, with a worldwide network of commodities traders. They could take down your pants and sell them before you could cry for help because traders have the incentive of a percentage of profits and work like animals eighteen hours a day.

Who are the principals of Integrated Barter? Well, I know one or two of them from the heady days of the sixties, when speculation was in the air—just like in the summer of 1983. Robert Goldsamt is the headman here, and he made his mark as a founder of American Medicorp in 1968, working intensively at acquiring hospitals. Bobby worked at this for four years, sold out too early, and then moved on to do a few things in the hospital-supply sector in Europe, later developing properties in Aspen, Colorado. Bobby owns 81,600,000 shares of Integrated Barter. The only other large shareholder that I knew briefly, again, in the breezy sixties, is Martin Solomon, who was a money manager then. I think he ran money for the Fund of Funds for a while, came to New York to manage some assets, then relocated back to London, and is now back in New York. Marty was a concept player then and still is consistent. Marty, Bobby, and a few insiders paid a total of $30,000 for 120 million shares. I could be wrong, but I remember that Bobby and Marty loved to work and loved to play, unlike the Phibro traders who just work and will kill for an extra nickel.

Who am I to say that such a talented promoter as Bobby Goldsamt won't implement this barter concept into another Phibro within time? After all, Bobby saw an opening in the hospital-management sector and went on the road with his partner for months at a time, buying up privately owned hospitals and forging them into a chain where the economies of scale and professional management bore fruit. He was hardly more than thirty years old then, and the entrepreneurial spirit never lies dormant too long. Word was that Allen & Co. was coming in for some mezzanine financing, providing $15 million to buy up barter operators. There are enough people on both coasts, in Aspen, London, and wherever, who itch to back Bobby. Bobby's name in the prospectus was enough for them, and they bid his goods up from 10 cents to a dollar, overnight. How many speculators read the prospectus carefully? Who knows? The urge to bet $2 to win on a long shot is a recurrent thing, and you give in, sometimes.

When I asked my trader to get me a prospectus, he punched out the price on his cathode tube—it was $25/32$s bid, and he wanted to know on the spot if he could buy 10,000 shares. All he saw was that the offering price was 10 cents and that I had asked for the prospectus—it was worth a $10,000 bet to him. Multiply the "hims" by just a thousand and you get 10 million shares. This is how a promotion feeds on itself until the facts eventually tell the story and the stock begins to relate to the same financial realities that govern the prices of IBM, General Motors, American Telephone, and other stocks. For the initial six months or year, nobody wants to know the facts. It was as though we were back in the Depression, when everyone bought an Irish Sweepstakes ticket that was supposed to take you out of the Bronx forever.

On or about the same time that Integrated Barter rose tenfold, Dennis Barnhart, the president of Eagle Computer, totaled himself a few hours after his company was underwritten by Hambrecht & Quist. At that moment, he was then worth $8 million on paper. Barnhart had crashed his Ferrari near company headquarters, in Los Gatos, California, legally intoxicated and accompanied by a yacht-broker friend on his way to buy a yacht, on his way to cash in on a good time. Eagle delivered a desktop microcomputer that did everything any big desktop model does for less money—that is, until IBM dropped its price another 20 percent. The underwriting was withdrawn at $13 a share and reoffered a few days later at $12. Initially, the offering gapped two dollars and the second time around, after the fatal car crash, the stock moved to a $5 premium and then peaked at $24 a few days later. The story had made every newspaper in the country and evidentally touched off a wave of speculation by people who would not have heard of Eagle Computer—ever. This was June 9, and the market smelled a little toppy, around 1250. By early July the market was 1200 and Eagle traded under $15. A few fingers had been singed, finally. Bruce, my restaurateur friend, was worried. Barter had ticked at $9/16$s and in a string of 90° days, his hi-tech joint was half empty. He had been told by buy Barter by ad-agency friends. I didn't have the heart to tell him then that his head chef, who had left the Palace, was not putting out. The entrées were passé.

The Return of the Jedi opened in New York early in June. Taxiing past the Loews 86th Street Theater around midday, I saw lines stretching around two city blocks—mainly blacks—the median age in the high teens. Maybe the welfare recipients and unemployed in New York were getting an afternoon of fantasy for four bucks. The film grossed over $6 million on opening day and was on its way past $100 million by the end of June. My five-year-old saw *Jedi* twice by month's end and knew the cast of characters—who killed whom and who were the good guys and the bad guys. How better for a kid (or for the unemployed black males) to gain a sense of omnipotence and act out fantasies of aggression against the adult world that frustrates them. My baby was working on Scott, his big brother, to take him to see *Superman III* for a second time. Five-year-olds are big on repetition.

In the late sixties, when the market peaked, pop art had its day. Andy Warhol had finished his distribution of his giant-sized Campbell Soup cans and Brillo boxes. Roy Lichtenstein had plastered the walls with blown-up comic strips of tearful dolls and Terry and the Pirates machine gunners. Claes Oldenburg worked in cloth, making soft toilets and toasters. Christo began wrapping Vespas in burlap, and Robert Rauschenberg planted a taxidermist's white angora goat cinched around his middle with an old automobile tire. The art of assemblage proliferated, and West Germans bought everything in sight. Their museums are full of it.

Art was challenging its public just as brazenly then as the underwriters in Hoboken who brought forth Integrated Barter. When the market crashed in 1969 and 1970, comparable underwriters like Charlie Plohn went out of business amid a squall of litigation. Almost all the goods brought out were either moribund or bankrupt. The lawsuits proliferated and were too costly to defend. Andy Warhol was a fashion illustrator before he probed the art world, and the word was that he sketched a wicked pair or patent leather pumps. Warhol's signed soup cans were an extension of his illustrator's facility. Then he went on to harness the Polaroid camera for his portraits of Mao, Marilyn Monroe, or anyone else who was sufficiently vain and had $25,000 to spend. A few shrewd critics denoted a subtle mockery of his subject, just as Goya and Velasquez had mocked the Spanish royal court. Andy has become the reigning painter for society these past twenty-five years. The rich and famous besiege his New York studio for portrait sittings the same way they press Kenneth's for a hair styling and armpit waxing. Our Hoboken underwriter had done no less for his constituency. The crisp phraseology of the lawyer's draftsmanship (probably Goldsamt's partner) had packaged another toy for the public to fantasize with and shortly thereafter disregard if and when it breaks down.

Nobody will dare give much thought to the arithmetic of such situations. Integrated Barter was packaged with too many shares for the insiders who paid next to nothing, and after the underwriting, there was minimal investable capital. If Barter earned a respectable 15 percent on its capital, it would come to $600,000—and this is spread over 180 million shares. It works out to a third of a penny per share. If we capitalize a third of a penny at the market multiple, of ten we arrive at the valuation of 3.3 cents! Or a 50 percent premium over its 2 cent book value. For all you guys who bought the stock at a dollar, I hope Bobby comes through for you. Everyone makes money with Bobby, right?

The pop artists revolted successfully against the abstract expressionism of the fifties, nauseated by the biomorphic forms of painters like Mark Rothko and Helen Frankenthaler, whose canvases seemed like multicolored clouds in suspension. The German Neo-Expressionists in the early eighties turned away from the painterly conceits of realism. Why paint flesh tones, pretty people, and colorist landscapes that reproduced nature? Instead, bloated bodies were inverted by Baselitz. Penck developed a new form of cybernetics: his figures were made out of the sticks of black paint, dots, circles, and rectangles. Young painters like Rainer Fetting dashed off nude couples in suggestive poses in swirls of hot colors, their bodies in hot greens and purples, their figures delineated crudely, almost in cartoon simplicity.

When we traveled through Germany the summer of 1985—Cologne, Aachen, Dusseldorf—we saw dozens of similar pieces, plastered like billboards in all the municipal museums. Too much of the work was cookie-cutter repetitive. The young Italian painters were the same story—many of them now working out of New York lofts. Chia and Clemente were flooding the market with new work. When I asked Leo Castelli, who was now dealing in these goods, what it all meant, he just shrugged his shoulders and said that he didn't understand it, but that the public could react emotionally to such aggressive pieces. Nobody had to think what it all meant. There was really very little explaining to do to sell this work, and for a dealer it was perfect mindless inventory—just like Integrated Barter. The vice-presidential limousine was stoned in Krefeld by young antimissile activists around this time, but George Bush pulled away unscathed.

Curiously, the one painter whose work I wanted to own, Anselm Keifer, was unavailable to me. There was a long waiting list for his pieces, and he hardly offered more than a dozen a year through his London-Amsterdam dealer, Helen Vander Mie. His lugubrious pieces with themes of scorched earth, almost cosmic disorientation, or of enormous empty interior rooms with light refracting psychedelically were highly sought after by collectors. Keifer would not expand his output to meet demand. This is integrity.

Across the river in Hoboken or down on Wall Street, for all that, underwriting issues expanded geometrically to satisfy all prospective buyers. This is a branch of investment banking, and it is excused as one of the excesses of the capitalist system's wondrous capacity to spawn new industries. In reality, it is pure whoredom. If you have a certificate of registration from the SEC, you can peddle your wares in the street. John Shad, chairman of the SEC, was formerly an outstanding corporate finance man at E. F. Hutton for twenty-odd years. After backing the Reagan campaign, John's prime priority was to facilitate the distribution mechanism for new issues, and he has been preeminently successful. You can come to market faster, cheaper, and with less paper work than anytime since the mid-twenties. More money was raised publicly in 1983—over $40 billion—than ever before.

By mid-1986, the new-issue market was heating up again. Despite the deluge of registration statements, the SEC was birthing new issues in four to six weeks. This is capitalism working overtime.

For all I know, the new-issue market, not the Federal Reserve Board, got us out of the 1982 recession and will have created hundreds of thousands of jobs and brought the cost of a personal computer down to the price of a portable radio. A new biotechnology outfit may find a cure for arteriosclerosis. The new-issue craziness can also turn into tulip mania, the dialectics for a crashing market when there are no takers. The OTC market itself is the most active barter market in the world. You can't get a hot stock from a broker unless you agree to buy an equivalent number of shares in the aftermarket. This is comparable to a theater producer's papering the house with freebies to make a show look hot. You may also have to take a cool secondary in a utility or a U.S. Steel preferred to get your allotment. Then you are not allowed to sell your hot stock until the broker says it's okay. The greatest capital-raising system in the world accomplishes its goals in as primitive a way as goats are traded in the Lebanese bazaars. Even some of the biggest, most respected houses are guilty of these "tie-in" scams.

Believe me, I know how hard it can be to trade. I am trying to sell a drawing back to my friendly dealer, Jean Aberbach. It is a nude of Dario Morales, and I paid $16,000 for it. Jean is telling me now, a few years later, how it is not a full nude. In fact, the piece is rather static, and his South American clientele want a kinetic nude. "Keep in mind, too, Martin, that it is a work on paper, not canvas, and it is done with pastels, not oils. I can take it back on consignment, but keep in mind that I will be forgoing a commission on one of Dario's new pieces if I have to sell yours first. I will do what I can." Jean Aberbach and his charming brother, Julian, were song pluggers in the fifties and built up a royalty library of country and western titles. I met Jean when I wanted to buy his royalty company for $30 million, and he was as difficult to negotiate with then as now. Song plugging, stock jobbing, art dealing—everyone who is successful in America is a promoter. When Atalanta/Sosnoff Capital went public in June 1986, I toured nine cities in seven days, including London and Toronto.

My friend, Jean Claude Farhi, constructs transparent rainbow-streaked cylinders and spheres of methyl methacrylate in stunning minimal simplicity. This is Plexiglas, and it is extremely difficult to work in, so few sculptors use it. There are perhaps two or three foundries in the world that can follow his instructions for the veins of color. One is outside Naples—Naples, which looks like the Bronx in the 1930s, with the laundry flapping outside the tenement windows. Farhi, a gesticulating Frenchman, rants at me. "It is crap! Crap! It is shit these Italians are making. I watched this coke head finish twenty paintings in one sitting. Twenty pieces. Boom! Boom! Bum! They are shipping all over the world and the collectors scream, 'Give me that, that, and that! I want that! I must have that!' "

Jean Claude has made his point with broad strokes. My point has nothing to do with aesthetics. When every cream puff in America scores in the market, it is time to prepare for tomorrow. Anyone can buy in French, but try selling in French—very few get by without a tie-in deal.

La Cage Aux Folles, a delightful Broadway musical, has run for three years—no small achievement. It took all of the initial year running at capacity for the limited partners to recoup their $5 million capital contribution. The magic word for theater angels is dilution. Not only do the general partners take half the net profits without contributing a penny of capital, but valuable ancillary rights such as film production are retained by owners and authors outside the partnership. Because general partners can continue to produce road companies even though they are unprofitable, the limited partners can suffer losses.

La Cage lost $3 million in its California road company. The authorship elements of a production don't worry at all about profits because they get paid a percentage of gross box office receipts, as does the theater owner. The director, choreographer, set designer, and producer are paid off the top, along with the owner of the property and the author. This percentage escalates to more than 28 percent of gross receipts and raises the break-even weekly budget to $255,000. If the theater is playing to anything less than 75 percent of capacity, its chances of breaking even are slim. Even at capacity, after all expenses are recouped, net operating profits are around $100,000 a week, and the general partner takes half. It would take three years for limited partners to double their money on a smash hit that was socko at the Boffo. Meanwhile, the "talent" is drawing over a $100,000 a week off the top. The number of productions that play for three years to capacity audiences can be counted on one hand, maybe a finger. Over the same time span, the turkeys could top a hundred.

Anyone who buys a limited partnership interest in a Broadway musical has about one chance in a hundred to double his money over a couple of years, odds more idiotic than state lotteries and certainly inferior to pulling a slot-machine handle or betting a long shot to show at the local racetrack. And yet, a charismatic promoter manages to round up 50 to 100 limited partners for participations of $50,000 to $100,000 time and again. Such craziness shouldn't exist.

As a serious dressage rider, I subscribe to several horse-show magazines which obviously sell their list to promoters. I am solicited by mail for limited partnerships in horse-breeding ventures that are equally seductive and dilutive to limited-partnership interests. Invariably, the cover in four colors depicts a gorgeous brood mare with her foal grazing in a velvety, verdant field studded with daisies.

The ways in which the general partner's interest departs from the limited partners are many and varied. Aside from the general partner's rising share in distributable cash, starting at 20 percent and going to 40 percent, the limited partner is diluted immediately by a 10-percent sales commission allocated to soliciting dealers, another 1.5 percent for organizational costs, 5.6 percent for credit insurance, and another 3 percent limited partnership interest for the G.P. There is 20 percent dilution from go, but keep in mind that the promoters also operate the breeding farm and reap payments for board, and bloodstock agent's commissions. Insurance for the partnership is purchased from an affiliate. These past ten years, only 114 yearlings sold at auction for more than $1 million, and during 1984 over 9,000 yearlings sold at public auction at an average price of $41,000—not much more than the previous year's average. (During the height of the breeding season, a stallion normally services two mares a day; the rules of the Jockey Club prohibit artificial insemination.) For a yearling to qualify for auction, its conformation and bloodlines must be exceptional, and there is no assurance the partnership's stock will qualify for the select summer sales. Meanwhile, the public auction prices have been declining for weanlings and two-year-olds. Except for the Keeneland sale, 95 percent of the auction crop for yearlings declined in price by 6 percent, year over year. The odds are getting very long by now, and we are nowhere near the starting gate. Nobody wanted to pay up for brood mares in 1985, either.

Like the theater, thoroughbred racing does not produce an economic return equal to its cost. During 1984 only 6 percent of all the racehorses coming out of the gate earned more than $25,000. You should know that a year's upkeep for one racehorse is also $25,000. The price trend for racehorses closely parallels the price of oil in the world. Foreigners accounted for more than half of all dollar sales at the Keeneland and Saratoga auctions. It is as true today as it was yesterday: racing is the sport of kings. Our partnership capitalized at $5 million will indulge itself with some hope for profits therein. (The odds are very long.) Our horses are boarded at farms owned by the general partners, and the general partner is booking management fees per annum at 6 percent of the gross partnership capital, inclusive of loans. For buying and selling our animals, our manager takes up to 5 percent in commissions. And the partnership's brood mares may be wed to stallions owned by these promoters who are busy syndicating and marketing coal, oil, gas, and real estate ventures in their spare time.

I will pass along the Emo Breeding Partnership IV confidential private-placement memorandum to anyone wishing to see how to construct a finely wrought partnership document that disenfranchises the limited partner in a methodical and carnivorous manner akin to an African crocodile.

Woof!

9 Sometimes the Fish Die

If buying equities seems the most hazardous and foolish thing you could possibly do, then you are near the bottom that will end the bear market.

————Joe Granville

WAS IT Integrated Protein Resources? I don't remember the name of the company, but a Florida-based operation was sure it could raise pompano to maturity and supply millions of pounds of succulent fish flesh monthly to the East Coast's quality fish houses. At $2 a pound—this was the 1960s—the arithmetic of the situation was mouth-watering on a capitalization of perhaps 2 million shares. The tanks, with controlled temperatures comparable with the pompano's natural ocean habitat, hatched the fry. Each day we called to check on their growth. Were they putting on weight? How much were our babies eating? Their formula was a grain mash from Ralston Purina, and they loved it. The analysts' slide rules slipped along in measured haste. (Desktop computers were fifteen years away.) If Ralston shipped unit trains of feed to Miami, the cost of raising our darlings could be brought down. What if Ralston couldn't supply sufficient grain soon enough? How rapidly could Integrated Whatever scale up its fish-tank incubators? The earnings breakout might be pushed back a year or more. The stock traded at $4, and we had extrapolated $5 a share in earnings a few years out—a fantasy of leverage.

Management was properly noncommittal, but were encouraged by the lively hatchlings darting in their tanks. Eager bidders for mature fish were lining up at the door, and the stock moved into double digits. The one thing analysts can do is multiply so many pounds of fish at X dollars a pound. A new industry of sea farming was born. Integrated Whatever made the newsletters of emerging technological growth companies, listed under oceanography, along with intelligent torpedoes and underwater ultrasonic detection

127

devices for mining the ocean bottom. I used to lie awake nights praying that Ralston would deliver its Rye Krisp on time. If my pompano multiplied exponentially, they might have to settle for half rations.

One morning I telephoned the President of Integrated Pompano. His voice sounded peculiarly flat. At first I thought the connection was bad, but then I heard clearly that trouble was brewing in the tanks. My darlings had stopped putting on weight. Actually, my babies had rolled belly-up during the night. Nobody knew why. The water temperature remained unchanged. There were no impurities in the filtration system, and the feed was homogenous. The fish just died! Here we were extrapolating unit trains of Rye Krisp and figuring out if the East Coast market could accommodate 2 million incremental pounds of pompano weekly. What would the wholesalers at the Fulton Fish Market do to us? None of us had dreamed the fish could die, but they did.

This is known as optimism. When people think nothing can go wrong, it is extreme optimism. When analysts and money managers extrapolate numbers covering several years in the future, it is the rationalization of optimism to justify presently high stock valuations. Neatness and order exist only in a computer printout. In reality, sooner or later, fish die. Sometimes it pays to know how many players believe the fish will die and how many think they will multiply till the end of time. Every technician in the world attempts to gauge the sundry indicators of sentiment in an effort to beat the pack at turning points. This bouillabaisse can be as mercurial and misleading as presidential polls, yet sometimes it is the only meaningful variable for securities markets. Everything else is already discounted, often ad nauseam. A few of the $10 billion money pools in the country will buy only out-of-favor markets and out-of-sync stocks. Good operators in the bond crowd cold-bloodedly plunk down billions of dollars for thirty-year Treasuries when everyone else is tearing his hair out as the demand for credit mounts each week and the government deficit pushes debt-service requirements into the wild blue yonder. The theory is simplistic: the fish have died and everyone knows about it. Therefore, there will be some event that will trigger a change in trend. Perhaps the fish tanks can be auctioned off at ten cents on the dollar, or the management concludes correctly that pompano are too temperamental, but that oysters are more adaptable. Thus, the cycle begins anew.

The amount of fluoroscoping that goes on totals millions of man-hours, including charts that plot hourly stock-market changes. God only knows why. Read, for example, the conclusion reached by one of the more solid technicians, who writes a twenty-page biweekly letter (*Marketrend*):

> Our short term Breadth-Momentum indicators are currently in oversold condition while our intermediate term Breadth-Momentum indicators are neutral to only mildly oversold. The present configuration points to the possibility of an upside oversold bounce but the current condition is not so overwhelmingly bullish to negate a short term downside break to new lows. But we must also note that if the market were to suffer such a breakdown a highly significant oversold [situation] would develop very quickly.

With this kind of Wall Street jitterbugging, you can cover all the eventualities—but can you make any money? Don't even try. How many technicians have made the Forbes list of 400 richest men? Before you take out a subscription to a market-letter writer, ask him for his income-tax return. If he has made millions, go with him. The few market-letter writers whom I know don't invest in the market. They buy tax-exempt bonds with their profits from client subscriptions. Smart. *Marketrend*'s sentiment scoreboard is comprehensive but unnecessarily complex. Of the thirty-five-odd variables it tracks, you can discount all but two. The percentage of investment advisers who are bearish is a convenient catchall for the mood on the Street avidly watched by contrarians who salivate as this index approaches 60 percent. The theory is that if 60 percent of the pundits are bearish, it is a contrarian's signal to be bullish.

Another indicator that gets respect is the amount of cash all institutional investors hold. When this percentage moves up near 17 percent, it suggests that the worst may be over. Again, the contrarian theory holds that by the time big money is concerned about serious losses, the money has been lost and there are no sellers left. All the other indicators should be totally ignored. Floor traders, specialists, and Big Board members scalp quarters and half-dollars on an hour-to-hour basis. They don't invest. The players of puts and calls and market-index futures are either

SENTIMENT SCOREBOARD

	Week Ending 2/28/86	4-Week Average	Bull-Bear Rating	Change From Previous Issue
NYSE Specialist Short Sales	44.8%	42.1%	Neutral*	Bullish
AMEX Specialist Short Sales	13.1%	15.6%	Bullish	
NYSE Public-Specialist Short Ratio	51.7%	53.5%	Bullish	
AMEX Public-Specialist Short Ratio	388.8%	403.7%	Bullish	
NYSE Member Short Sales	76.7%	77.6%	Bullish	
AMEX Member Short Sales	48.9%	42.8%	Bullish	
NYSE Public Short Ratio	23.3%	22.4%	Bullish	
AMEX Public Short Sales	51.1%	57.2%	Bullish	
NYSE Public Short Ratio	2.24%	2.09%	Bullish	
AMEX Public Short Ratio	.92%	1.43%	Bullish	
NYSE Total Short Ratio	9.66%	9.43%	Bullish*	Neutral
NYSE Public-Member Short Ratio	30.2%	28.7%	Bullish	
AMEX-OTC Speculation Index	66.6%	64.5%	Neutral	
Investment Advisors—% Bearish	15.5%	18.1%	Bearish	

Indata All Equity Institutional Cash Levels	6.4%	6.5%	Bearish	

Debt Market Sentiment Index	71.0%	63.5%	Neutral
Insider Buy-Sell Ratio (8-Week Moving Average)—3.44			Bearish
NYSE Odd Lot Index (10-Day Moving Average)—2.34			Neutral
AMEX Short Interest Ratio—2.35 February vs 2.22 January			Bullish

Source: *Marketrend*
          Butcher & Singer, Inc.

arbitrageurs or scalpers of eighths on a second-to-second time span. The average age on the floor of the Chicago Options Exchange equates with the median for fighter pilots on our aircraft carriers, and their net worth is comparable: no more than $50,000. Everyone knows that money moving into stocks or out of stocks determines prices, and thus the press for early warning indicators. Note the distinguished contrarian record of the sentiment index of leading investment services. In every recent cycle, when this index hit 60 percent bearish, the market made its bottom for that cycle. Conversely, when the index recedes to only 15 percent bearish, the market tops out.

Who are these 80 market-letter writers whose temperature is

taken weekly by Investors Intelligence of Larchmont, New York? Are they major think tanks with hundreds of scholarly analysts and billions of dollars under management? Hardly. Many are solo practitioners operating out of their back yards. If you can convince 5,000 subscribers to pay you $200 a year for your poop sheet, you gross a million dollars and net perhaps $950,000. Notice the farflung P.O.'s of our remittance men.

The Granville Market Letter—P.O. Drawer, Kansas City, MO
The Dines Letter—POB Belvedere, CA
Smart Money—Six Deer Trail, Old Tappan, NY
Major Trends—6971 N. Beech Tree Drive, Milwaukee, WI
Deliberations—POB Adelaide Street Station, Toronto, Ont
Kon-Lin Research & Analysis Corp.—Rocky Point, NY
Market Timing Intraday Demand/Supply Analysis—Madison Avenue, New York, NY
Dow Theory Forecasts—Hammond, IN
The Holt Investment Advisory—Westport, CT
Technical Comments—Dallas, TX
The Cabot Market Letter—Salem, MA
The Astute Investor—Paoli, PA

Newsletter prose leans hard on metaphor. "While the bearish camp awaits evidence of a wholesale capitulation by the bulls—in the form of white knuckles and fear in the eyes—the NYSE has had every opportunity to fall apart, but still the February lows have held." How many bulls does Ian McAvity know who have been bred for white knuckles and fear in the eyes? Mexican bullfighters? Maybe. Spanish? Impossible. I guess if you put all 80 of these soothsayers in one room, you would have an equally good picture of what the market opinion would be for a group of 80 money managers, securities analysts, or nursery-school teachers. Are the medicine men entitled to their opinions? Have any of them ever said they don't know what the market is going to do tomorrow, next month, or next year? Or that it is too tough to call most of the time? In fact, they really have zero talent for making money—except from their subscribers. Their readers lose and lose and lose.

There is an essential foolishness in market letters. Many offer 800 hotline numbers service to their subscribers for an extra hundred bucks. Yet aren't highbrow investment strategists, with their forty-page quarterly essays, just as silly to rely on as 80 guys writing biweeklies on the surface of their wives' ironing boards, to discover when to go against the grain? I know chief investment officers at multibillion-dollar money pools who rely on this sentiment indicator more than on their staffs of forty analysts, ten investment managers, and three economists. Joe Granville makes the front page of *The New York Times* when he triggers a one-day downdraft with a bearish telegram to his hotline subscribers. Every broker in the country knows the contents of this message within minutes and acts accordingly. Volume is good for brokers.

It may be amusing to think bearish or bullish as a market-letter writer does, but it isn't if you are on the firing line, managing billions of dollars. In my early years, I ran paper portfolios to learn the art of managing money. I lost no sleep when paper profits disappeared. Yet how do I face the treasurer of Princeton, or the Vatican, or the Ford Foundation and tell them that their institution's capital has been schmeissed in half its original funds. Anyone can talk bullish or bearish. I can give you fourteen reasons to buy stocks and fifteen reasons to sell stocks any day of the year. It's only what I do with my money that counts.

It is easy to analyze the motivation and behavior of the *dramatis personae* in the American securities markets. There are links to each category of investors that are symbiotic yet Darwinian. Put simply: There are those who eat and those who are eaten. Pre-1929, the pool operators sold the public their inflated goods. In the postwar World War II years, the public cashed in war bonds and bought stocks. From 1946 until 1950, there was no competition from the professional investor. Most of the fiduciary funds were domiciled in bank trust departments. In 1946 the prevailing consensus of economists and money managers was that the country was headed for a postwar recession that would curl your hair. Stocks yielded more than bonds, selling at 4 times earnings. The recession never arrived; the public made money. It was the last great investment opportunity. The professionals chose to stick with bonds for five long years when stocks were a giveaway. By the early 1950s, the mutual funds promoted and caught the public fancy as repositories for savings. Thus the performance game was spawned. Mutual funds publish changes in net asset value daily. If your asset value increases faster than your competition, money flows into the fund from the public and from brokers, who earn fat commissions. The dynamics of the performance game is essen-

MARKET LETTER
SENTIMENT INDEX

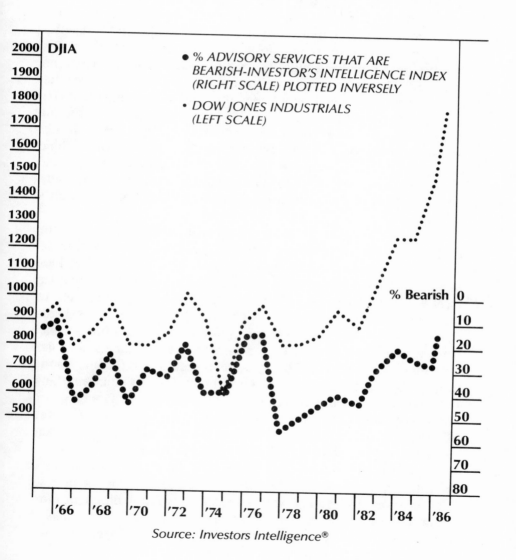

Source: Investors Intelligence®

tially that speculation becomes institutionalized. Everyone looks for the company selling a new and better mousetrap.

Discount all the sentiment indicators that affect the public, if for no other reason than most of the public's money is invested by proxy by the institutions—not only mutual funds, but also insurance companies, bank trust departments, and investment advisers controlling hundreds of billions in pension and profit-sharing trusts. What does it matter that margin debits are $22 billion? It is just petty cash; likewise, if odd lotters are buying or shorting. The public doesn't make trends, but simply accentuates whatever is going on. The same holds true for foreign investors. Their money arrives here only when they believe the dollar will remain strong. By then the market has already made its move. Because institutional activity in stocks determines stock prices, understanding the *modus operandi* of each class of investor is important. How will each act during a market's cycle? The institutionalization of the stock market today is a given as shown in the next chart. Block trades dominate the market, compared with just a 3-percent share during the mid-sixties.

There was a time when banks like the Morgan were on the leading edge of the investment world, but they forgot how to sell overvalued stocks; and today they, and many of the other bank money pools of $10 billion to $25 billion, are just purveyors of trendy off-the-shelf goods. Much of the money-center banks' investment capital is earmarked for index funds, which are chosen by passive investors like state and municipal pension funds which want a piece of the market at a very low management fee. The remainder of the banks' assets are targeted for income funds, growth funds, technological growth funds, foreign stock markets, emerging growth funds, venture-capital pools, et al. The banks, in short, are nothing more nor less than the stock market. Very few of them know how to get out of the way of a declining market. They are almost always more than 80 percent invested in assets oriented toward equities. Despite their mediocre performance record, banks still manage hundreds of billions, the lion's share of stock-market money. The Morgan has the same $30 billion or more under management that it had fifteen years ago. Obviously it doesn't get much new money. Perhaps the reason Morgan holds on to its $30 billion is that there is not enough new capacity in the country available to General Motors and its ilk.

Life-insurance and fire-and-casualty underwriters also invest some of their assets in the stock market, yet they are cut from the same bolt of cloth as banks. If anything, they are less venturesome with their assets, which are invested largely in high-yield securities, principally long-term bonds. Because they pay their investment people modest wages, there are, with few exceptions, no trend setters in the crowd. Institutions like Loews and American Financial are controlled by the managements who own these companies and use them as fiefdoms for personal investing, and also as tax havens. Savvy insurance operators invest a minimal percentage of the $100 billion or so of equities controlled by underwriters. The composite portfolio of the industry looks like the Fortune 500.

We have just dealt with all the trend setters except mutual funds and privately held investment-management companies. Mutual funds are the greyhounds, but certainly not the thoroughbreds, of the investment scene. Like the dogs at the races chasing a mechanical rabbit, they know how to run. Almost all the mutual funds are committed to the market 365 days a year, albeit with various schema. There is over $100 billion chasing stocks of all description. If you want to know what stocks are fashionable, check the inventory of a large growth mutual fund. Because it takes a lot of losses before a fund will raise cash much above 10 percent of assets—a meaningless amount—it helps a money manager to know when the professional is scared. It's a meaningful index of professional investor sentiment. For me, when growth-mutual-fund cash mounts above 15 percent as it did in 1982, it means that the fish have died. Everyone knows it. Now it's time to start a new game of musical chairs.

Because many privately owned investment management organizations are controlled and managed by a few principals in each organization, they tend to be very sensitive to market risk. They stay fully invested throughout a cycle only if performance is positive. Many have compacts with their clients stating that they will not overstay down markets. There are virtually two dozen privately run counseling firms in the country which have the best long-term records for investing billions. They will not jeopardize the compounding of their assets under management if the investment setting is too chancy. These organizations tend to raise much more cash than mutual funds do, and when the number goes above 17 percent, it usually signals that everyone who has wanted to sell

BLOCK TRADES AS A % OF TOTAL VOLUME

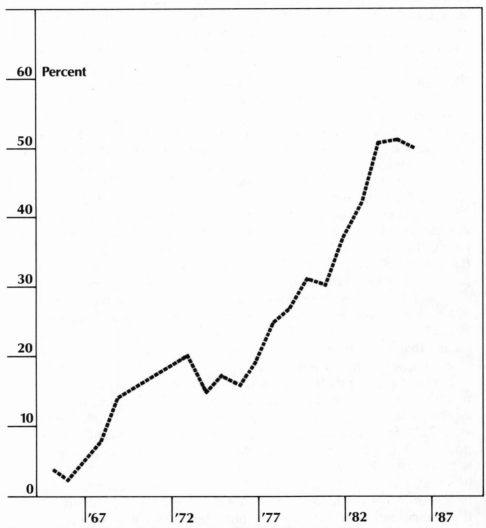

Source: New York Stock Exchange, Data Plotted Through 3/86

down to the sleeping level has done so. Several of the $10 billion plus money pools also run index funds and bond money, as well, so the reading can sometimes be very murky. How do you know how much equity money is parked in two-year Treasury notes? Is it really equity money? You don't know, but you make a judgment based on anecdotal experience. It's probably the highest-quality indicator of a market bottom. Obviously, when the numbers are reversed—when cash for mutual funds and pension fund managers falls to 4 or 5 percent—there is little incremental demand that can fuel stock prices. The market is sold out when growth mutual funds cash rises above 12 percent of assets. With few exceptions, stock mutual funds stay fully invested except for a cash reserve of 4 percent or 5 percent kept for redemptions.

The most reliable indicator of speculative excess is the new-issue market. A year after Eagle Computer went public at $12, it fell under $2. The company was in deep financial trouble. Aside from a $10 million operating loss in its latest quarter, it dropped a line of personal computers shortly after IBM pressed patent-infringement charges. Creditors were solicited for extended terms. It took IBM precisely one year to put the hood on the Eagle as a contender of substance. Eagle Computer had been underwritten by a very respectable high-tech house, Hambrecht & Quist. For a few months, at least, it was considered to be one of the more promising technology plays by speculators in emerging growth stocks. Underwritten at $12, its net tangible assets were 35 cents.

In every market cycle peak, new equity financing expands to accommodate all takers. The dynamics of the new-issue market can be compared to television network programming. There are producers and packagers of sitcoms each new season, basing their product on what was successful last season. If the market is buying personal computers, floppy disks, and biotechnology, there are enough new deals in the mill at venture-capital firms, which package the companies for the Wall Street underwriters, which then price the new issues at a composite average of similar companies already public. It takes a good promoter a little more than a year to put together a 50,000-square-foot facility with a nucleus of production-oriented engineers with some me-too products, copied or adapted from the extant technology of the day. Of the hundreds of deals going public each year, maybe a handful are legitimate speculations that are fairly priced to the public. As a barometer of rampant

GROWTH FUNDS

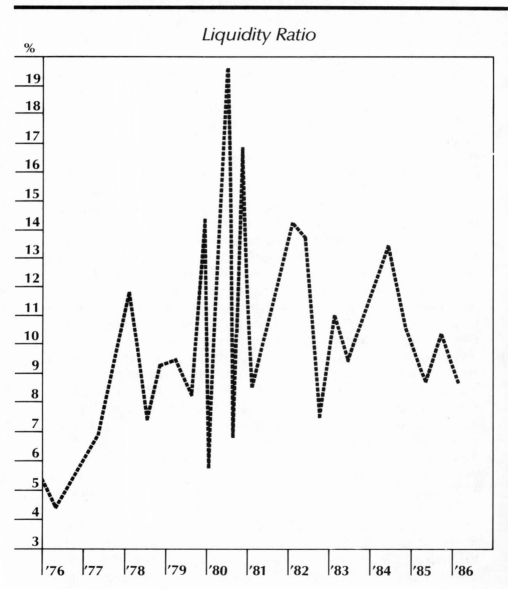

Liquidity Ratio

Source: Investment Company Institute

optimism and public, if not institutional stupidity, there is no index more revealing than new-issue activity.

The stock market is a giant present-value-discount machine. The valuation of a dollar's worth of current earnings declines when inflation and long-term interest rates rise. Conversely, if interest rates are lower and growth of earnings is along the historic 3-percent trendline, price-earnings multiples tend to rise. Look at 1985–1986. Today, under financial deregulation, everyone bids for money and arbitrages it profitably. If a bank issues floating-rate notes and reinvests the money in floating-rate bonds at higher levels, it runs no risk except liquidity and the possibility of a financial debacle by the issuer. Today interest rates are more volatile than stock prices. Therefore, the sentiment in the bond crowd is just as critical to stock performance as is the amount of cash raised by equity players.

For the past twenty years, Market Vane, a Pasadena, California, advisory service, has taken the temperature of commodities-futures advisers, including hard-money boys, currency and interest-rate strategists, and Treasury bond and T-bill traders. When only 20 percent of the bond crowd is bullish, experience suggests that the bond market is about to bottom out, barring a default by the U.S. Treasury. In the summer of 1982 when Fannie Mae bonds yielded over 16 percent and my analysts were questioning the ultimate solvency of this government agency, it was time to buy them. Fear had overcome faith in the perpetuation of the credit agencies of the federal government. Although the stock market bottomed synchronously with bonds, in 1982 more money was made in fixed-income paper.

I have already observed that some of the most conservative investment pragmatists commit billions to bonds based on a timely reading of this index. The rationale applies to stock-market sentiment. The index represents a boiling pot of all the negative variables extant in the investment advisory community. There is nothing more to crank into the negative forecasts; therefore, things will soon get better. The Federal Reserve Board will eventually stop worrying about inflation; the price of oil will decline, or the economy suddenly will sustain a zero-growth quarter for GNP. In the summer of 1984 we began to buy bonds again because we believed all of the above were possible. The sentiment index helped reinforce our Micawber-like optimism. How much is such a temperature reading worth? Sometimes a lot. And think of all the boring economic forecasts you don't have to pore over.

The major problem always is the quality of sampling. Who is *Tiger on Spreads? Market Master?* Is *Tony Henfrey's Gold Letter* the real thing? There is *Common Sense* and *Common Sense Viewpoint.* I have heard of none of the above. Are they Wizards of Oz, or true participants in the bond sector putting billions of their own money and their clients' assets on the line? And what about the *Financial War Room Information System?* Have they won the battle for investment survival? I have somehow managed to get along without reading these soothsayers. If the Federal Reserve Board and the economists in the country, with computer power monitoring 104-odd indicators, can't be right in their predictions, who can? The answer, my friends, is blowing in the wind. Bob Dylan had it right.

Sometimes a consensus of two or three firing-line operators is revealing. On the eve of the introduction of computerized games, we bought almost 10 percent of the capitalization of Mattel after seeing its Intellivision black box and comparing it with Atari, whose graphics were inferior. The stock moved from 10 to 30. We exited Mattel in the high teens, after a ride that lasted less than a year. While many analysts on Wall street projected a machine in every household, Mattel and Warner Communications were scaling up production capacity. Meanwhile, I was observing a declining frequency of play in our household. Scott, the sixteen-year-old, was coaching Jason, the five-year-old, in Frogger, and then Scott stopped playing. A few months later, the hand-held directional signal box lay in a heap of tangled wires among the baseball bats and gloves. Jason discovered checkers and chess. The TV was tuned into the baseball games at Shea Stadium. It was more than a year before managements on Wall Street wised up. Mattel and Warner eventually lost hundreds of millions. They wrote off inventory and shut down plant facilities. Where was their market research? All the directors of marketing had only to poll their kids at home. They would have told them that the party was over.

The White House, Hollywood, and Wall Street seek fervently to divine the word-of-mouth consensus, the most potent of all market forces. After all, the lack of a consensus ended Lyndon Johnson's presidency, blew the whistle on the Continental Illinois Bank. A new constituency made Steven Spielberg a very wealthy

NEW EQUITY FINANCING

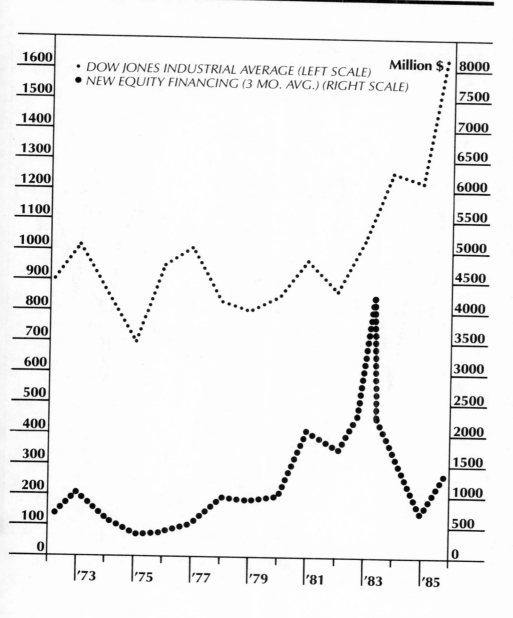

BOND MARKET SENTIMENT

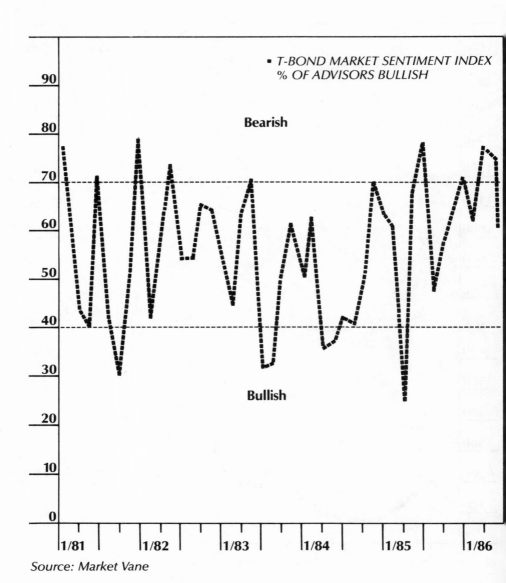

Source: Market Vane

purveyor of fantasy. Jason, now seven, knows more about who's great in films, popular music, and games than I or any group of professional market researchers know.

"Jason, who do you like better—Superman or Michael Jackson?"

"That's easy, Daddy. Michael Jackson."

"Why Michael Jackson?"

"Michael Jackson sings and dances, Daddy. Superman can't sing and dance."

"Have you seen *Gorilla?*" I asked.

"Not *Gorilla,* Daddy. *Thriller.*"

"Okay, *Thriller.* It didn't scare you?"

"I've seen *Thriller* ten times. Scott gave me the cassette for my birthday. I love it."

And so it goes. As soon as Michael Jackson loses his constituency of seven-year-olds, it is all over for him.

The ultimate contrarian, in painting, is Georg Baselitz, whose upside-down figures confound the viewer who cannot sight-read his work. Like contrarians, Baselitz's people seem isolated and discomforted by their encapsulations. The artist forces gravity to function for him in a subjective way. Although his canvases have painterly brush strokes, they are primitive in execution. There is an unstated rejection of a classical art form and symbolism of rationalism, of the classically influenced Western world. The German Neo-Expressionists, like Baselitz, have abandoned the mathematicians, the minimalists. Just as much of the sixties belonged to the minimalists, the Neo-Expressionist work is dominating the eighties with its potency and defiantly antiestablishment attitudes. Minimalist work, like much of security analysis and economic forecasting, looks puny and academic next to the primeval qualities of Baselitz, the contrarian painter.

It is no accident that Mike Milken, the antiestablishment champion of unrated bond paper, operated for years behind an unmarked door in Beverly Hills. The worst excesses in conglomeration during the sixties were perpetuated by West Coast operators. Equity Funding, the greatest financial scam of the seventies, was concocted on Wilshire Boulevard. California is definitely a leading indicator of revolutionary tendencies among financial operators.

On a clear day in June, I stood on top of a 750-acre hilltop

Georg Baselitz. Frau am Strand. *Woman on the Beach*. 1981 Oil on canvas. 200 × 250 cm. (Collection of Toni and Martin Sosnoff).

bordering Beverly Hills, overlooking streaming traffic on the San Diego Freeway. It was the last sizable parcel around, and the Stanford Research Institute found it for the J. Paul Getty Trust. By 1991, a few hundred millions would create a new arts center for the growing Getty collection, with housing for art historians, conservators, and technicians in art restoration. The trust's money managers, encased in two Jeep Wagoneers, had bumped their way up the fire road to the summit, purposefully involved in the gestalt of successfully nurturing the Getty's nest egg. Fittingly, Harold Williams, a former chairman of the Securities and Exchange Commission, would oversee the implementation of Getty's legacy that was so enhanced, trebled, by the pressing needs of Texaco's management to buy proven oil reserves. The money managers, chosen for their consistency of performance and generalized stability, would strain to provide additional wherewithall.

Joe Kearns, the trust's chief financial officer, had a more pressing problem. The caretaker rattled up in his ancient black pickup, accompanied by a battle-hardened short-haired mongrel who had a long history of biting. We were told to stand clear. The Getty Trust, with its $2 billion in assets, a powerful lawyer, and a savvy financial man, had fought the old caretaker to a draw. In return for the continuation of his squatter's rights (on a hilltop in Beverly Hills), he would consent to installation of a telephone for communication with security personnel and would reduce his dogs from five to two. He would be allowed to continue to feed the fauna on the hillside with discards of restaurant lettuce and other herbaceous growths, the same heaped on his truck bed for the daily feeding.

Back in the museum bordering the beach at Malibu, the curators unlocked many doors for us, and we were treated to their most pressing problem in authentication. A creamy marble torso of a young man, life-size, lay on a pallet in a basement room. Track lights shone on his elegant head and on the separate fragments of feet and hands. Aside from a blunted penis, the statuary reposed in unblemished serenity. A book of classical antiquities lay propped against the torso, placing the piece around 600 A.D. Its frontal, stolid rendering bridged the stylistic gap between Egyptian and Greek statuary. A hazy provenance over fifty years forced a decision to bore a hole in the marble and probe the specimen for mineral leachings. The laboratory test had just come back and was positive. After eight months of analysis, the Getty Museum had to decide whether to spend several million dollars for this marble specimen. Despite the test bore, some staff members were unconvinced of the sculpture's authenticity. Stylistic anomalies of the extremities, perhaps. Joe Kearns was more concerned over the millions asked by the European owner of the piece. And for me, it was an old story of how fragile a consensus exists, even among the *cognoscenti*.

When we moved upstairs, I called the office.

"You won't believe what's going on," my trader said. "The bond market's collapsing again, and stocks are down ten points. The preliminary figures on second-quarter GNP were just released. How much do you think they were up?"

"Around 4.5 percent," I said.

"Almost 6 percent, and they just revised up the first-quarter GNP to 9.7 percent. When are you coming back? I put another 8 percent of our cash into bonds with five years' duration, and we have a fast loss."

Anxiety needs company. "I'll be in the office tomorrow morning. Don't do anything more for now."

As I drove into the Los Angeles Airport, I observed a Western Airlines 727 taxiing into line for a takeoff spot beyond a Braniff 727. They don't make any money, I mused. Western's management keeps diluting shareholders. A bankruptcy will come in the next recession. Braniff, resurrected temporarily by the Pritzkers, is losing millions each month. In the distance, a squat billboard building, perhaps twenty-stories, had the institution's proper name imprinted near the roof line in six-foot lettering. How many customers knew or cared that this bank was almost a basket case? Then, as we pulled up at the Regent Air terminal, an operation backed by the Perlmans (departed recently from Caesar's World), there was the ultimate Beverly Hills statement. A dozen pearl gray stretch limos with their black-capped drivers stood at attention in a perfectly aligned rank. Each trunk door gaped open in reptilian omnivorousness to receive its allotment of deplaning luggage. Hopefully, the Chinese and Russians will never see this, to conclude that Nero's Rome has overtaken the U.S.A.

Is the statue of the archaic Greek youth real or fake? Do the fish die or grow and multiply? Will there always be a shifting consensus? Some will say yes and others no.

10   Napoleon, Rubber Tires, and Craps

WHEN ROBERT Rauschenberg placed the automobile tire around the angora ram's tummy in his 1959 assemblage called *Monogram,* contemporary art broke free of the pure canvas mode of representation. A predecessor of Rauschenberg was Marcel Duchamp, whose antiestablishment constructions littered the 1920s. There are always sources, conscious and unconscious. Contributing to the genealogy of this work were the collages and constructions of cubism, constructivism, dada, and surrealism. There is the tie that binds—trying to create total harmony out of disparate elements and free association. Who would have dreamed that in 1984 Rauschenberg would slip back more than a century and reformulate Delacroix's young Napoleon Bonaparte on a rearing white charger. Rauschenberg's reference point of the automobile tire was almost a personalized stamp, set above his signature in the lower left corner of the huge canvas.

In 1959, as a young analyst covering electronics, I watched silicon transistor technology exploding in a dozen companies on both coasts. Boeing was test flying its 707 jet. Color television broadcasting was in the takeoff stage. And Polaroid couldn't keep up with the pre-Christmas demand for its cameras and film. Technology was moving in all directions, and the stock market was to begin a ten-year run.

But in 1986 computer manufacturers were going out of business. The last in, the first out, as we have seen, was Eagle Computer. The country appeared oversold with cable-television channels. IBM's valuation moved closer to a manufacturer of toilet seats, whose demand increased only with the proliferation of backsides. Michael Jackson and Steven Spielberg now owned the country as purveyors of fantasy. Michael with his "moonwalk" dancing had captivated everyone in the country from five to twenty-one. Much of nineteenth-century art represented comparable escapism, but for the establishment. The succulent reclining nudes were there to

Robert Rauschenberg. *Able Was I Ere I Saw Elba*. 1983. (Japanese Recreational Claywork Series). High fire ceramic. 106¼″ × 91″. Courtesy of the artist and Leo Castelli Gallery.

feed the sexual fantasies of the males in power, and the many salon paintings of politicians in conquering poses was abject flattery by the artists for financial gain.

The Neoclassic quotations that contemporary painters are putting into their work evoke cultural memories, a reference to the inherited art of the Western world. Rauschenberg leaves his mark on a classical painting, like graffiti. His work becomes the fragment rather than the reference point, and maybe, unconsciously, he is self-deprecating, saying that his work may be viewed historically as more ephemeral than the museum pieces of the nineteenth century. Rauschenberg virtually re-creates the entire Delacroix canvas. Does nineteenth-century art have more historical value, or is the painting another of his indirect commentaries on the role of memory enriching new work? The Neoclassical movement in art that was beginning to take hold in 1984-1985 subliminally seems a defeatist point of view that maybe there is something to classical antiquities after all, not to mention Renaissance painting. As the movement draws powerhouse names like Rauschenberg, does it say it is time to slow down the new and take stock of the old?

For me, the Neoclassic movement signaled that financial markets were about to tone down their psychedelic jitterbugging. The world needed a respite from the adventures of the big banks and the leveraged speculators who had pushed the utilization of money past the point where the human condition begins to suffer. In mid-August of 1984, Financial Corporation of America, the biggest savings and loan in the country, started to lose depositors. This $32 billion institution run by former Wall Streeter Charlie Knapp was mismatched precariously. Its short-term liabilities exceeded long-term assets. It could no longer meet the liquidity demands of its depositors or fulfill the statutory requirements of the Federal Home Loan Bank Board. Rather than the bad-loans syndrome of Continental Illinois, Financial Corporation was about to be sized down for excessively leveraged speculation in government bonds with funds derived from outbidding other institutions for jumbo deposits from the corporate sector. By the middle of 1986, it was still writing down mortgages and losing money.

That banks should run their businesses so helter-skelter and still retain the facade of respectability in investment circles must be a sign of institutional obtuseness. The reciprocal attitude of looking down one's nose at certain categories of equities is equally silly.

Gambling casinos, for example, are on the proscribed lists of many investors who consider them little better than dens of vice. But the legalized-gambling industry is a part of the hostelry business and has, for many operators, provided an outstanding return on invested capital. It took my seven-year-old, Jason, to introduce me to Circus Circus in Las Vegas, where a mezzanine of game booths and circus acts above the casino floor entertains the young at heart. While I stayed at Caesar's Palace and tried to figure out how this huge facility was structured to get its share of a resurging market, Jason and his nanny were busy at Circus Circus with coffee cups full of quarters, throwing darts at balloons and shooting at rotating ducks. I went to meet them and noted the crowd on the casino floor although it was midafternoon. Back at Caesar's Palace, the crap tables napped along with the slot machines and blackjack tables. Why was Caesar's empty and Circus Circus mobbed?

Well, they have a completely different format than Caesar's, which is a high-roller's emporium. Circus Circus gives the rooms away for $25 and hopes everyone goes down to the casino, where the house can make it up. Circus has the best buffet table in town for $3.49, and the city troops there for lunch. All through the recession, Circus's room occupancy hovered at 100 percent while many casinos in Las Vegas saw occupancy ratios decline 20 percentage points, and there were several bankruptcies. Wall Street didn't know Circus Circus—all the analysts' focus was on Atlantic City, where Circus's management has so far stayed out. Yet Circus Circus is a big and very profitable money-making machine. Its total casino capacity is second only to Holiday Inns, which bought out Harrah's a few years ago for a lot of money.

Nobody in the business even comes close to the 25 percent return on equity of Circus Circus. Note that Holiday Inns' rate of return is half that of Circus's and despite all the debt leverage utilized in the business for building facilities, the return on equity for many operators is unexceptional.

I had to meet the management. With a debt-equity ratio of 2 to 1, an exceptional return on assets and ownership by the two principals, Messrs. William Bennett and William Pennington each spoke for 39 percent of the company. In the spring of 1985 nobody on Wall Street knew they existed. Despite impressive financial credentials, the valuation awarded Circus Circus was lower than other operators with mediocre financials. Was Circus another Metromedia, falling through the cracks of analytical scrutiny, or just a lucky company that had put together a five-year string of good years? I bought half a million shares for myself to whet the appetite, and the underwriters, Drexel, Burnham, arranged a meeting with Bennett, the Las Vegas headman.

It wasn't easy to find the chairman of the board. I jostled my way through the slot crowd and was directed by uniformed guards to push buttons on unmarked doors. Then, I stated my business to a series of receptionists and secretaries. Somewhere in the guts of the buildings, in an unmarked office, was my man. After climbing a staircase, some button pushing and intercom conversations, I met William Bennett, molded from the understated, staid, silver-fox kind of businessman. He was installed behind a twelve-foot mahogany desk that must have weighed a ton. We talked about how you manage a casino and about growth.

"Hell, you got to be on the premises to do well here. I don't know how anyone can manage a property from Beverly Hills or New York. We get our figures every day." Bennett riffled a sheaf of papers with statistical returns from every single slot machine on the casino floor. "If one machine goes off trend, we know it and can trace the shrinkage."

I liked this. Bennett reminded me of a Grand Rapids furniture manufacturer who repeatedly toured his showroom and delighted in the goods. We talked about plans for growth. Each facility was due for expansion: Las Vegas, Reno, the Colorado River. Some 2,900 rooms were going up to 5,000. Circus would releverage itself with a $100 million debenture offering. It was still too expensive to find a way into Atlantic City. Bennett wouldn't bet the net worth of the company on a $250 million facility there. Here is Circus running 100 percent occupancy, almost doubling its capacity. How could I know if it would work? But management, the parent, was betting its major stake in the company, worth over $200 million. Shareholders like me were minors, just taken in hand. By mid-1986, all the rooms were in place. The Circus stock had doubled during the past twelve months.

I liked my investment even more after the meeting with Bennett. How many investors in the world ever heard of Circus Circus? Everyone knew Caesar's World, but Caesar's almost bankrupted itself after buying out the previous owners, the Perlmans, at an enormous premium. I later became a major shareholder in Caesar's, but my investment was less successful. Management owned a token amount of equity. Henry Gluck, for all his studious application, was enscounced in Beverly Hills. Bennett, who had a $100 million stake in Circus virtually lived in his unmarked office in the bowels of the casino. There were too many wrinkles in Caesar's: the liberal granting of credit, the poor play at the tables from convention bookings, and the strong dollar that decimated its Mexican and South American clientele. At the height of Caesar's prosperity in 1980, few Americans sat at the baccarat tables. The faces were Oriental, Arabic, and Latin. The baccarat circle looked like the variegated ship crew of the whaling vessel *Moby Dick*. By 1984 the baccarat section had emptied out, except for a few middle-aged female shills in black cocktail dresses. Where was Mr. C., Mr. S., and Miss Y. who circled her chair three times and then placed a $10,000 rectangular chip on the bank line? Circus Circus just kept putting out a buffet for breakfast, lunch, and dinner for a couple of bucks. It filled all its rooms with Middle-American guests who were content to play the slots hour after hour, their campers locked up in the parking lots. Circus Circus was a manufacturer of money.

The best investments are always those with the simplest format. If you can run a hotel at 102 percent occupancy during a recession, how bad can it get when business is better? Would you rather own a company whose management owns the business and minds the store twenty-four hours a day, or would you invest in a New York City bank or a Fortune 100 company with a board of directors of two dozen insiders and passive outsiders, none of whom will ever own more than a token percentage of the equity? Look at Bank of America. For all I know, the two principals of Circus Circus will bury their company through the use of leverage and the enormous expansion of rooms. One of the principals almost buried himself in a capsized speedboat on Lake Tahoe. He was brought up from eighteen feet of water after five minutes on the bottom. But if you own $100 million worth of something you will work your heart out to make it good. Meanwhile, the faceless bankers in New York who could panic the financial system—if not the country and the world—insist they have done no wrong. "The growth of the world will take care of the doubtful loans," they say. This is like a precocious deflowered virgin insisting that with a little luck her hymen will grow back.

When Bill Bennett came to visit me in New York, the first thing he saw on the wall in the reception area was Andy Warhol's *Dollar Sign*. "I should have something like that in my office," he said.

"Well, I can get you one, Bill," I said. "But it's going to cost you thirty thousand bucks."

Bennett passed on the Warhol.

11   David vs. Goliath

THE NIGHT Joe Louis floored Billy Conn in the thirteenth, I was outside the Polo Grounds waiting to sell a bunch of papers. For three cents you got the final edition of the *New York World-Telegram.* If I sold ten papers, a dime was mine. Fats, the newsstand dealer, pegged me as a ten-paper kid. I was all of seven years old and couldn't muscle my way up to the gates to meet the crowd for "the break." My brother George, who had three years on me, got twenty papers, and he fought the other hustlers for a spot at the bullpen gate, where the bleachers emptied out. Don't ask me why, but everyone wanted the late paper to read on the Jerome Avenue El that shuttled you home in the steaming summer nights of pre-air-conditioned New York. The art of folding your paper with one hand in the few inches of air allotted each rider may be lost by now. All the bars in the Bronx were Irish during the Depression, but there was little to celebrate late that night. The way the papers had it, Billy was ahead on rounds, but waded in for the knockout. Joe caught up with the dancing Billy and peppered him until he folded. The consensus in the bars was that if Billy was Jewish he would have danced away from Joe during the last two rounds and won the title.

Forty years later, I sat next to one of the gray-haired dowagers of the Arthur Hays Sulzberger family, publisher of *The New York Times.* We were at a dinner party in a Carlyle Hotel suite, where Jean Aberbach was about to launch the career of a young Colombian painter, now a Parisian: Dario Morales. When I gently informed this lady on my right that Dario's work was erotically oriented, that every piece had a generous dab of pubic hair defined punctiliously, she turned to her companion, Richard Zeisler, a serious-minded collector-bachelor and said, "Oh, dear! I think we may not want to go next door to the gallery after all." This sums up the bourgeois "Our Crowd" reaction to titillating work. Years

Dario Morales. *Woman on mattress*. 1982. Pastel on canvas. 150 × 150 centimeters. Collection of Toni and Martin Sosnoff.

later, at a second exhibition, a group of Madison Avenue coop owners pressured Jean to remove a certain canvas of Dario's from the show window next to Parke-Bernet. The spent nude sprawled over a mattress was too much for Upper East Side sensitivities. The eroticism of the female and the plasticity of the mattress which undulated sympathetically with the curvaceous lady outraged the neighborhood.

The thematic linkage between Dario's nude and Edouard Manet's *Olympia,* painted in 1863, is their antiestablishment intent. Manet's prostitute outstares all comers and brazens it out. Salon audiences couldn't deal with this cardboard cutout figure. They were used to the receptively pink and fleshy reclining nudes surrounded by winged cupids. According to Robert Rosenblum in his book, *19th-Century Art,* even Gustave Courbet, who claimed not to flinch at reality, found the pressing closeness of *Olympia* disquieting, commenting that "it looked like a Queen of Spades getting out of the water." Manet's aggressive modern female provoked the same anxiety in salongoers as did Morales's piece more than a hundred years later. The sexual revolution had bypassed the Upper East Side Manhattan enclave as late as 1981.

Uncovering a great investment idea sometimes is a by-product of comparable negative attitudes. We had studied the network broadcasters in the early eighties and had come away puzzled at the charisma that Paley and CBS retained. The corporation had thrown its money away on mindless acquisitions of book publishers, band instrument manufacturers, and toys—an odd assortment of second-rate properties. Its recorded-music business peaked with the arrival of cassette recorders. (Teen-agers learned how to pirate disks effortlessly.) Meanwhile, ABC was spending shamelessly for Monday-night football and the 1984 Olympics. But the country had its full of low-scoring inept teams like the New York Giants, and the Nielsens flickered worrisomely. Management told us they were spending $600 million on the Olympics to shore up their network affiliates' allegiance. They had no idea whether they could make any money, but it was a necessity. Beverly Hills producers of sitcoms and specials continued to up the ante each season by 15 percent. Costs for creative products were out of control, the business almost as crazy and unpredictable as film-studio production, with none of the residual asset values of an extensive film library.

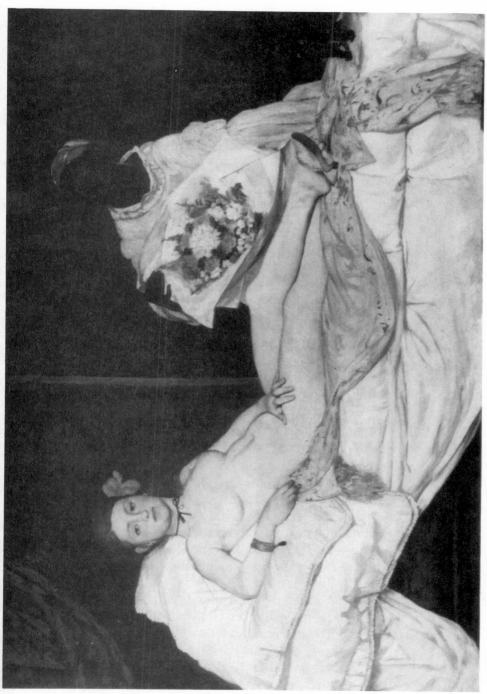

Edouard Manet. *Olympia*. 1863. Oil on canvas. 51″ × 74¾″. The Louvre, Paris.

When I'm in an airport, I buy at least four magazines before boarding. The fear of running out of something to amuse myself with is costly: ten bucks at the newsstand for *Playboy, Penthouse, Esquire,* and *The New Yorker.* Ten years ago, the same four "books" cost about 25 cents apiece. It is from such mundane strands of experience that my focus sharpened on newspapers as a prime investment medium. Subconsciously, I wanted to get my money back. Gradually the perception permeated my consciousness that newspapers during the eighties were one of the last remaining amenities that could be had for next to three cents. Where can you get entertainment delivered to your breakfast table for next to nothing, for the price of a packet of chewing gum? Even *Time* magazine, a glorified joke book, costs almost 2 bucks at the newsstand. If *The New York Times* is 30 cents, the disparity between it and the slick magazines must close over time. The marketing people call this phenomenon "pricing flexibility," and Wall Street money managers translate it into an inflation hedge.

A well-run newspaper is not only an inflation hedge because you can periodically raise advertising and newsstand rates, but it is a deflation hedge as well. Circulation doesn't disappear even in a depression—everyone has 3 cents for a paper. Advertising linage is cyclical, but you can choose to reduce the ratio of editorial content to advertising and stay afloat. Even if you're just printing flower-club winners and Little League scores, pricing flexibility is not just limited by the rising cost of newsprint. The umbrella of television's programming inflation provides a comforting cushion for newspapers. The disparity in cost-per-thousand-audience delivery remains constant. The Dow Jones Company, publisher of the *Wall Street Journal,* understands the impregnable nature of its national franchise. Management has escalated its subscribers gently to 50 cents a copy—on its way to 75 cents—and they will lose few subscribers. It is a rare year that advertising rates don't increase about 8 percent.

A newspaper that dominates its marketing territory is an extraordinarily profitable business with substantive net free cash flow. Once you have a modern printing plant and a supply of newsprint, there is very little more you can spend money on except talent; and so many aspiring journalists come up each year that the best paid earn little more than an executive secretary or auto mechanic. *The New York Times* would not make my friend Bob Lenzner an offer better than $57,000 to fill a prime financial columnist seat. Punch Sulzberger, present publisher of *The Times*, was born into the right family. *The Times*, run as an institution, a printer of record for all of the twentieth century, has succeeded thereby in burying a dozen or more metropolitan dailies which printed the ninth-race, in-the-money horses at Jamaica and little else. Its competition today is the *Daily News* and the *New York Post*, both marginal operators. *The Times* has a near-monopoly on the upscale demographics, and that's what advertisers pay for. The unemployed steamfitter reading his *Daily News* on the stoop of his Queens two-family rabbit hutch is considered worth reaching only by local supermarket flyers. Aside from good Long Island competition from *Newsday*, which dominates its market in Suffolk County (*Newsday* is owned by the Times Mirror Corporation, a smart media conglomerate), *The Times*, in my generation, has put away the *Daily Mirror*, the *Sun*, the *Journal-American*, the *World-Telegram*, the *Herald-Tribune*, *PM*.

Whenever you can, you try to invest in the best just as long as you don't overpay. The world-class operator never goes out of business, generally has an impregnable balance sheet to weather recessions, and is the first to come back in an economic recovery. The dominant player also stands as the buyer of last resort for prime properties that come on the market. Today *The Times* has about fifty profit centers: a stable of suburban and metropolitan dailies in the Sun Belt that in time may approach the profitability of its Big Apple paper.

The focus of any sane investment philosophy is that you always want to own properties that trade on the Big Board for much less than their economic value. Value is what a private investor would be willing to pay for control. This was our rationale for Metromedia, which sold at less than 30 percent of its economic value when we bought it and had a 40 percent reinvestment rate—practically the highest return of any company in our universe of 600 stocks screened by computer. Metromedia paid no dividends and earned 40 percent on its equity. It had a price-earnings ratio below the market and half of the media sector multiplier, largely because analysts were afraid of John Kluge, who wouldn't talk to them. They considered Metromedia a one-man operation. From the bottom of the recession in 1974, the stock moved from $8 to over $500 nine years later, when Kluge took the company private. So much for an efficiently priced investment universe. When they come up for sale, monopoly newspapers draw enormous bids from dozens of media conglomerates. Everyone is willing to pay 20 times earnings five years out because they know these earnings are growable and will be there forever as a source of net-free cash flow to the parent company.

After tripling between 1981 and 1983, *New York Times* stock split two for one, and then rose another 150 percent by mid-1986, and then split two for one. An indicator of the "Our Crowd" mentality of the Sulzberger family was the sale, in the spring of 1983, of 800,000 shares at one-third of its present price. Instead of selling shares to diversify, they should have pressed to buy in publicly owned shares and reduce the capitalization. That is what Kluge did and he, too, owned over 20 percent of the capitalization of Metromedia. Not only was *The Times* selling at a valuation discount compared with prime media properties like the Times Mirror and Gannett of at least 20 percent, but its operating profit margins were exploding in 1983 while the others were under pressure as advertising linage flattened out. The decades of covering the news first and worrying about profits later finally had begun to pay off. The *Daily News* and *New York Post* struggled to stanch the flowing blood—and were marginal, at best, after years of losing tens of millions.

Twelve months of a bull market prompted all kinds of longings. I decided to look around for a few good Henry Moore sculptures during 1983, particularly the work of the late forties and fifties, when the female figures proliferated in phantasmagoric sensuous forms in wood and bronze. But Moore was pushing eighty-five and the word put out by the big dealers like Marlborough was that he had only a few years left to work, and the very rich were hoarding all the good pieces. There must be at least 10,000 Moores extant in the world—almost all being editions of seven—and I couldn't find an important piece for under $1 million. Three dealers in New York had marked up their inventory 100 percent and were charging 50 percent commissions for locating pieces in Europe. I had missed my market.

The impressionists and Old Masters market is where a couple of hundred men in their seventies and eighties who want to own the world regain their manhood for a few seconds in an orgiastic bidding ritual. For the rich old *machers,* art—not power—is the ultimate aphrodisiac. As Jean Aberbach has cautioned me, as soon as a piece crosses the $250,000 mark you are dealing in a narrow stratum of the art community where indulgence—not price or connoisseurship—may be the motive force. So far, I have not paid more than $250,000 for a canvas; the valuation thesis applies in art as well as equities. If you can't discover through your own connoisseurship what you want to own early on before it sells at the equivalent of 30 times earnings, look at the work in the museums. Compounded rates of return, even for Old Masters when viewed century-to-century, yield less than Treasury bills.

When the Sulzberger trust sold 800,000 shares, I decided it was time for us to make ourselves a little better known. In the few periodic meetings we had in the course of a year, operating management treated us with evenhanded aloofness. Walter Mattson, the president, answered our questions in a perfunctory manner that shed little more insight on operations and policy goals than one could glean from an annual report. We were treated like run-of-the-mill security analysts though we owned for ourselves and clients over 10 percent of the capitalization. I personally owned approximately 300,000 shares worth $25 million. Walter Mattson owned 43,000 shares. On paper, the board of directors for the New York Times Company looked like a family circle and smelled like a geriatrics ward. It included the daughters of Iphigenia Sulzberger, her son, Punch, a sprinkling of professional directors like Cy Vance and William Scranton, who owned token amounts, and Richard Gelb, the only distinguished businessman, headman of Bristol-Myers.

My conclusion was that the operating management had sold the board a diversification package over the past ten years that brought forth a litter of stillborn mice. The buzzwords of the decade—teaching machines, gossip magazines, book publishing, and cable TV—consumed a couple of hundred million and contributed next to nothing. The newsprint joint venture with a lot of off-balance-sheet financing made no money in 1983. Cable television, a modest system in New Jersey, was in its investment phase and could have no meaningful impact on total corporate results. Losses in book publishing and mediocre results in TV and radio broadcasting suggested that management's talent lay solely in newspaper pub-

NEW YORK TIMES COMPANY

Relative P/E History

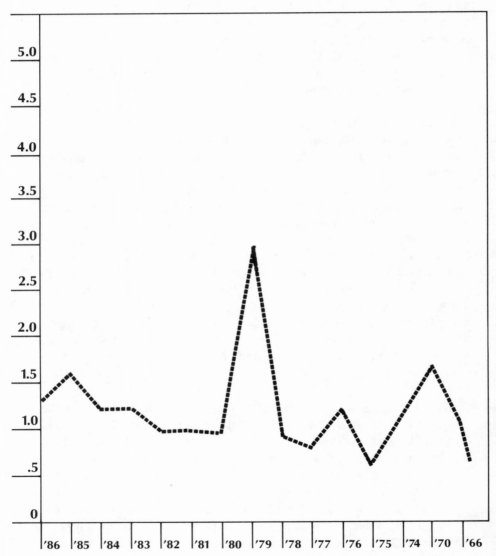

lishing. The buildup in Sun Belt newspaper acquisitions had a sizable impact on earnings and made sense. In the early seventies management had traded Cowles more than 2 million shares—over 20 percent of the equity in the New York Times Company—for an undistinguished group of magazines like *Family Circle* that never contributed materially to operating momentum. When the Times stock was grossly undervalued, management would have done much better for its shareholders utilizing cash flow and even borrowed money to shrink the capitalization. In the early eighties, management leveraged the balance sheet instead to buy Irving Kahn's cable system for $100 million.

Admittedly, criticism of past diversification efforts contains much second-guessing, but it does suggest the state of mind of a management more interested in proliferating profit centers and skipping around in a corporate jet than maximizing the price of their stock through more discriminating employment of cash flow and debt leverage. Does *The New York Times* have energizing management? Up until now, not yet. I wanted the company to sell off all these investments that had consumed hundreds of millions and had skimpy returns. The money could have been used better to buy back undervalued shares. Why didn't the company bid on the Sulzberger block of 800,000 shares? The answer I received from Mattson was feeble. The board considered it and decided it wasn't ready as yet.

The insensitivity of the management—namely Mattson and Sulzberger—to the underlying economic values of their property was seconded in the Cowles situation. After trading away a good part of the Times capitalization for magazine properties, the board slept through an opportunity to buy the Cowles block of 2 million shares that were distributed to Cowles shareholders. The decision not to consider this action seriously at a time when the debt burden was minimal and management had sharp-penciled its forecast of a net-free cash flow surplus mounting rapidly through the late-eighties suggests that the name of the game—maximizing share prices— was not exactly on anyone's mind. Punch Sulzberger was busy playing newspaperman, sitting by his cathode-tube console and helping shape the coverage of the day's leading stories. When I first saw him, he was preoccupied with the von Bulow guilty verdict of murder that had just broken. Because there are four family beneficiaries of the trust's 2-million-odd shares, no one scion holds a sufficient equity interest to care excessively about stock prices from year to year. There was no Gordon Getty with 40 percent of the equity straining at the leash.

For a hundred years the Sulzbergers have concentrated on making the *Times* a better newspaper, and they have succeeded. In the late seventies, the paper was sectionalized into four parts: news, financial, sports and amusements, and home care. The additional editorial content attracted incremental advertising linage and increased the *Times* share of the metropolitan market to about 60 percent. The *Daily News* belched black blood, and the *New York Post,* even under Murdoch, who successfully doubled circulation, was losing more than $1 million a month. Who gets the credit for this masterly decision to upgrade the paper? Did the impetus come from the business side or from the editors? The word is that the editorial side pushed the product upgrading and sold it to top management. Wall Street, impervious to such qualitative changes in the delivered product, still condemned management as sleepy nonbusinessmen just when the *Times* was on the verge of an explosion in profit margins.

Contrasting the *Times* with Metromedia, there was no other conclusion than that John Kluge fulfilled everything an investor could ask of a chief executive officer. Mattson and Sulzberger, as yet had missed or passed up several critical decisions in the corporation's development and had to be labeled also-rans. Kluge traded up a handful of insignificant broadcasting properties, leveraged his balance sheet to buy in his stock, saw an opportunity in an emerging new industry—cellular radio communications—eschewed cable properties, and sold his billboard operations as a $450 million tax shelter. Finally, he bought out all his public shareholders. The stock appreciated 5,000 percent in a decade while CBS, ABC, and others floundered around in sterile diversification efforts.

We had made a costly mistake in underestimating Kluge's genius in convincing Bear, Stearns to package his outdoor advertising properties as a tax shelter and thereby raise $450 million for stock repurchases and beeper acquisitions. The original investment in the billboard properties was perhaps $20 million. When Metromedia hit $175, we sold back to the company almost 5 percent of the capitalization only to watch the stock soar irrepressibly to over $500. Then the broadcasting business softened in mid–1983 and the stock weakened to $250, at which point we decided to move back in. But we were preempted by Kluge, who that very day decided to offer the equivalent of $400 to outside shareholders. The stock opened up for trading the next day at $350. When I had questioned Kluge, a few years earlier, when the stock was $90, why he didn't take the company private, he mumbled something about personal tax problems. The only mystery for me was not what Metromedia was worth, but why Kluge took so long to make up his mind. The answer I came up with was that he wanted to draw his fourth and fifth cards. The fourth card was Bear, Stearns's packaging the billboard properties, and the fifth the success of several cellular-radio-franchise consortium bids where Metromedia now held sizable percentage interests. By year-end 1983, Kluge had positioned his company for the 1990s in a business that would have enormous cash flow, competition from nobody but the local phone company, and a very low tax rate. Kluge would later sell his broadcasting stations for top dollar to Rupert Murdoch and reinvest the proceeds at a much higher rate of return. The capacity of energized management to surprise you consecutively never ends. By mid-1986, Kluge was considering bids on his cellular radio properties, again at a heady price.

While the old generation of network broadcasters slept, John Kluge had traded himself up to a billion-dollar fortune. Contrasting his behavior and actions with the typical custodial managers—most of the Fortune 500—the marginal differences boiled down to guts, brains, and a single-minded determination to advance the price of his stock based on improving the fundamental economic values of the underlying properties. At year-end 1985, U.S. Steel was still writing off plants for hundreds of millions that had become obsolescent decades ago. The custodial managers of Getty Oil fought a desperate but losing battle to hold off Gordon, John Paul Getty's son. Management had failed to replace its oil in the ground, and the most imaginative corporate gambit made in years was the acquisition of a reinsurance business at a premium price: a field as far removed from geological exploration as you could get. The subliminal message is "Yes, oil is a lousy business, but we want to hold onto our salaries."

By year-end 1983, and again in late 1985, I was under enormous pressure from my partners to sell out 1.3 million shares of *The Times*. We all sit at a round table during investment meetings, and the symbolism is that everyone is equal. Whoever puts the most meat on the table should prevail. My partner, Osh, had come well prepared with computerized charts of relative price-earnings ratios for the prime media properties. The charts suggested that the years of undervaluation of *The Times* had finally been closed by mid–1986 and that the property had approached the average multiple for the media group of 1.5 times the Standard & Poor's Index. Although Dow Jones sold at a premium to the market of 100 percent, it had a national franchise second to none and subscription and linage growth that was secularly meaningful. Gannett, which sold at 1.6 times the market, had a stable of suburban monopoly papers with enormous profit margins. *The Times,* operating in metropolitan New York, couldn't ever equal such profitability. I then asked for a respite to have Bob Kobel, our director of research, study the operating-profit-margin trends of the major newspaper properties. The numbers below show that *The New York Times* margins had finally turned quite respectable. The leverage of low newsprint prices, of advertising linage increases of 12 percent per annum, and controlled labor escalations had largely run its course. Only classified advertising, the newspaper's most volatile profit center, had to recover. Margins on classified advertising can run 80 percent or better.

NEWSPAPER OPERATING MARGINS

	New York Times	Times Mirror	Knight Ridder	Gannett Co.	Gannett Without USA
1980	8.4%	17.8%	15.2%	26.8%	26.8%
1981	8.9	15.9	14.8	27.6	27.6
1982	9.5	13.1	13.1	25.4	27.8
1983E	16.1	17.8	14.8	23.5	29.5

The focus sharpened on the company's operating statistics, and the pressure mounted for me. I then asked for a comparative analysis of year-end projected balance sheets and net-free cash flow estimates for 1984 and 1985. My case rested on meaningful qualitative differences. Depreciation for *The Times* exceeded $50 million a year, a sizable sum on a 13-million-share capitalization, compared with other properties. Additionally, I knew from conversations with Walt Mattson that after 1984, net-free cash flow for *The Times* would be approaching $100 million a year and that the balance sheet would have no more than vestigial remnants of low-coupon debt.

1984–1985 CASH FLOW FOR MEDIA COMPANIES	Net-Free Cash Flow (in Millions)	Cash Flow Per Dollar of Market Capitalization
New York Times		
1984	$ 84	8 cents
1985	120	12 cents
Gannett		
1984	$115	3 cents
1985	128	4 cents
Knight Ridder		
1984	$ 84	5 cents
1985	94	5.5 cents
Times Mirror		
1984	$112	4 cents
1985	145	5.6 cents

So I fought my people for time. If we all agreed that a cyclical recovery in linage was just around the corner and that the net-free cash flow for *The Times* was mounting significantly, why couldn't we hold tight and wait and see? Grudgingly, I received a reprieve of six months. If the cyclical recovery in linage became impressive during 1984, we could see the consensus estimate of $7 a share move up, pushing the stock higher. (This is exactly what happened.) I also agreed that the capacity for Mattson and Sulzberger to surprise us was a remote bet, at best.

My periodic meetings with Walt Mattson almost invariably fell flat. There was nothing expansive or spontaneous in his responses to my questions. Quite directly, I was notified that the intelligence system of the corporation had focused on me. We had made a pension-fund presentation to the mail deliverers' union. Mattson had a copy of our statistical packet. The hostile profile on me in the *Washington Post* had been clipped by their service and placed on Mattson's desk. At the cigar stage of our lunch, I got down to business.

"Walter, I'm tired of being a number on a broker's ledger. I want to be on the inside looking in, not on the outside looking in. Your board of directors looks like a geriatrics ward. Aside from the family, no one owns any stock. I think I can make a contribution as a director." Walter puffed his cigar a little faster.

"I don't want to impose anything but I want to be heard." Poker-faced Walt finally informed me that they were not contemplating any additions to the board for the present.

"Walter, I want to be heard. I know it doesn't mean you will listen to me. If I can't make a contribution, I will go away. I want you to know that my partners are pressing me to sell out our clients' holdings of a million shares. My 300,000 shares are not for sale—for many reasons."

Walter perked up a little. "Will you tell us if you decide to sell a million shares?"

"Yes, Walter. We will give you a shot at it if you care."

The lunch was drawing to a close. "You know, Martin, I live on Long Ridge Road and you're in New Canaan. We should get together for some weekend tennis."

"I would love that, Walt. Are you in the phone book?"

"Yes. Of course."

I began to understand the message. Whenever we lunched, Walt suggested we get together for tennis. My children and close friends consumed my tennis hours, but the message was there for me to act on. "If you want to be considered for a board seat, we have to get to know you. . . . If you're socially acceptable and we like you, there is the possibility that someday we will entertain your request. Otherwise, forget it."

I have labored on Wall Street for twenty-five years, and my successes have been measured empirically by rising stock quotations. Our money-management performance is measured in raw statistics, not tennis balls. In the corporate sector it is not a question of who is right or wrong, but of control; and if I wanted to move out of the role of passive investor, another set of attitudes and behavioral patterns must evolve. My ambivalence became indecision because I hadn't the faintest notion of whether I would end up on the tennis court with Mattson and the Sulzbergers. When I got back to the office, I sat down with my partner.

"Osh, they want me to play tennis."

"You want a board seat? That's what you have to do."

"The company is still a sleeping giant."

"What makes you think they will listen to you?"

"I can see another double if they sell off all the crap and do a shrink. Just from the cyclical recovery they should have eight up quarters."

"How many profit centers do they have?"

"Fifty, and Mattson does 'em all with the corporate jet."

"A company with fifty profit centers is not in a shrinking mode. You are wasting your time."

"So what should I do?"

"If you start thinking about board seats, it's the beginning of the end. You'll never sell out the goods when it comes time." The feet went up on the round table, and Osh crunched the ice cubes in his Coke. "Don't get yourself locked in by relationships. Then you can own the world. I'm curious to see what you do with all your money. That is how I'm going to judge you."

"Yeah, but I still don't know what I'm going to do now," I said.

As he exploded out of my office, still crunching on ice cubes, Osh said, "So think about it a little longer."

Yes. Think about it a little longer. If the goods stop being pieces of paper and turn into badges of honor, what next? I glanced at the black marble table and noticed that I had chewed off the top of a blue plastic ballpoint pen. I remembered what Larry Roose, my analyst, had said to me after he read *Humble on Wall Street*. The psychoanalytic interpretation is the story of David and Goliath. The little guy against the big guy. You are David slaying a giant with your slingshot. Ten years later, it was no longer clear whether I was a simple David. Were Goliath's thoughts dancing in David's head?

The New York Times Company underperformed the market during 1985. Management made a number of dilutive acquisitions of broadcasting and newspaper properties, leveraging the balance sheet by hundreds of millions. There was no tennis but we did see Mattson socially and got to like him. In the end, this enormously successful investment gave me heartburn. The Sulzbergers weren't Kluge. They acted consistently in character. I'm sure they will do so for the next hundred years.

12   Stress Cracks in the Marble Pillars

THE worst investment I ever made—the one that violated every precept assimilated over twenty-five years of painful trial and error—was in Gibraltar Financial, a California savings-and-loan holding company. Fortunately, I bought over a million shares close to the bottom of the market in the summer of 1982, when interest rates broke 500 basis points in a matter of weeks. Two years later, I sold out at not much more than I had paid. The carrying costs on the investment had wiped out any profit. At one point, I owned almost 8 percent of the company. Management, a man named Herbert Young, owned under 100,000 shares. He had been an officer of the company for twenty-five years. The remaining officers and directors owned just over 100,000 shares.

I had bought the stock hoping to get an inside look at a financial intermediary with $6 billion in assets and minimal earning power. Perhaps I could convince Herbert Young, its chief executive officer, to put me on the board. Perhaps, there was a way for us to help Gibraltar make the big calls on the trend and direction of interest rates, which is vital to the health of a savings and loan. I thought there was room for me on the board of directors. The listing on page 173 illustrates what a kept group is. Note the seventy-year-old homemaker with 1,000 shares (a $6,000 investment at market). Then there is a professor with 315 shares and a manufacturer of bedding components with 200 shares (a $1,000 investment).

Do the professor, the homemaker, and bedding producer know more than I do about the investment setting? Of course, anything is possible. Yet do I want these three directors with a collective stake in Gibraltar of under $10,000 watching over my $8 million investment? Jesus, no! Then there is the case of Jay Janis, a former chairman of the Federal Home Loan Bank Board, with 1,000 shares. What is Jay doing on this board? Is it right for a former regulator of savings and loans to transfer his allegiance to a regulated entity? Maybe. But is it right that Jay should also be a paid consultant to Gibraltar at $75,000 per annum? The practice of chief executive officers surrounding themselves with loyal little-league players and high-powered paid consultants is outrageous. When is the SEC going to step in and outlaw board members being retained at substantive honorariums as consultants? Would you expect a paid consultant to vote against management proposals? Not if he wanted to hold on to his consultancy. Did Herbert Young want me on the board? Never. When we met, he suggested feebly that it would be better for us to communicate regularly on the phone. In other words, I should keep at least 2,500 miles between him and me.

The questionable tactics of holding out directorships to public figures and promptly putting them on retainer is all-pervasive. Amax, a faltering natural-resource operator in which the officers and directors owned under 1 percent of the equity, had elected Gerald R. Ford and Harold Brown, Jimmy Carter's former Secretary of Defense, to the board. Both had consulting contracts of $90,000 and $67,000, respectively. By the end of 1983, Gerald Ford was serving on eight corporate boards, possibly spending eight working days a month in boardrooms, thus trading golfing time for a handsome income. Pierre Gousseland, now ex-chairman of Amax, had been instrumental in turning down a $78.50-a-share offer by Standard Oil of California. Amax's net loss for 1983 through 1985 reached $1.2 billion, or approximately $21 a share. The stock, in the low teens, hit a ten-year low. In the interim, Gousseland leveraged the balance sheet with poorly conceived acquisitions and investments. He owned about 10,000 shares of Amax and earned $600,000 a year. Standard Oil of California sits with almost 13 million shares. It has three of the fifteen directorships with slightly more parity than Messrs. Ford and Brown with their token holdings.

Because Gibraltar Financial typifies everything that can go wrong under the deregulation of financial institutions, particularly if management isn't of genius calibre, its operations and balance-sheet posture are worthy of examination. During 1983 Gibraltar pressed ahead into corporate and consumer banking, stock brokerage, insurance, mortgage banking, and real estate development. Management diluted the equity of shareholders over 20 percent with $56 million in equity-related securities to do so. But its most recent five-year operating history suggests that perhaps it should have learned more about its basic business of lending money profitably to homeowners. Between 1979 and 1983 Gibraltar lost money cumulatively, and its stated book value moved down from $14.95 a share to $10.19. There were no dividends paid since 1980. By 1986 book value had just recovered to 1979's level.

A few years ago, Herbert Young had changed the complexion of his company without alluding to the risks he was taking. The 1983 annual report is a typical document of corporate obfuscation. Only a footnote reveals that trading government securities had become a sizable commitment. There was a paper loss of $42 million in bonds—about 25 percent of net worth. Gibraltar, in fact, had become an engine of speculation, carrying $621 million in bonds and moving higher, almost 4 times its stockholders equity. As interest rates moved up 100 basis points between year-end 1983 and mid–1984, unrealized losses on investments mounted. Nowhere in Gibraltar's financial reports does it mention the most crucial data for a financial institution: the matching or mismatching of its assets and liabilities. By mid–1984 Gibraltar was about 10 feet underwater if you marked to the market its asset and liability structure. On $8 billion in assets, we estimated a mismatch of half—or over $4 billion. With a fourteen-year life on its assets and an average yield of 11.54 percent, a current blended yield would approximate 14.90 percent.

Gibraltar would sustain a haircut of $800 million on marking its portfolio to market, from par to about 82 on its loans and investments. Additionally, with most of its savings deposits maturing in less than twelve months, Gibraltar had subjected itself to a sizable earnings squeeze if the yield curve turned negative, with short rates moving up faster than longer maturities. This was exactly what was beginning to happen during the summer of 1984. I should point out that the composition of earnings had changed markedly by 1983. If you set aside gains on securities and loan sales, the institution would have reported no earnings. Yet management chose to report earnings despite its sizable unrealized losses and paid $20 million in income taxes. Herbert Young was unlikely to report the fact that his institution was underwater by $800 million. Despite the long bull market in bonds from late 1984 through the spring of 1986, shareholders got very little market appreciation for their holdings. Half the time, Wall Street's financial analysts are smart enough to smell a loser.

GIBRALTAR FINANCIAL'S BOARD
(partial listing, 1983)

Nominee	Business Experience During Past Five Years	Age	Director of GFC and Gibraltar Since	Shares of Capital Stock Beneficially Owned
Herbert J. Young	Chairman of the Board and President of GFC and Gibraltar Savings ("Gibraltar"); Officer Since 1959	52	1959	99,980
Houston I. Flournoy	Professor of Public Administration and Special Assistant to the President of Government Affairs, University of Southern California	54	1975	315
Bernice H. Hutter	Homemaker	70	1975	1,000
Jay Janis	Financial Consultant (since October 1982); President, California Federal Savings and Loan Association (January 1981–October 1980); Chairman, Federal Home Loan Bank Board (September 1979–December 1980); Under Secretary, U.S. Department of Housing and Urban Development (February 1977–September 1979)	51	1982	1,000
Melvin P. Spitz	President of Bedline Manufacturing Co., a manufacturer of Steel bed mechanisms	54	1979	200

The Gibraltar Financial case is just one of hundreds of prospective trouble spots. Under financial deregulation, financial intermediaries can go into the marketplace and bid for money, investing substantial percentages of their assets in unrelated businesses: stocks, unrated bonds, whatever. Managements of financial institutions with insignificant equity stakes in their companies speculate wildly in the bond market, trading huge sums that involve leveraging net worth as much as 100-to-1, in some cases. Essentially, the government has created the basis for a 1929-ish financial panic without even blinking an eye. In the late 1920s the public was induced by stock jobbers to trade on 10 percent margin. Today, the Federal Reserve Board, U.S. Treasury, and the Congress induce institutional speculation that is already out of hand. Many financial institutions—banks, savings and loans, and insurance companies—have figured out that the only way they can overcome the unprofitability of old investment portfolios embedded in a lower-interest-yielding stratum is to bid for money in the marketplace, increasing assets and liabilities at a multiple of their current base.

This is wonderful if it works, yet how many managements are good enough to do it well? How many more could screw up and jeopardize multibillion-dollar liability bases with losses on investments? If interest rates move up from 8 percent to 13 percent (for whatever reason), financial institutions that are mismatched and speculating will run out of accounting conventions to forestall writing off enormous losses that dwarf their net worth. How many conflagrations of $4 billion proportions can the regulatory authorities put out before they deplete their reserves? Very few.

A surrealistic quality pervades almost all of the financial-services businesses. Not only are these institutions not what they are supposed to be in their charters, but accounting conventions and net-worth statements are often total misrepresentations of earnings capacity, dividend-paying capability, and true book value. When Continential Illinois folded because it could not keep its liabilities (its CDs) from running off, no other banking institution would bid for its asset base. The "official" delinquent loan total of $2 billion turned rapidly into a $4 billion shrinkage. It wiped out the loan loss reserve and net worth. Until large depositors fled, the bank continued to pay dividends and report sizable earnings to shareholders. Characteristically, the regulatory authorities, accounting firms, and auditors played along in this charade of public reporting. They would have preferred to continue to do so for the next twenty years to preserve public confidence in the banking system.

So much has been written about the quality and magnitude of foreign loans our money-center banks hold that I think it's worth examining how they got there, and whenever they will be able to dig themselves out. The wholesale banks (big corporate lenders) were forced into the foreign-loan business because their corporate accounts were raising money in the commercial-paper market. It's worth observing that nonbank commercial paper outstanding has quadrupled over the past ten years. Bank business loans have only doubled. Not only did commercial paper cut into the banks' traditional market, but it compressed loan rates. The banks looked abroad, where loan spreads and fee generation were enticingly higher. Subliminally, top management pressed its loan officers for asset growth to fulfill promises made at Wall Street luncheons for 15 percent compounded growth in earnings extending to the end of time.

Walter Wriston of Citicorp was the premier practitioner of heady growth forecasting, and he was emulated by chief executive officers of the top twenty-five banks in the country. Problem loans did not emerge overnight. They had been compounding at a snappy rate for many years. BankAmerica is a good example. Its admitted problem assets almost equaled its equity of $3.8 billion, but didn't include over $8 billion loaned to the shakiest foreign debtors: Mexico, Brazil, Argentina, and Venezuela. At the average rate of reported earnings for BAC, it would take more than twenty-five years to rid the balance sheet of past mistakes. And 34 officers and directors own under 200,000 shares worth about $3 million.

COMPOUNDING MISTAKES AT BANKAMERICA

	Loan Losses (in millions)	Nonperforming Loans (in millions)	Foreclosed Real Estate (in millions)
1985	$1,599	$3,423	$470
1984	982	3,851	344
1983	707	3,675	361
1982	439	2,577	173
1981	248	1,263	40
1980	207	414	18

Citicorp, which led the thrust into foreign lending and years ago implemented the concept of a bank-holding company radiating out into all financial-services businesses, is the paradigm of aggressive bank management. Despite its elephantine proportions, the comparative profile is not too dissimilar from the near-basket cases in the banking system. Incidentally, no officer or director owns more than 0.3 percent of the outstanding capitalization, and the entire board owns only 1.7 percent of the stock. Despite all the problem loans pervasive in the system, executive incentive compensation participation was generous, in comparison to extant salaries for the top five executives.

By year-end 1985, Citicorp sat with an equity base of $7.8 billion, less than 5 percent of the $174 billion in assets. The international scope of its commercial lending is double domestic outstandings, or almost $40 billion. Loans to Brazil, Argentina, Mexico, Venezuela, the Phillipines, and other trouble spots are twice the stated net worth of Citicorp. This is no mossbacked savings bank in Maine, making bulldozer loans to farmers.

DETAILS OF REFINANCING COUNTRIES

	Adjusted Total Cross-Border and Foreign Currency Outstandings	Cash Basis Loans[1]
	(billions)	(millions)
Argentina	$ 1.4	$ 116
Brazil	4.7	99
Chile	.5	13
Dominican Republic	.1	10
Ecuador	.4	14
Jamaica	.1	—
Mexico	2.8	52
Morocco	.1	10
Nigeria	.1	1
Panama	.2	2
Peru	.1	47
Philippines	1.8	182
Poland	.1	101
South Africa	.7	4
Uruguay	.3	3
Venezuela	1.2	295
Yugoslavia	.2	—
All Other[2]	.2	117
Total	**$15.0**	**$1,066**

Source: Citicorp Annual Report, 1985

Citicorp's 1985 total net provision for possible losses on a commercial-loan portfolio of almost $60 billion was $377 million, up substantially from the previous year. The generalized deterioration in Third World debtor nations was reflected in losses more than doubling in overseas offices. Citicorp's loan-loss reserve reached only 1.06 percent of total loans, a skimpy ratio when compared to other lenders like the Morgan, which had built up loss reserves to above 2 percent of outstandings. The geographic sector which includes Latin America accounted for 24 percent of reported earnings, and the Less Developed Countries contributed 11 percent of net profits. In short, 35 percent of Citicorp's reported earnings were of questionable geographic derivation and unpredictable viability.

The next table suggests that there are no distinctive differences among the five major money-center banks of New York. (We have excluded J. P. Morgan because of the comparative soundness of its assets and reserves.) They are one bank in terms of leveraging of net worth to total assets of about 20 to 1. Loss reserves are skimpy, relative to total exposure to Latin American loan defaults of one kind or another, averaging only 12 percent of those loans, and loans south of the border are almost twice the net worth of these banks. We are talking about five banks with $445 billion in assets under their management. The Continental Bank's assets were only $40 billion. There is no way for regulatory authorities to deal with a crisis in confidence focused on the biggest money-center banks in the country. The infusions of money into Continental never exceeded $10 billion on the part of the Federal Reserve System, but the only difference between Continental and its New York brethren was $1 billion in bad loans to the oil patch. It was enough for foreign and domestic corporations to yank out their uninsured deposits. During 1985 Bank of America wrote off $1.5 billion in bad loans, thereby wiping out reported earnings. When asked what the special problems were, the president, Sam Armacost said, "Have you got a globe?"

An examination of Citicorp's interim 1985 form 10-Q reports to the SEC showed several precancerous loan problems and a marked decline in the quality of reported earnings. Cash basis and renegotiated loans, $2.2 billion, showed little improvement from the previous year despite continued worldwide economic recovery. About half these problems originated in the Third World sector. Real estate acquired in settlement of loans rose $66 million, and this was all domestic. Credit-card chargeoffs were rising, and there was a generalized deterioration in the consumer-loan portfolio.

THE FINANCIAL CONDITION OF 5 MAJOR NEW YORK CITY BANKS

Year-end 1985

	Total Assets (in Billions)	Net Worth (In Billions)	Loan Loss Reserves as a Percentage of Loans	Loans to Latin America as a Multiple of Net Worth	Total Loss Reserves as a % of Latin American Loans
Citicorp	$174	$ 7.8	1.1	1.9	11 %
The Chase Manhattan	87	3.8	1.5	2.0	14 %
Manufacturers Hanover	76	3.5	1.4	2.1	11%
Chemical N.Y.	57	2.7	1.4	1.7	12%
Bankers Trust	51	2.3	1.7	1.4	13%
TOTAL	**$445**	**$20.1**	**Avg 1.4%**	**Avg 1.8x net worth**	**Avg 12%**

Source: 1985 Annual Reports

BANK LIQUIDITY AND CAPITAL

Citicorp
(formerly National City Bank)

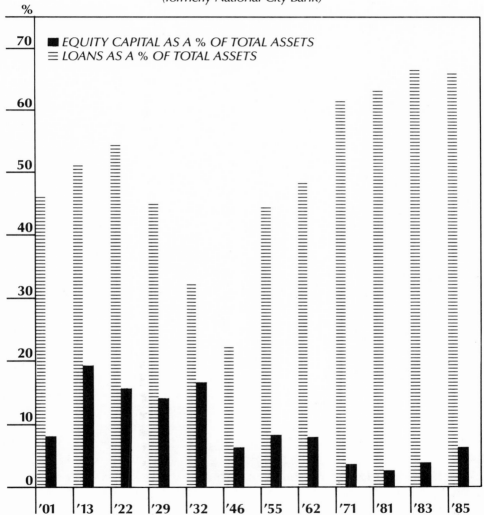

EQUITY CAPITAL AS A % OF TOTAL ASSETS
LOANS AS A % OF TOTAL ASSETS

Source: Comptroller of the Currency

Profits reported from securities trading and foreign-exchange transactions rose, and management decided to book a very large profit from the sale of aircraft lease residuals. Without these special credits, domestic earnings would have shown little improvement. Sooner or later, even a bank Citicorp's size can run out of special items to shore up earnings.

Around midyear we decided to reduce our position by almost a million shares despite the buoyant action of the stock. The 10-Q report just had the wrong ring to it this far into the economic cycle. Throughout 1985 and well into 1986, all the money-center banks moved higher. Money managers like us were enthralled with the apparently low valuations of bank stocks relative to the rest of the stock market. However, a close textural reading of their financial reports showed no progress in reducing nonearning assets. Loan chargeoffs were rising domestically but nobody was writing off any of the questionable global paper. The only bank that looked anywhere near-kosher was Morgan. Its loan-loss reserves exceeded non-earning assets and bad-loan chargeoffs were a small percentage of earnings. At Manufacturers Hanover, loan chargeoffs exceeded reported earnings, which were infused with all kinds of nonoperating gains. Characteristically, all the New York banks' annual reports averaged close to a hundred pages and were totally unreadable, except for Morgan, where the presentation was logical. The others suffused their reports with pages of charts and tables in small print that explained little about how the bank was earning or losing money, division by division.

During the 1930s, virtually every bank and insurance company in the country was technically bankrupt and insolvent. The mortgage loans and real estate owned by the marble-pillared institutions were unsalable at any reasonable approximation of book value. In the best interests of the country, the administration kept the system going, and ten years later, land values recovered and consumers came back and paid off their delinquent loans. Solvency returned to the system. It is one thing to get in trouble providing single-family mortgages to Middle America at the onset of a depression. It is another story to electrocute oneself in a period of economic recovery providing Latin American politicians (many in jail) with capital to squirrel abroad. The ex-mayor of Mexico City is my neighbor in rural Connecticut, where he surrounded himself with the longest dry-wall barrier on the East Coast. Tens of billions in

of debtor nations stretches to the breaking point. After all, bread riots fueled the French Revolution and changed the course of history. Street demonstrations in Mexico by its citizens made homeless by the earthquake are the early signs of unrest and frustration.

In 1960, when I was a securities analyst at E. F. Hutton with a corner window facing lower Broadway, I was given my quota of a carton of confetti to shower on the Republican candidate, Richard Nixon. His rival, John Kennedy, with a movie-star tan masking his Addison's disease, got nothing when he rode by in an open convertible. Wall Street spent fifteen minutes on politics and then went back to its stock jobbing. Later, when Vietnam was a gut issue on the streets of New York, I had moved my work uptown. One day I got a call from my buddy, Joe Rosenberg, then director of research at The Bank of New York. "You won't believe what's happening down here," he said. "The construction workers are running loose in the streets, clubbing the peaceniks, reporters— anyone with a beard or a camera is in big trouble. The country is coming apart at the seams. I'm selling everything."

It was too early and too late to sell. Markets moved higher, but missed the perception of the financial consequences of the Vietnam spending. The inflationary impact was to last into the eighties and wasn't broken by the Federal Reserve Board until the summer of 1982, when the strain to financial markets and business precipitated near-bankruptcies for corporations like Chrysler and International Harvester, and the end of Continental Illinois Bank.

How is young Tom Spiegel going to handle his successes in bond trading? Is he going to cash in his gains and reduce the leverage? So he says. Anyone who takes a shell of a savings and loan and turns it into an open-ended investment company of $7 billion almost overnight may be fixated on adding a long row of zeros to his account: $100 million becomes $1 billion and then $10 billion, and the fantasy of a $100 billion institution congeals. After all, Citicorp got there even if it took most of the twentieth century. Spiegel may try to cut the timing down to a decade. Welcome to the financial olympics! Does Tom become the Carl Lewis runner of securities markets, or does he go down in flames? Wait till 1990 and you'll know.

13 The Enduring Rape of Shareholders

These managements need shaking up—they're horrendous. They take money from the peasants and then hire mercenaries [lawyers] to protect their castle, mainly by browbeating the peasants. So we attack the castle.

Wait. I don't want to call shareholders "peasants"—don't put that in the article. Call them an "oppressed majority."

——Carl Icahn

YEARS AGO, I negotiated seriously to buy a public savings and loan association. The stock sold in the marketplace below book value. The price quoted to me to acquire a controlling block was 1.5 times book value. Nobody could justify the rationale for the price, except that's what it was. Sometime, somebody sold control of an S&L for 1.5 times book value, and that obviously created a precedent for everyone to follow. Considering my cost of financing, the price was too high, and I walked away.

The concept of the market as an anomaly of value may well be the most productive investment thesis of the eighties—provided that interest rates remain low enough to finance takeovers. Note the table on the media sector. Most of these well-heeled conglomerates in broadcasting and newspaper publishing sell far below "going private" market value. This is after appreciation on average of 100 percent from mid-1985 to mid-1986. Few had leveraged capitalizations until 1985, and all have undedicated net-free cash flow: money generated from earnings and depreciation each year burns holes in management's pockets. You might think that management would toss restlessly in its sleep, pondering how to narrow the gap between market value and economic value. Don't.

Corporate managements want to control the game. In media, *The New York Times*, *Washington Post*, and *Boston Globe* have two classes of stock: theirs, Class B, and ours, Class A. They are

188

Darenfort. Illustrating the Contemporary Conception of the Corporation in the 1890s.

BROADCASTERS AND NEWSPAPER PUBLISHERS
ESTIMATED PRIVATE MARKET VALUES

Company	Estimated Private Market Value Per Share (dollars)	Closing Price 6/16/86 $	Stock Price as a % Of Private Market Value (Percent)
Broadcasters			
Belo, A.H	90	56	62
Capital Cities	400	243	61
CBS	200	134	67
Multimedia	80	41	51
Taft Broadcasting	130	105	81
Newspaper Publishers			
Gannett	120	82	68
Knight Ridder	90	55	61
New York Times	115	75	65
Times Mirror	120	68	57
Tribune	115	76	66
Washington Post	280	172	61

Source: Atalanta/Sosnoff Capital Corporation
Estimates based on 10 times cash flow, minus debt

quick to rant and rave about freedom of the press, yet they have disenfranchised their shareholders. Management wants to use cash flow to build plants and make acquisitions. Outsiders believe they can do this better. Maybe you strip away layers of incumbents making millions on minimal performance. Management fights back. Who will rehire a sixty-four-year-old making $1.2 million a year? There are few options open to someone who has worked thirty-four years at the same company, except early retirement. Then power and influence are gone. There is no reason to wear a navy blue suit to put out the garbage at night. So the men in blue suits fight the group behind unmarked doors, whose telephones are answered by secretaries announcing only the last four digits. (Today, buyers frequently wear black suits with gold watch chains on their vests. Open collars are out.)

Somewhere along the line, the shareholders, who are everyone else but the management and the bidder, may get buried. Any annual report that starts with the words "your company" should be thrown out immediately. It is not your company; it is management's company. Anyone who talks about shareholder democracy should be jailed. The shareholder's vote is about as powerful a voice as a referendum in Afghanistan after the Russians have landed. The individual shareholder spends usually five minutes with an annual report. The chances are that the proxy statement is discarded unread and the proxy card never signed or mailed. The professional investor who devours annuals and proxies is certainly less passive, yet equally powerless. More than fifty years ago, Adolf Berle and Gardiner Means wrote: "The proxy machinery has become one of the principal instruments not by which a stockholder exercises power over the management of the enterprise, but by which his power is separated from him."

Institutional ownership of the Fortune 500 is growing. In many instances, we own more than 50 percent of the outstanding capitalizations, but we don't get to vote many proxies. The banks—the master trustees for the underlying pension funds—are instructed by the trustees of the funds, or are left on their own to vote. Except in rare instances, management votes for management. In the sociology of ownership—half the public and half institutional investors—it is impossible for shareholders to win. The public doesn't vote. Half the institutional holders vote with management. On every substantive issue detrimental to shareholders, management wins 2-to-1. So much for shareholder rights.

Company managements are not above gloating in public. Full-page ads (repeated on consecutive days) are placed in the *Wall Street Journal*. Al Neuharth, the feisty chairman of Gannett, railed against junk-bond raids by "shady folks," a small cartel of very sharp wheelers and dealers. Yet his shareholders approved anti-takeover amendments that will do nothing but inhibit the price appreciation of the stock. Shareholders cast proxy votes disenfranchising themselves, so they are patted on the head by management. Al Neuharth owns a token 59,348 shares of Gannett and earns $1.25 million. There are over 80 million shares of Gannett in public hands.

During 1984–85, the stock market attracted well over $200 billion in cash bids for listed companies. Many of the takeovers—particularly the oil companies—were unfriendly bids, some were friendly leveraged buyouts, and some, management buyouts. It's a mistake to extrapolate the privatization of the Big Board. Corporations have learned how to strike back with amendments to the corporate charter, staggered terms for directors, and fair-price clauses. In *Unocal* vs. *Mesa Petroleum*, the Delaware

SEVEN-YEAR SUMMARY (1978–1984) OF CHANGES IN U.S.
OIL EQUIVALENT RESERVES OF SELECTED COMPANIES
(million barrels)

	Start of Period	Revisions	Improved Recovery	Extensions & Discovery	Production	Purchases	End of Period	Percent Change in Reserves
S&P Domestics								
Amerada Hess	523	68	43	84	(344)	0	375	(28.4)
Amoco	3,348	754	301	1,000	(2,052)	0	3,351	0.1
Atlantic Richfield	4,892	814	526	958	(2,056)	(6)	5,127	4.8
Phillips Petroleum	1,288	202	56	271	(785)	281	1,313	1.9
Shell Oil	2,878	153	471	1,269	(2,039)	831	3,564	23.8
Sohio	5,403	(284)	174	469	(1,706)	9	4,065	(24.8)
Sun Company	1,443	(53)	37	434	(938)	277	1,200	(16.9)
Unocal	1,623	(21)	42	560	(865)	0	1,339	**(17.5)**
Other Domestics								
Crystal Oil	16	(10)	1	63	(32)	1	38	143.9
Diamond Shamrock	210	(42)	4	141	(146)	4	171	(18.4)
Mesa Petroleum	238	22	2	130	(142)	4	254	6.8
Kerr McGee	200	(16)	1	108	(140)	0	153	(23.4)
Pennzoil	314	54	30	184	(308)	5	279	(11.2)
S&P Internationals								
Chevron	2,362	193	375	534	(1,360)	(12)	2,092	(11.4)
Exxon	6,999	453	262	1,414	(3,433)	0	5,696	(18.6)
Mobil	2,137	308	103	609	(1,497)	731	2,390	11.8
Texaco	4,517	(1,443)	116	536	(2,229)	1,481	2,977	(34.1)
Total	38,389	1,152	2,543	8,762	(20,072)	3,606	34,382	**(10.4)**

Source: Annual Reports

Supreme Court ruled that a corporation, within the context of a proxy fight, can discriminate between shareholders and offer the passive shareholder a deal that excludes the aggressor's shares. This was upheld by the court as a "valid business judgment" with which courts shouldn't interfere. Lower courts had ruled against Unocal's offer on the ground that all shareholders had to be treated alike.

Unocal then proceeded to make an offer to shareholders to exchange 29 percent of its stock for $72 in debt securities, thereby leveraging itself more than Mesa's offering promised to do. In effect, Unocal's chairman, Fred Hartley, was willing to swallow his company live rather than surrender to Boone Pickens. By its offer, Unocal reduced its earnings and raised debt to 77 percent of its capitalization, up from 16.5 percent before the offer. Pickens correctly called attention to the poor record of oil-company managements in replacing oil and natural-gas reserves. Many of the major oil companies have been in a phase of involuntary liquidation. The Unocal record of reserve enhancement is one of the industry's poorest, down 17 percent during the years 1978 to 1984. Nevertheless, Fred Hartley felt he had earned the right to preside over the partial liquidation of Unocal.

Do these "paper" transactions do the country any good? Does the releveraging of corporate America create jobs, lead to bigger research and development budgets, and rising capital expenditures? It cannot. If you're worried about servicing a lot of debt, you don't overspend. Nevertheless, the past thirty-five years suggest that most corporations have been living within their cash flow in terms of capital spending.

Not only has the oil industry been in partial liquidation, but immediately after the Unocal releveraging, management fired thousands of its employees. There are other "noncompetitive" sectors like steel, where the industry has been "downsizing" for years. At Bethlehem Steel, employment rolls have been halved. It symbolizes the condition of the majority of Fortune 500 corporations. Few provide employment opportunities for new entrants in the workforce largely because they are also-rans in world competition.

Just to reassure you that I haven't stacked the deck, compare two first-class competitors: General Electric and Hitachi. General Electric shows a consistently high 19 percent return on equity for

BETHLEHEM STEEL—THE DOWNSIZING OF OPERATIONS, 1977 VERSUS 1985

	1977	1985	Percentage Change
Annual Capacity (Millions of Tons)	242	175	− 28%
Officers	39	19	− 51
Sales Offices	81	39	− 52
Corporate Staff	3,500	350	
Labor Management Participation Teams	0	74	
Blast Furnaces	25	10	− 60
Open Hearth Shops	13	7	− 46
Basic Oxygen Shops	9	7	− 22
Electric Furnaces	15	12	− 20
Salaried Work Force	25,000	12,500	− 50
Hourly Work Force	75,000	45,000	− 40
Total Employees at Capacity	*100,000	*57,500	− 42.5
Employees Per Thousand Tons	41	33	19.5

Source: Corporate Annual Report
 * 43% cut

the past five years. Its average world-wide employment is down from 404,000 to 304,000. Notice that GE was virtually a fully deleveraged company, until it bid for RCA. Long-term borrowings formed an insignificant 6 percent on an equity base of $13.9 billion. Capital spending showed no upward bias these past five years. Even after its acquisition of RCA, GE's debt to equity ratio will be just average for a corporate industrial.

GENERAL ELECTRIC COMPANY
(dollars in millions)

	1985	1984	1983	1982	1980
Net earnings per share	$5.13	$5.03	$4.45	$4.00	$3.63
Net earnings on average share owner's equity	17.6%	19.1%	18.9%	18.8%	19.1%
Short-term borrowings	1,297	1,047	1,016	1,037	1,17
Long-term borrowings	853	753	915	1,015	1,059
Share owners' equity	13,904	12,573	11,270	10,198	9,128
Return on average total capital invested	16.5%	17.9%	17.5%	17.1%	17.4%
Property, plan and equipment additions	2,038	2,488	1,721	1,608	2,025
Average Employment— worldwide	**304,000	330,000	340,000	367,000	**404,000

Source: Annual Reports
 ** 25% decline

DEBT/EQUITY RATIO

Hitachi, Ltd.

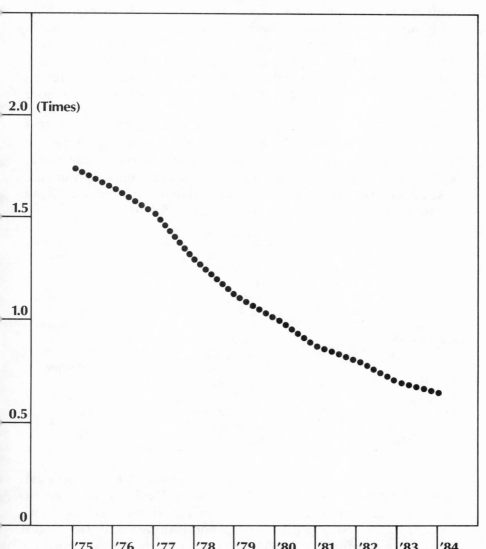

Hitachi is an interesting example of a Japanese corporation that has employed debt leverage successfully. From the mid–1970s until 1980, Hitachi had more debt than equity. Thereafter the debt-equity ratio tilted the balance sheet to a more respectable ratio of 70 cents of debt for each dollar of equity. This is still much higher than in a typical American corporation, which feels uncomfortable with more than 35 cents of debt for each dollar of equity. Hitachi stockholder's equity has tripled over ten years. Very few well-managed American corporations have done as well. Hitachi management's present conventional stance now suggests a future performance not unlike that of GE. Japanese companies are more Americanized.

Corporate boardrooms take care of their own. The typical chief executive is in his early sixties, with a tenure spanning thirty-odd years. Unless he is a founder of the company, he owns little stock, except those shares that have been awarded under option programs. Usually compensation bears no relationship to performance. Some of the high men in executive compensation follow:

EXECUTIVE COMPENSATION INCLUSIVE OF STOCK RIGHTS

NVF	Victor Posner	$4.5 million
First Executive	Fred Carr	4.5 million
Ford Motor	Philip Caldwell	4.1 million
IBM	John Opel	3.8 million
Exxon	Clifton Garvin, Jr.	2.6 million
Emerson Electric	Charles Knight	2.1 million
General Electric	John Welch, Jr.	2.0 million
General Motors	Roger Smith	1.6 million
Kimberly-Clark	Darwin Smith	1.6 million
First Boston	Peter Buchanan	1.6 million
Gannett	Allen Neuharth	1.5 million
New York Times	Arthur Sulzberger	0.85
Loews	Laurence Tisch	0.60
Hartford Steam Boiler	Wilson Wilde	0.25

The table above raises questions. Is Caldwell of Ford worth 2½ Roger Smiths of General Motors, and is Neuharth of Gannett worth 2 times Sulzberger of *The New York Times*? Probably not. I could make a strong case that General Motors and *The Times* have more comfortable long-term franchises than either Ford or Gannett. Exxon is one of the few oil operators that took care of its stockholders during 1984 and 1985 by using a stock-buyback program out of net-free cash flow. Subsequently Exxon's stock appreciated 50 percent. Ford went nowhere. Why shouldn't management compensation be tied to stock performance—or, at the very least, to the extent that they exceed the norm for their industry? If the average rate of return for a sector is 14 percent on equity, and corporate management delivers 50 percent more, it should share in the profits. Yet the extra compensation ought to be in stock, not cash. Forcing management to take half its compensation in equity can only help bridge the disparity of interest between the boardroom and its passive public investors.

Before I reach Victor Posner, note the low salaries. Larry and Preston Tisch pay themselves $600,000 a year, but they own plenty of Loews stock. By keeping their salaries low, they force everyone else to take less. Loews has been a consistent achiever in the market, attracting enough outside management talent to run its cigarette and insurance businesses at levels far above industry averages. I accidentally ran across the Hartford Steam Boiler Inspection and Insurance Company while analyzing the insurance industry. Aside from a name a lot longer than Exxon, it is a model of New England morality and frugality. Its board is strongly Yankee in flavor with presidents of New England companies and academicians from Harvard and Wesleyan University. Its president earns $250,000 a year. The remuneration of the entire management group is $878,622. Hartford's incentive-compensation policy is a model of fairness. Key employees can earn an additional 60 percent of their base salary if the corporation attains 150 percent of its annual budgeted earnings. Wilson Wilde earned nothing extra in 1984 and $98,544 during 1983. At the bottom of the insurance cycle, early in 1984, Hartford bought 35 percent of its common stock. A year later, the share price had risen over 50 percent. Unfortunately, such morality and frugality is not a common part of our corporate culture.

My only exposure to the Posner family, who control Sharon Steel, NVF Company, Pennsylvania Engineering, Birdsboro, Southeastern Public Service, National Propane, Wilson Brothers, Alaska Gold Company, DWG, APL, Evans Products, and Salem Corporation, came from an excited third party's introduction to Steve Posner, Victor's forty-two-year-old son. Steve was about thirty-two at the time and made his headquarters on the penthouse level of the Plaza Hotel in New York. Daddy preferred Miami

Beach. Steve is now vice-chairman of all the above alphabet soup, and Victor is chairman. If their corporate empire is not comprised of recognizable names or well-known properties, don't feel uninformed. Evans Products is bankrupt, and Sharon Steel, the holding company for many of the properties, has defaulted on several hundred millions of debentures. Mike Milken of Drexel may possibly salvage this one.

From the top of the Plaza, Steve was Daddy's eyes and ears, scouting prospective acquisitions, primarily by fielding calls from brokers, analysts, and the downtown corps of corporate finance men. What I recall about Steve was that he drank a lot of coffee—there were trays of stale black coffee cups littered all over the floors and tables. Steve loved to talk on the telephone (there was a snake pit of one-inch telephone cables undulating and connecting all the rooms in the suite), and he loved acid rock. His sound system pervaded every room, including the bathroom. The decibels beat a snappy counterpoint to the Wall Street jitterbug that floated up:

"I can deliver a block of 15 percent of XYZ. Management is sleepy. There's another 45 percent in street name, and you can probably acquire arithmetic control under ten."

Steve would pull the "yellow sheet"—the Standard & Poor's summary of the corporation's history—and open up a file on the target company's financials. There are those who eat and those who are eaten. In this case, the eaters chose second-rate capital-goods operators because they were easier prey and had hefty book values. Being a steel manufacturer, when the industry operates at 55 percent of capacity and importers land steel here 20 percent below cost, is to be in a business in which you can lose a lot of money.

The Posners have lost a lot of money both as stock-market operators and as managers of companies. At the end of 1984, Sharon Steel had a negative net worth of $105 million. By the summer of 1985, the Posners were writing their third offering circular to bondholders in an effort to ward off bankruptcy proceedings. By the spring of 1986, they were up to their fourteenth offering circular. Tens of millions of dollars of unpaid interest had accrued on debenture coupons at 13½ percent and 14½ percent. The bonds had traded at 30 percent of face value and attracted the usual gang of high-risk bond players and arbitrageurs. The purpose behind an exchange offer is to wipe the slate clean of accrued interest. It forces bondholders to accept lower-yielding paper, zero-coupon bonds, and common stock. In addition, future interest payments are often denominated in common stock—at management's option, of course.

The buyers of these bonds have changed markedly: from passive high-yield investors to aggressive professionals who marked their positions almost to zero when Sharon defaulted on its interest payments. If you're an arb who bought the bonds at 50 and then marked them down to 10 on your sheets, you know that Christmas bonus may be smaller this year. You have nothing further to lose except your job, so you go for the jugular. Either the Posners make you whole, or you put them into bankruptcy. The first thirteen offers were turned down. Posner could not obtain the consent of 80 percent of bondholders to tender their "bad" paper for the new and improved Chinese money.

The arbs and pros made a smart threat. The Posners actually might not want to seek the protection of the bankruptcy courts. Victor was also offering a second-priority security interest (the second lien) in much of the plant, property, and equipment of his company—especially the Victor Posner Steel Works in Farrell, Pennsylvania. The banks had the first lien, securing nearly $200 million in debt, which exceeded the book value of the properties in question. It was debatable whether the second lien had as much value as Confederate money.

The offering circular, half the length of *War and Peace*, suggests a number of good reasons for the Posners to renegotiate with The Street. Victor was imitating the Rothschilds, who, in early postwar years concentrated on natural resources—with equally poor results. In the postwar years, consumer-related operators outperformed the heavy-industry sector, now called the Rust Belt. Baron Philippe is better known today for Chateau Mouton-Rothschild, the first-growth Bordeaux, than for his nickel investments. Victor is not known for much beyond his litigious personality. For the Posners, fabricating steel, copper, and brass, mining coal, copper, and gold, and refining lead did not lead to the alchemist's dream. Yet there have been other inducements to continue along the same path, although cash flow from operations for the last several years was insufficient to meet cash requirements. Along the way, the Evans Products bankruptcy led to over $100 million in writedowns by

Summit Securities, its investment arm. Evans was a manufacturer of railroad cars. Over 82 million shares of Sharon are listed on the American Stock Exchange, trading at ¹³⁄₁₆s, which is where imminent bankruptcies reside. Some $400 million in debt is on the balance sheet. This is not a potential bankruptcy of a corner luncheonette. Some major banks hold $129 million in Sharon's paper.

THE RAKE'S PROGRESS AT SHARON STEEL

	1985	1984	1983	1982	1981
		(in thousands except per share amounts)			
Selected Income Statement Information:					
Net sales and operating revenues	$ 799,790	897,527	820,815	692,886	911,973
Income (loss) from operations	$(51,134)	18,658	23,452	(70,218)	25,378
Debt costs	$ 78,534	96,793	94,092	111,590	101,135
Net earnings (loss)	$(64,340)	(144,911)	(68,785)	(105,636)	20,777
Per share data:					
Primary net earnings (loss)	$ (.78)	(1.77)	(.84)	(1.29)	.25
Cash dividends	$ —	—	—	.09	.36
Book value at year-end	$ —	—	.38	1.34	2.71
Market price at year-end	$ ½	1¼	2¾	2¼	5⅜
Selected Balance Sheet Information:					
Current assets	$ 255,565	379,176	439,063	402,373	527,692
Current liabilities	$ 665,858	754,742	434,094	405,178	399,521
Working capital	$(410,293)	(375,566)	4,969	(2,805)	128,171
Total assets	$ 627,336	771,434	914,632	1,053,716	1,199,091
Long-term debt	$ 41,796	43,046	364,842	467,322	473,527
Total stockholders' equity (deficit)	$(162,119)	(105,794)	31,515	109,732	222,753

Source: *Sharon Steel* 1985 Form 10-K

You might think that by now the Posners would have been dispossessed and thrown out on the street with all their furniture. Wrong. You might also conclude that Wall Street houses wouldn't touch the Posners. Wrong again. Drexel Burnham Lambert is advising Sharon on debt restructuring and will receive a cash fee of $2.25 million plus 2,333,333 shares in the company. DBL makes a market in Sharon's securities. They have had a long association with the Posners, both in underwriting and investment banking. Money has no smell.

Let's now look at the real world. Victor Posner's works in Farrell, Pennsylvania, are busy keeping the U.S. Environmental Protection Agency (EPA) and the Pennsylvania Department of

Environmental Resources (DER) at bay. They are both concerned about the discharge of the industrial wastes that date back to 1971. The total valuation of prospective penalties is $194 million. Sharon's basic oxygen furnace is apparently polluting the air. The EPA and the DER have served notice on Sharon of violations in disposing of nonhazardous solid wastes and of poor recordkeeping on hazardous waste material. Sharon is now appealing a decision of the West Virginia Circuit Court on a matter of disposing hazardous wastes within the city of Farmont, West Virginia, at Sharon's coke facilities. In other actions, Sharon has been accused of polluting states and townships as far west as Shasta County, California, and Midvale, Utah, where 10 million tons of its mill tailings contain high concentrates of lead, arsenic, cadmium, copper, chromium, and zinc. This site is ranked among the top 49 hazardous sites in the country by the EPA. State and local officials report elevated levels of heavy metals in food grown on site by residential gardeners.

According to generally accepted accounting standards, Sharon lost almost $100 million from its operations during 1984 (after interest expenses) and $19.3 million of corporate overhead. Let's examine this corporate overhead number, while keeping in mind Hartford Steam Boiler—its total bill for executive compensation was under $1 million. Keep in mind that the Evans Products caper burned Sharon for $120 million odd bucks, and its Chesapeake Financial Corp. (an offshore insurance company controlled by the Posners) dropped $10 million by reinsuring surety bonds to Evans creditors. Also note Sharon's other transactions with related parties such as SCOT, a distributor of Sharon's steel products generating over $1 million a year in commissions. DWG, a Posner entity, received $4.7 million for "substantial management services." Sharon purchased $5 million in engineering and construction services from Pennsylvania Engineering Corporation, another Posner operation. Sharon secures the major portion of its property and liability insurance coverage through an insurance agency controlled by Victor Posner and Son. Chalk up another $2.5 million, but consider Chesapeake Insurance, domiciled in Bermuda, another affiliated company, whose premiums for insurance coverage of Posner entities amounted to nearly $18 million for 1984. Leasing transactions with related parties added another $2.3 million. In the securities business, as long as there is full disclosure, you can do anything and everything.

For a company on the verge of bankruptcy, Sharon was extremely generous to its executives. Incentive compensation was $1.7 million in 1984, and its Senior Executive Achievement Recognition Plan cost another $550,000. "The Plan is designed to retain, encourage, motivate, and recognize the extraordinary efforts of members of designated senior executive management whose decisions have resulted in significant and measurable contributions to the short and long range growth and success of the corporation." There are five Posners among the senior management of Sharon, starting with Tracy, aged twenty-three, a vice-president. Steven's executive compensation reached $476,000 during 1984, while Victor, benefiting from the Executive Achievement Plan, had cash compensation of $3.55 million, up with the top executives of IBM and Ford. Posner's salary does not include additional compensation from affiliated companies such as NVF, APL, DWG, et al. Sharon also leases office and apartment space in Miami Beach, Florida. The building is owned by a Posner trust, the beneficiary of $1.54 million in rents during 1984. It is no surprise that aircraft and yacht expenses run about $700,000.

Adolf A. Berle, Jr., coauthor with Gardiner Means of *The Modern Corporation and Private Property* speculated in the preface about whether the corporation will dominate the state or be regulated by the state, or whether the two will coexist with relatively little connection. "This is a question which must remain unanswered for a long time." Well, the answer is in. The two exist side by side with scant connection. This is how two-year-olds play, side by side with little connection, and they have to be watched carefully so that they don't hurt themselves, or each other. Arthur Andersen & Company, the auditors for Sharon, examined its 1984 balance sheet and income statement and found it impossible to express an opinion on Sharon's financial condition. Meanwhile, the Internal Revenue Service has charged Victor Posner with income tax violations for the years 1975–79. An indictment was issued by a federal grand jury, and a jury trial in the summer of 1986 found him guilty. On appeal he was granted a new trial.

Mike Milken started his Wall Street career as a specialist analyst in unrated bonds. The early conglomerateurs flocked to his Beverly Hills office because they had heard that he could make them money on their personal investments. After all, a rated AAA bond can only go down. At least a BBB piece of paper has a chance at improving its credit rating. Later, Mike helped Messrs. Riklis, Lindner, Steinberg, et al., go private. He sold their debenture paper and preferred stocks to institutional investors, who then traded in their common stock. It was just a small step to further utilize the distribution network of Drexel Burnham to mount hostile takeovers of major corporate enclaves like Unocal and Phillips Petroleum. The targeted companies were usually poor, underleveraged performers. The newly leveraged entities are run by high-metabolism achievers. Boone Pickens talks like Yogi Bear, but he ain't Yogi Bear. Some of them are prudent businessmen, others are wild men. The country will survive them all.

Mike, the guy behind the unmarked door, did more for the stock market during 1985 than all but a few of us will admit to. The market rose 30 percent on no increase in earnings. By financing hostile takeovers, he forced the gap to close halfway between market value and economic value for broad sectors of industry. The arbitrageurs and leveraged buyout specialists played a supporting role, but Mike made it happen. Now the Federal Reserve Board has stepped in, and the market is much higher. I give Mike credit for adding at least half a trillion dollars to the Big Board's value. The level of shareholder consciousness of Fortune's 500 has been raised forcibly. Hundreds of managements now know that even the FRB still can't protect them from an all-cash tender offer, so they'd better close the gap between market value and economic value. It shouldn't take them more than another fifty years.

If Ted Turner is the prototype of J. R., I can inform you that everyone in France thinks J. R. a genius. The French wish they could summon an equivalent mixture of his malevolence, street smarts, wealth, and good looks. "Dallas" is a religiously viewed hour on French television. Plutocracy exists. Yet it is a tight island conclave of men who control their fiefdoms. Henry Ford and John D. Rockefeller, Jr. were the exceptions. But even Rockefeller had to wage a proxy fight to oust the management of Standard Oil of Indiana, and he controlled 15 percent of the issue. The likes of Steinberg, Pickens, Posner, and Icahn may have been initially excluded from the establishment boardrooms on religious or personal grounds, but these "persons of uncertain heritage," as defined by the men in green sports jackets and plaid trousers, may eventually control everything. It's because they possess carnivorous entrepreneurial instincts.

Posner used the wrong schemata for the assets he chose to control. Although he compensated himself and his family overgenerously (to the tune of tens of millions), his was not a stock the professional investor had to study. The chief executive at Getty Oil tried to block Gordon Getty from realizing 3 times on his money—several billions—and the headman of Amax cost his shareholders equivalent billions in unrealized profits. Amax shares tick along in the low teens. It recently omitted its cash dividend. Standard Oil of California offered about $80 a share for Amax at the top of the natural-resource cycle.

Who is the keeper of morality in business? Some outside members of the Amax board were also paid consultants hired by the company they were supposed to be shepherding in the interest of shareholders. Why have both the SEC and the New York Stock Exchange slept while greenmail transactions cost passive shareholders billions in lost profits? Why have managements like Unocal remained unchallenged for their two-tiered shareholder exchange offer? It's the very thing regulators and targeted companies have condemned as unfair. What reasoning kept the Federal Reserve Board or the Comptroller of the Currency from speaking out on the excesses in junk-bond financing? Should banks be permitted to finance hostile takeovers? All this regulatory obtuseness and venality was seconded by the New York State legislature, which rushed to support CBS efforts to ward off Ted Turner's raid with antitakeover legislation. At least the White House understands the problem, deciding for now to allow the laws of the jungle to maintain the balance of nature on the corporate hunting grounds.

What fascinates me about the Berle and Means work of fifty years ago is how little times have changed. The public is forever the bystander. The number of shareholders was estimated at 5 million in 1928. Today there may be 26 million. This is not a significant per-capita increment. As late as 1983, a New York Stock Exchange survey showed that only 14 million college graduates owned stock directly, or through mutual funds. The median portfolio was just $5,000. Middle America has less money committed to paper assets than to furniture and fixtures.

It is no wonder that corporate privilege goes on and on.

14 The Case Against Custodial Management

THE flagrant insensitivity on the part of corporate managements and politicians as to what is acceptable conduct reminds me of the crass materialism and vulgarity of the Second Empire when the combination of grossness and opulence was symbolized by the layers of corsets and petticoats—the yards and yards of fabric that upper-class females burdened themselves with. This predilection for ostentatious display embraced Victorian England as well. Ingres's portrait of Mme. Ines Moitessier, painted in 1856, wallows in a glorious inventory of things. Note the oversized bracelets and brooch. The plump forearms and the acres of fabric, bows, and ribbons cascade over the tufted damask sofa. Pomposity was the mid-nineteenth century vogue, and its equivalent is the way the multinational corporation reports to its shareholders. Hundred-page annual reports are filled with charts, graphs, and photographs—a glorious inventory of things without rhyme or reason. Imelda Marcos, exiled in Hawaii, between sobs, said she had heard enough about the 3,000 pairs of her shoes found in Malacanang Palace. "I don't throw anything away, even old slippers. Those are shoes added up over almost 21 years." The Associated Press reporter had done his arithmetic: 143 pairs a year or a new pair every 2½ days.

The slavish subservience of French salon painting to the establishment is captured aptly in Cabanel's *The Birth of Venus*. The painted female nude during the Second Empire assuaged the need of upper-class males for fantasies of romantic sexual conquest. This painting was coveted by Napoleon III, himself, and he bought it. Note the double standard of erotic conventions. Cabanel's Venus is powdered and depilated, yet she reclines in a odalisque pose of total abandonment. Similarly, the twentieth century multinational corporation provides the trappings and conventions of shareholder voting control, but, in practice, the tightly knit executive committee uses the corporation as a female appendage to satisfy their personal venal cravings.

Ingres. *Mme. Moitessier*. 1856. Oil on canvas. 47¼″ × 36¼″.
National Gallery, London.

Alexandre Cabanel. *The Birth of Venus*. Salon of 1863. Oil on canvas, 52″ × 90″.
Musée d'Orsay, Paris

Today, prominent law firms like Skadden, Arps, Slate, Meagher & Flom are the equivalent of the 19th-century salon painters. They pander to the need of entrenched establishment corporations to perpetuate the disenfranchisement of their shareholders. Several horrid examples of gross corporate aggrandisement pervaded the oil industry during 1982–83. Looking backward from 1986's perspective, with oil futures ticking at $10 a barrel, U.S. Steel and duPont, the big buyers, must feel just a little foolish.

Within three crowded years, four oil companies, U.S. Steel, and duPont swallowed up half a dozen brethren for $50 billion. Between 1981 and 1984, Gulf, Getty, Superior Oil, Conoco Marathon, and Cities Services disappeared. Shareholders of the companies acquired were paid in cash with premiums over preacquisition prices ranging from 50 to 100 percent. The acquirers justified such premiums by explaining that they were buying energy reserves at less than it would cost them to replenish their own. So the leveraging of balance sheets was rationalized. The transfer of wealth to shareholders was deemed appropriate. After all, major corporations plan the repositioning of their assets for a decade; if energy prices kept up with inflation, the prices they paid would seem reasonable by 1990. The ferociousness of the legal infighting by companies outmuscling their adversaries in oil deals is best illustrated by the litigation between Pennzoil and Texaco. Texaco outbid Pennzoil after Pennzoil thought it had a deal to buy Getty. The Texas court sided with Pennzoil, a Texas-domiciled oil operator. The judgment against Texaco was a world record $11 billion.

What were Pennzoil and Texaco fighting over? The last annual report published by Getty showed approximately 2 billion barrels of oil in the ground. Not only had Getty's oil and gas reserves diminished year-to-year, but they had been singularly unsuccessful in discovering new fields. Oil production was averaging 150 million barrels a year, compared with discoveries averaging 22 million barrels. During 1982 alone, Getty's oil reserves declined 120 million barrels. Petroleum exploration that year totaled $640 million, up from $482 million during 1981. To its credit, management spent more to replenish its dwindling stock of raw material, but it found less oil. Actually, Getty spent over $1.1 billion in two years and discovered just 35 million new barrels of new oil and some gas. If we translate cubic feet of gas into barrels of oil, it was costing Getty approximately $9 a barrel to add to its reserves.

GETTY OIL'S NET PROVED RESERVES

(Oil in millions of barrels, gas in billions of cubic feet)	Total		
	Oil	Gas	
1982			
Proved reserves			
Beginning of year	2,066	2,782	declining
Revision of previous estimates	13	43	reserves
Improved recovery	2	1	
Purchases of minerals in place	1	3	
Extensions, discoveries and other			puny
additions	16	245	discoveries
Production	(151)	(328)	
Sales of minerals in place	(1)	(5)	
End of year	1,946	2,741	
Proved developed reserves[1]			
Beginning of year	1,743	2,572	
End of year	1,670	2,591	
Oil applicable to production-sharing contracts[2]	6	—	
1981			
Proved reserves			
Beginning of year	1,914	2,824	a bookkeeping
Revision of previous estimates	263	(48)	entry
Improved recovery	19	7	
Purchases of minerals in place	1	—	
Extensions, discoveries and other			puny
additions	19	327	discoveries
Production	(150)	(327)	
Sales of minerals in place	—	(1)	
End of year	2,066	2,782	
Proved developed reserves[1]			
Beginning of year	1,721	2,648	
End of year	1,743	2,572	
Oil applicable to production-sharing contracts[2]	6	—	

1 Included in proved reserves.
2 Not included in proved reserves.

It was difficult to sense any disappointment in such operating results by reading management's letter to its shareholders, written in the usual uplifting corporatese. "In short, Getty is continuing to move forward, adhering to its traditional values, basing business strategies on prudent financial management, careful planning and, when required, bold initiatives in areas of opportunity."

In fact, in 1982 and 1983 Getty moved backward. Gordon Getty's brooding frustration was understandable. The son of John Paul owned 40 percent of Getty. Another 11.8 percent was controlled by the Getty Museum, run by Harold Williams, former chairman of the SEC. With the stroke of a pen and $10.1 billion, Texaco doubled its U.S. liquid reserve base and increased domestic gas reserves by 45 percent. Getty Oil as a stock closed out 1982 at $49. Getty Oil, the acquisition, went out on February 17, 1984, at a price of $128. Between the Pennzoil price of $110 and Texaco's $128 was a step-up of approximately $1.4 billion. Texaco's eagerness to add to its reserves is easily understandable. It had spent $1.2 billion for exploration from 1980 to 1983 and had discovered mice-sized, rather than elephantine fields.

If we adjust earnings for the reduction in reserves, earnings disappear. Quite aside from the decline in gas reserves, proven oil reserves dropped 120 million barrels. At a finding cost of $9 a barrel, Getty's earnings of $691 million were actually a loss of over $300 million. In short, the company went through the motions of an operating company, but its return to shareholders was a return of capital, not of earnings.

Characteristically, oil companies that don't find significant new oil publish this fact with no interpretive text, usually as a statistical supplement buried on page 45 of their annual reports. Texaco earned over $1.2 billion during 1983. If we adjust Texaco's earnings in terms of its decline in oil and natural gas reserves, an alarming 194-million-barrel shrinkage, the company would also have shown a loss of approximately $500 million for the year. Most analysts, if they want access to management, don't write about such basic issues as the quality of earnings.

Questions. Questions. Why didn't Texaco buy its own stock with the $10 billion instead of diluting its earnings by an estimated 10 percent in 1984? There are 259 million shares of Texaco extant, which were selling at year-end 1983 at around $35. If Texaco could have offered its shareholders perhaps $45 a share for 100 million shares—spent $4.5 billion—it would have reduced its capitalization by almost 40 percent. At a rate of 12 percent, interest expense would have risen $540 million. Ah, but earnings per share would have increased more than 25 percent from the $4.80 a share reported in 1983. On 100 million fewer shares, the savings to the company on dividends paid would have been $300 million, or

GETTY'S INCOME STATEMENT

	1983	Years ended December 31 1982	1981
		(In thousands except per share amounts)	
Revenues			
Sales, including consumer excise taxes of $210,198 in 1983, $138,458 in 1982 and $150,481 in 1981, and operating revenue	$11,810,222	$12,109,188	$13,037,841
Interest and other income	122,358	190,547	148,894
Equity earnings of unconsolidated companies	84,448	95,912	64,825
	12,017,028	12,395,647	13,251,560
Costs and expenses			
Crude oil and product costs	5,765,815	5,683,717	6,329,027
Operating expenses	1,790,661	1,972,182	1,882,918
Selling general and administrative expenses	391,599	355,780	282,686
Exploratory costs, including dry holes, geological and geophysical, and undeveloped lease amortization	441,627	*666,361	506,112
Depreciation and depletion	823,463	798,045	621,804
Interest expense	171,928	162,269	78,905
Excise, property and other operating taxes	716,852	940,632	1,205,185
	10,101,945	10,578,986	10,906,637
Income before special provision and income taxes	1,915,083	1,816,661	2,344,923
Provision for crude oil pricing and related tax issue, including interest	344,000	—	
Income before income taxes	1,571,083	1,816,661	2,344.93
Income taxes on income before special provision	1,170,769	1,125,071	1,488,058
Income tax credit on special provision	(94,000)	—	—
	1,076,769	1,125,071	1,488,058
Net income	$ 494,314	$ **691,590	$ 856,865
Income per average common share	$ 624	$ 861	$ 1042

*They spent as much as they earned and came up with nothing.
**A return of capital, not earnings.

approximately the after-tax cost of carrying the debt to shrink the equity base. Texaco would not have spent one cent out-of-pocket.

The average age of Texaco's executive officers is fifty-five, with an average of thirty years in service. Corporations usually publish ten-year financial records in their annual reports. Not Texaco. They issue a five-year summary. It's understandable. Texaco earned twice as much money in 1979 as in 1983.

During 1983 Texaco earned 8.6 percent on equity—about half of what a well-managed corporation earns. Texaco's return on average assets of 4.6 percent can be dismissed only as dismal. Despite doubling of the dividend payment ratio to almost two-thirds of earnings, shareholders voted with their feet. More than 15 percent departed since 1979. With $57 a share in net assets, one would think that management might have considered purchasing their own stock at substantially under book value; but with the Getty acquisition, they chose to dilute shareholders' equity instead.

You can reach two simplistic conclusions. The oil business is a lousy business, and for thirty years, Texaco's management have been feeble custodians of the corporation's assets. The proxy statement clearly discloses the custodial nature of Texaco's management. It is a profile typical of 98 percent of corporate America. It explains exactly why big corporations get in trouble. They overexpand capacity at peaks of cycles and are not at all bashful about overbidding for acquisitions. Right before oil prices collapsed early in 1986, U.S. Steel bought another oil company, Texas Oil and Gas. Manager egos are enthralled in growing bigger rather than growing more profitable. Unless you buy these stocks near the bottom of earnings cycles and sell 'em out short of the earnings peak, you never make serious money on companies with custodial managers.

A few years later Texaco's stock ticked in the twenties, missing an enormous bull market. Meantime, the price of oil moved from the high twenties to the low teens. Strategically, management couldn't have made two greater errors: overpaying for reserves and sustaining a court judgment against itself that approximated its net worth. The directors and officers of Texaco together owned about 0.3 percent of the outstanding stock. Despite the subpar returns on equity and assets, the executive officers received $7.4

million in remuneration, including more than $2 million in bonus payments. In their 1983 income statement, management went to great lengths to protect themselves from a takeover by requiring an 80 percent shareholder vote for a business combination. Yet they purchased 25 million shares from the Bass family and Sid Richardson at a premium price of $50. The passive shareholders of 230 million shares were stuck with stock worth $40. They were made no equivalent offer and were thus deprived of $2 billion in market appreciation. The SEC is often worried about some poor proofreader who trades based on inside information, making $1,000; but they have chosen to ignore the injustice done to stockholders by management's strategies for self-perpetuation in office. There have been many "takeouts" of hostile blocks in the past few years in which remaining shareholders have been deprived of tens of billions in realizable capital gains.

A typical outside director on Texaco's board owned a token amount of stock. Frank Cary of IBM—1,000 shares. Willard Butcher, headman at Chase Manhattan Bank—300 shares, Elvis Mason, formerly chairman of the board at Interfirst Bank in Dallas—500 shares. Where were they when shareholders needed their collective wisdom? Is it any wonder that Chubb and other insurance carriers are charging major corporations $1 million for officers' and directors' liability insurance policies?

I asked Leon Levy what he had learned from his unsuccessful proxy fight to force the management at TWA to spin off its airline to shareholders so that the earning power of the Hilton International and its other viable properties might be more recognizable in the marketplace. He noted that through the coercive power of TWA's lawyers and bankers, many major shareholders were threatened with losing credit lines if they voted with the dissident group. Leon's group did receive about a third of the vote, and the moral suasion of such numbers subsequently persuaded management gradually to divest itself of the airline which was losing serious money during the period of economic recovery. My personal experience in owning blocks of up to 10 percent of a company's capitalization is that it provides you with little more than a hot but mediocre lunch in the executive dining room. If you own anything less than a 25 percent equity ownership in a major corporation, management will fight desperately to keep you off its board of directors.

Caesar's World did it to me, a 13 percent holder. In the spring of 1986, Caesar's World issued $100 million of convertible debentures through Drexel Burnham Lambert. As far as I could tell, Henry Gluck, chairman of the board, didn't need the money. Cash flow was exceeding capital spending. A close textural reading of the prospectus uncovered the real reason for this underwriting. The convertible debenture was an insidious poison pill aimed at me. Artfully designed by Skadden, Arps, Slate, Meagher & Flom, the creator of poison pills, the debenture effectively disenfranchises major shareholders. The conversion privilege is abolished if conversion by a holder would result in his holdings exceeding 25 percent of the outstanding stock. Not only have law firms already disenfranchised shareholders, but they are now getting away with the disenfranchisement of debenture holders.

Where are the SEC and the New York Stock Exchange in this issue? I guess they are studying the situation for the next five years, maybe forever.

In addition, management can reduce the conversion price of its debentures if there is a change in control defined as 30 percent ownership by an outsider. Caesar's can reduce the conversion paid by any amount—down to the par value of the common stock, which is 10 cents. In effect, management could voluntarily dilute shareholders (the pill). Stepping back from my personal interest in Caesar's, the basic interest of shareholders has been impaired. Lawyers like Flom are being allowed to subvert the rights of active shareholders. Common law says that all shareholders are equal. Beverly Hills and Big Apple legal mills continue to bastardize shareholder rights, and our institutions side tacitly with the advocates of entrenched management. I intend to fight this all the way to the Supreme Court. It's going to cost hundreds of thousands, but what the hell—somebody has to do it.

If you have caretaker management, you get caretaker results. The International Paper Company has revenues of $5 billion and earning power of just $100 million. It ranks as one of the Fortune 100. Twelve directors owned collectively 74,740 shares of the approximately 50 million outstanding. No nominee owns as much as ¹⁄₁₀ of 1 percent. Why should they? The return on stockholder

WHOSE COMPANY IS THIS ANYWAY?

Return On Common Share Owners' Equity

Answer: International Paper Company
If you have caretaker management, you get caretaker results.

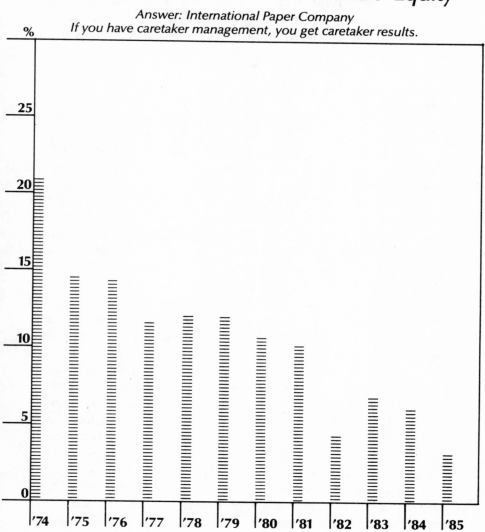

equity has flowed downhill for the past ten years, averaging less than 7 percent in the past five years, and just 3 percent in 1985. This deadly combination of management's negligible equity stake, a deleveraged balance sheet, and the poor returns to shareholders is a paradigm for many of the 500 largest corporations. Stay away.

The profile of an energized management is the exact reciprocal of the custodial operators. Dow Jones is a good example. There is no other product like the *Wall Street Journal*. It could charge almost anything, and few subscribers would drop out. Keep in mind that this is a family-controlled business. They tend to be frugal operators, like The New York Times Company, Loews, and many others, where a high percentage of stock is owned by management. When my friend, Joe Rosenberg, went to work for Larry Tisch as a money manager, he had a hard time convincing Larry that his office needed a coat of paint. Not coincidentally, Tisch was appointed to the Getty board by Gordon Getty. He was instrumental in squeezing the last couple of dollars a share out of Texaco's headman (total: $200 million), who wanted Getty at almost any price. Larry Tisch and his brother Preston took salaries of $600,000 a year. The Texaco president earned $1.1 million. Tisch, one of the smartest and most productive businessmen in the country, is asked to serve on very few boards of major corporations. Nobody wants him around. Larry can't abide managers who don't deliver enough to shareholders.

The Dow Jones financials clearly illustrate a frugal management group that delivers a lot. Dow Jones's rate of return on equity consistently hits the mid-twenties, double what the average industrial corporation delivers, and substantially more than what other media enterprises reach—19 to 20 percent being the norm for a well-managed newspaper or broadcasting chain. Note the upward bias in operating profit margins and the doubling of shareholder equity in four years. Because the earnings on reinvested capital are so high, dividends are minimal. Nobody at Dow Jones earns more than $600,000 a year. In its heyday, Metromedia sported 35 to 40 percent returns on equity, an unheard of number even for a technology enterprise at the top of its field. Yet Metromedia's John Kluge wasn't afraid of leveraging his company with $3 of debt for every dollar of equity. He owned over 20 percent of Metromedia until it went private in 1985, by his initiative, and then he owned almost the whole company.

The Bancroft family controls 56 percent of the equity in Dow Jones. They intend to keep it in the family to the end of the family line. Who wouldn't? Sidney Peterson, chairman of the board of Getty Oil, owned .0043 percent of Getty—yet he fought bitterly to hold off Gordon Getty from recognizing the intrinsic value of his 31.8 million shares, which turned out to be worth over $4 billion to Texaco. The president and chairman of the board of Getty together owned 7,400 shares, yet they averaged over thirty years service with Getty-related corporations. Where were their entrepreneurial instincts? Did they give a damn for passive shareholders?

Let's now look at a good proxy statement that shows an energized management with substantial equity ownership. Loews is controlled by Laurence and Preston Tisch, who together had owned roughly

DOW JONES & COMPANY
A WINNER'S FIVE-YEAR PROFILE

Profit margins high

	1985	1984	1983	1982	1981
PER SHARE AMOUNTS					
Net Income	$2.15	$2.01	$1.79	$1.39	$1.14
Dividends paid	$ .78	$ .72	$ .60	$ .54	$ .46
Dividends declared	$ .78	$ .72	$ .60	$ .54	$ .46
OTHER DATA					
Operating income as a percent of revenues	23.4%	23.8%	24.3%	20.5%	21.1%
Net income as a percent of revenues	13.3%	13.4%	13.2%	12.1%	11.1%
Net income as a percent of stockholders' equity	23.1%	25.5%	27.4%	26.4%	26.5%
Long-term debt as a percent of total capital	29.2%	4.0%	3.9%	9.5%	15.6%
Average shares outstanding	64,396,000	64,212,000	63,966,000	63,459,000	62,605,000
Newsprint consumption (metric tons)	224,000	227,000	215,000	194,000	189,000
Number of full-time employees at year-end	6,924	6,834	6,273	5,893	5,394
Capital expenditures	$154,589	$142,792	$84,948	$73,572	$77,084
Total assets	1,176,697	803,539	780,207	594,741	532,075
Long-term debt	248,104	21,020	16,793	35,083	49,696
Stockholders' equity	600,200	505,601	416,814	333,995	269,663
Cash dividends declared	50,228	46,232	38,377	34,289	28,802

Employees grow   **Management uses debt leverage**   **Shareholder equity doubles in under 4 years.**

40 percent of the company. The Loews Corporation shows a return on equity of about 20 percent, far above average for its corporate sectors split between insurance and tobacco. Despite the high return on equity, the Loews' fourteen-man executive group is paid half the compensation of the Texaco management. The Tisches could easily take $6 million, but they don't. It's ironic that Loews falls into the category of an interdisciplinary security analysis problem: cigarettes, fire and casualty insurance. Nobody has bothered to analyze and write about the company. The annual report is a black-and-white printing job with no fancy lithography, but there are sufficient statistical exhibits to cause more than enough excitement for anyone who takes the time to read it carefully. The enormous accretions of net-free cash flow so far seem to have been used wisely.

LOEWS EXECUTIVE COMPENSATION

		Cash Compensation
Curtis H. Judge	President, Lorillard Division	$ 409,314
Bernard Myerson	Executive Vice President; President, Loews Theatres Division	352,684
Edward J. Noha	Chairman and Chief Executive Officers of insurance subsidiaries of CNA	534,004
Laurence A. Tisch	Chairman of the Board and Chief Executive Officer	605,338
Preston R. Tisch	President and Chief Operating Officer	605,338
All executive officers as a group (14 persons including the foregoing)		$3,782,727

The ultimate example of custodial management is the Continental Illinois Bank, which destroyed itself with ill-advised loans to domestic oil operators in 1982–83. On an equity base of $1.8 billion, over a billion dollars of domestic oil loans went bad. The bank's return on equity averaged 5 percent during 1982–83. J. P. Morgan does four times better. On a 40-million-share capitalization, management and its directors owned slightly more than 1 percent of the equity. Despite the Continental's enormous burden of bad oil loans, there were Poland, Zaire, Nicaragua, Argentina, Mexico, Brazil, and Venezuela to consider. Total nonperforming credits of

$1.9 billion exceeded the net worth of the bank. There was also an additional $2 billion in loans to Latin America—questionable, at least as to ultimate payback. By any definition of sound accounting standards, the bank was technically bankrupt, but yet solvent. Despite these problems, management was unsuccessful in holding down salaries, wages, and employee benefits. They rose an inexorable 10 percent during 1983, despite a modest decline in the head count. In fact, management thought it necessary to offer profit sharing to its executive officers and employees. When we met with them, their most pressing thought seemed to be the prospect of restoring profit sharing and incentive compensation.

We asked how $1 billion worth of poorly appraised oil-patch properties could elude their loan committees. They answered that decentralization of lending by industry sector left top management without any supervision over lending criteria. It wasn't until the loans turned bad that they finally received executive committee cognizance. When the Federal Deposit Insurance Corporation took over Continental Illinois, the first act was to fire the top management and get rid of the useless board of directors. By year-end 1985, the FDIC wrote off an additional $1.8 billion in bad loans.

The seventh largest bank in the country had contributed mightily to the excesses in domestic oil-patch drilling and exploration. It had joined readily in consortiums extending foreign credit to underdeveloped countries and their nationals. Continental Illinois had done its part in bringing the domestic banking system to its knees, helping to outline the profile of a world-wide financial panic. Yet in Chicago, it didn't seem to matter. Management insisted on preserving its $2 per share dividend, even though its timely passing would have conserved a badly needed $80 million after taxes. This move would have shored up equity or could have been used to charge off doubtful loans by further appropriations to loss reserves. A pretax charge to earnings would have helped, too. Instead, management was dedicated to preserving a semblance of business as usual. Reported earnings were buoyed by asset sales, and $18 million in income tax was paid out. Management claimed that a crisis in confidence would take place if it cut the dividend or eliminated it.

In practice, creditors are more interested in cash flow than bookkeeping earnings. It is difficult to see how the elimination of dividends would have hurt the bank. In 1985 Bank of America eliminated its dividend, and nobody even blinked. Wall Street had discounted the stock from the mid-twenties to twelve. The market had also halved Long Island Lighting as well as a bunch of other electric utilities with unfinished nuclear-power-generation stations, suspended when municipalities refused to countenance cost overruns of up to 1,000 percent. Utilities, like banks, are not rich in energized executives.

Many paths crossed as the Continental Bank remained in cramps from the heartburn of bad loans. We bought 1.5 millions shares toward the end of 1982 on our macroeconomic projection of cyclical recovery for the country. The macroeconomics was correct, but the bank couldn't earn any money. Its costs soared and earnings assets fell—something we had not foreseen—so we sold the stock for approximately what we paid for it: $21 a share. Meanwhile, the stock market rose over 60 percent. Quite probably, our block of Continental was bought by Batterymarch Capital as a contrarian play in the financial services sector. In May 1984, Larry Tisch telephoned me, wanting to know if he had bought our block of stock at $15 a share. Tisch, another bargain hunter, must have been turned on by the stated asset value of Continental: $45 a share. The bank was capitalized in the marketplace for under $500 million. It had over $45 billion in loans outstanding, but a loan-loss reserve too skimpy to provide investors much comfort.

By mid-May, Continental's stock sold off heavily on rumors of major customers defecting. Its cost of CDs was running half a point above that of other reserve city banks. South of the border, Argentina's finance minister was brooding publicly over the sharp increases in Yankee interest rates, and even Paul Volcker was pressing our banks to lower their interest rates to Third World debtors, or risk default. Continental management doggedly held the dividend at $2 a share, even though the stock was selling at $12. The bankers all wore conservative suits, white shirts, and silk rep ties, but they were the weakest link in a banking system that persistently denied that their Latin American loans were a serious problem. Soon thereafter, Continental passed its dividend, but only after its large corporate depositors cashed in CDs to the tune of $7.5 billion. By the end of May, the bank was a basket case. They sought a merger partner under the guidance of the FDIC, but there were no takers.

Morris Shapiro, an old and wise market maker in bank stocks used to say, "There are more banks than bankers in the world." I heard him say this twenty years ago, before the demise of the Franklin National Bank of New York. Unfortunately, for Continental Illinois and its investors, it was still painfully true.

Long ago, when I sifted through my senile mother's effects in her steamer trunk, under the knotted chokers of glass beads I found mildewed stock certificates of Texaco, Ford Motor Company, and U.S. Steel—all odd lots. I can still hear my father cursing the market: "The sonofabitch motors and steel. The damn oils. They never go up."

15 The United States of Leverage

SHOULD we care deeply about the course of securities markets, or is the market just a rich man's odalisque? When the market was cracking in November of 1929, the New York Stock Exchange begged all the blue-chip corporations to buy back some of their stock that had dropped so precipitously. (The motivation of stock-exchange officials was to create a more orderly market, not increase earnings per share.) Few managements made any attempt to support their underlying equities. If only there had been a buyer of last resort, like the Federal Reserve Board, which guarantees the success of every government underwriting in the bond market!

Berle and Means noted that in 1927 only 516,000 individuals with income over $5,000 reported the receipt of dividends. The American Telephone & Telegraph Company, even then sporting the longest list of shareholders—424,000—reported that 37 percent of its stockholders owned five shares or less and received an average of $25 in dividends. There were approximately 20 million stockholders of record, and since many owned stock in several corporations (assuming an average of four stocks per player), there were perhaps 5 million shareholders in pre–Great Crash America. Shareholders of American Telephone, the people's choice, at the end of 1985 approached 3 million, compounding at 3 percent per annum since 1931. U.S. Steel's shareholders—about 182,000—hardly increased at all for more than fifty years. It delivered very little, and the public stayed away.

Another way to look at securities markets is to estimate the percentage of net worth in securities on consumer balance sheets. The Federal Reserve Board's most recent survey of consumer finances—1983—showed stocks and bonds as an insignificant total when compared with homes and land values. Homes, net of mortgages, form 50 percent of consumer net worth. Stocks represent no more than 12 percent of equity. Ownership has declined since the 1970 survey. Almost 55 percent of the families surveyed reported zero to negative financial wealth. The top 2 percent of American families control more than half the financial wealth in the country. The top 10 percent controlled 86 percent. From these statistics, it is not difficult to understand the lure of lotteries, bookmaking, crap tables, and automatic teller machines, for Blacks, Hispanics, and poor whites.

The middle-class investor has a different problem. He is sucked into the market, actively and passively. Solicited by brokerage houses and mutual funds, he is a mark for the ambitious but inexperienced broker who follows his research department's recommendations. Every broker recommends at least 50 to 100 stocks—his "approved" list—which represents a compendium of a number of analysts, each contributing a few recommendations. Usually, there is no unifying theme to the recommended list. The stocks are random picks, and the "contact" is programmed for mediocre performance. Sooner or later, the poor dentist figures out that he might as well sink more money into his home—which seems to appreciate each year—or in a mutual fund, again, recommended by a salesman.

Without recognizing it, a large percentage of everyone's money is being managed by proxy. The results are mediocre. When you buy a life insurance policy or a variable annuity, your rate of return is "arbitraged" by the insurance underwriter. He is using your money, investing it to obtain a spread between what your policy guarantees and the insurance carrier's profit. On your automobile insurance, the underwriter prices your policy to give him a reasonably high return on the invested capital. A good percentage of this money is invested in the equity market. During the early seventies, a typical fire-and-casualty underwriter kept as much money in the market as he had in his capital-and-surplus account. After the 1973–74 market debacle, these carriers deleveraged themselves and put more money into bonds. If an insurance carrier has above-average investment results, it can be more competitive on policy rates. Few can boast more than an average investment experience. Many are still mired down in low-coupon bonds bought decades ago and never sold.

Aside from corporate profit-sharing funds, from which participants receive the benefits of stock-market performance, almost all pension plans are defined-benefit programs. This means that you're guaranteed a stipulated retirement sum, unadjusted for inflation and investment performance. If the plan does well in the market, the benefit goes to the employer, who can reduce his annual payments to the fund, or even withdraw substantial capital—hundreds of millions, in some instances—especially if he can prove to his actuaries that the plan is overfunded. Incidentally, in a profit-sharing plan, if an employee happens to retire during a down year in the market, he could lose a decade of performance simply because participants' equity is geared to the market upon the date of withdrawal.

It is a mistake not to believe that the quality of life is unaffected in the long run by the course of securities markets. If rates of inflation are low, the federal government's debt-service problems are eased. Just note the doubling of the interest bill in a few years, out to $235 billion. If the embedded interest rate is 8 percent instead of 10 percent, it represents a saving of almost $50 billion a year in debt service: money which would be used elsewhere in the federal budget.

A sharply eroding trade balance and a rising trend of inflation destroy confidence in a nation's currency a lot faster than the wholesaling of its gold reserve.

This table shows the total irrelevancy of gold as the underpinning for currency in circulation, or even for a country's debt. Japan has virtually no gold, but has a strong currency. Italy has three

INTERNATIONAL FINANCIAL STATISTICS

Country	Gold Stock Position[1] Amount (mil. ozs)	Value (000) ($42.22/oz.)	M1 ($ bn)	Gold Reserves As a % of M1	Gov't Debt ($ bn)[2]	Gold Reserves As a % of Gov't Debt
France	81.85	$3,455.7	$115.58	2.99%	$237.5	1.46%
Germany	95.18	4,018.5	96.77	4.15	242.7	1.66
Great Britain	19.00	802.2	0.74	1.08	235.7	0.34
Italy	66.67	2,814.8	120.65	2.33	326.9	0.86
Japan	24.32	1,026.8	335.7	0.31	752.4	0.14
United States	262.70	11,091.0	581.6	1.91	1,734.1	0.64

[1] Source: International Monetary Fund
[2] Source: O.E.C.D. Main Economic Indicators. Merrill Lynch Int'l Economic Research Dept. Data is for total government sector, including all national, state, and local units.

THE VICIOUS CIRCLE

1985-1988

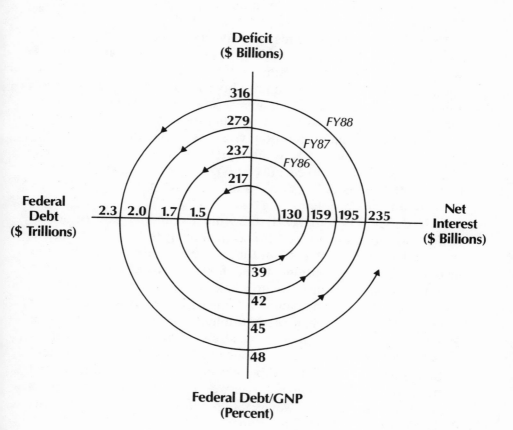

Source: Congressional Budget Office. Budget of the United States.
Our adjustments & estimates.

times more gold than Japan and Great Britain, but a weak lira. We have more gold than the five largest economic entities put together, but a horrendous trade deficit, and, recently, a declining dollar. The amount of gold backing government debt for all the Great Powers is insignificant. When gold was $800 an ounce, perhaps we could have sold $100 billion dollars worth of gold-backed bonds, saving $10 billion a year in interest expenses. The Treasury Department and Congress slept through it all.

The Social Security funds are invested solely in government bonds, so they are deleveraged in terms of performance. States and municipalities, which traditionally put little money in the stock market, are now increasing equity investments. In the past, these pension funds were used to invest even in local bond issues, thereby assuring their success. During the New York City fiscal crisis, teachers' and sanitation workers' pension funds bought hundreds of millions of new high-yielding MAC paper from the city, a move which staved off New York City's bankruptcy. The fact that the funds didn't need to invest in the tax-free paper was incidental to the problem.

It is difficult not to reach the conclusion that governmental bodies, in the last resort, will use their invested assets to insure the well-being of the state—not for good performance, which could lead to increasing retirement benefits for its citizens, or lower interest rates. The only country taking an equity position with governmental pension funds is Singapore, a virtual city-state (comparable to an Italian Medici domain). Singapore is run by a Harvard-trained strongman with a streak of mercantilism down his back. It is obviously too early to look at results, but the Government of Singapore Investment Company is capitalized at $15 billion and is an equity-oriented investor. A tax on employees and employers raises 45 percent of total wages. Such enforced savings represents 12 percent of GNP. This is an incredibly benevolent intrusion of the state into the private sector.

For the consumer, the cost of an auto loan or a mortgage is directly tied to the embedded interest cost of the bank or savings and loan making the loan. If interest rates are high, the consumer's interest costs may be too large relative to his disposable income. Everyone knows when he can and when he cannot take on more debt. High interest rates can defer the new car purchases for half the nation's families. The marvel is that interest rates are never a gut issue in the public's consciousness; only unemployment and inflation seem really vital.

The growth of money-market funds to over $200 billion during the past few years confirms the fact that the public feels that the securities markets are too tough to fathom. In France, a few years ago, the government gave its taxpayers a credit for investing new money in the stock market. The idea was to stimulate economic growth. Getting the stock market going could facilitate underwritings and enhance capital spending. France got the Bourse humming, but there was no surge in the country's growth rate. The French economic problems were too deep-seated in the labor sector and aging fixed investments in plants and capital equipment—a phenomenon most of the Western world is experiencing.

The combined fiscal deficit of the seven major industrial countries has risen 2 percentage points of their GNPs since the late seventies. This suggests a substantial claim on the private savings of all of us with, potentially, higher interest rates and erratic currency gyrations. The investor not only must pick stocks miraculously well, but also anticipate in which country to invest his money, while watching national interest rates, which affect the valuation multiplier for stocks. You could be correct on a stock purchase but lose money because of a downward earnings multiple revision, or a 10 to 20 percent swing in currency parities. An example: I bought Rupert Murdoch's News Corporation, denominated in Australian dollars, just before the Australian currency dropped from 86 cents to the dollar, to 65 cents, in a few months.

But keep in mind that the average real interest rate in the Western world during the eighties has been 5.5 percent, with long-term rates slightly higher. If you are a borrower, borrowing is more costly now than during the sixties and seventies, by a factor of 5 percentage points. In the United Kingdom, from 1868 to 1914, the average yield on undated bonds (Consols) was 2.9 percent. This was a time when there was little or no change in the cost of living. To the extent that government policy creates inflationary expectations, we all pay more for our money as borrowers. Using a "worst policies" scenario for the federal deficit—rising from $200 billion in the mid-eighties to $350 billion by 1990—it is therefore easy to project a weak dollar, rising interest rates, recession, and uniformly poor investment results for both stocks and bonds.

MAJOR INDUSTRIAL COUNTRIES: FISCAL IMPULSES

*1982-85 and 1986-87**
(In Percent of GDP/GNP at Annual Rates)

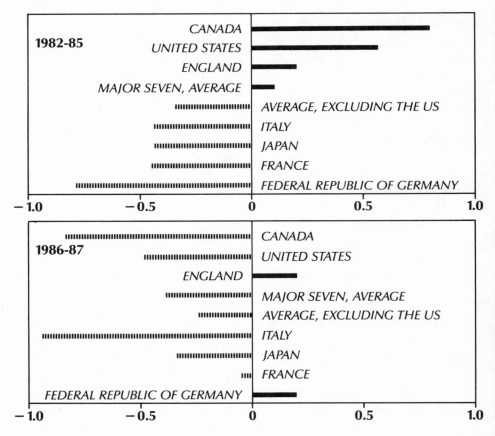

*General government, that is, central and local authorities plus social security. Data are on a national accounts basis. A positive fiscal impulse indicates injection of a stimulus; a negative impulse indicates withdrawal of a stimulus.

Source: World Economic Outlook, April 1986

In medium-range forecasting, it is crucial to know whether we are in a deflationary or inflationary environment. This should interest everyone who invests, except short-term traders. The composite GNP deflator in the Western world is as low as it has been since the mid-sixties. (The deflator is the adjustment for inflation in the country.) Then stock-market multiples boomed far above economic value because of the high confidence level and an orderly growth scenario. With oil prices on a downward course, it is difficult to project a GNP deflator of more than 4 percent the next few years. It could even fall lower if the administration and Congress get their act together. Remember that the unemployment rate in Europe probably won't decline below 9 to 10 percent by 1990 simply because most countries cannot afford further fiscal stimulation. The role of government is peaking in European countries. With comparatively higher inflation rates than the United States, any further rise in European deficits as a percentage of GNP would shuffle currency parities and aggravate inflation.

We have seen the upward drift of debt burdens for the corporate and private sectors. Debt normally declines during periods of expansion. However, this cycle is distinguished by a steady climb in leverage. Many economists shake their heads at this increased debt, suggesting that it is the beginning of the end. They think that business debt service has reached punitive levels and that the consumer-debt burden requires spending retrenchment, which is right around the corner. In the real world, aside from financial corporations who are normally heavily leveraged players with layers of junior and senior debt, the typical industrial's earnings power is affected by only about 1 percent for every 1 percent change in interest rates. So long as the earnings cycle is not in contraction, corporations are likely to maintain—or even increase—debt burdens, in an effort to leverage earnings power. The use of debt to buy in equity as a protective measure against would-be predators appears likely to continue.

If the country remains in a disinflationary mode, consumers and corporations will borrow more, disregarding historically high "real" interest rates. A borrowing consumer prefers not to look at real rates, but rather at his monthly debt-service burden as it relates to his take-home paycheck. A major error economists make is focusing on the "flow" economy, rather than the asset-based economy. They relate debt to income, rather than to just asset wealth. We are, after all, in the early stages of unwinding the inflation-hedge mentality of the seventies, beginning with oil and including farmland and other tangibles. If there is a credit crisis in the private sector, it will be asset related. More real estate and oil wells will have to be liquidated to reflect lower economic values. The current write-off of major natural resource plays—steel mills, copper mines, oil acreage—is the beginning of the deflationary unwinding. The major wholesale banks are still experiencing rising defaults on their real estate, and natural resource portfolios, including tankers forlornly waiting to be torched or scrapped. The 1985 annual reports of banks take 100 pages to explain all this.

In its annual June survey of financial and tangible assets, Salomon Brothers catches the deflationary concept dramatically. During the past five years only one tangible asset, Old Masters, showed a gain in excess of inflation, and that's esoteric enough to be suitable for only a few hundred professional players. Nothing comes close to the performance of financial assets. If inflation creeps along at 2 to 4 percent, financial assets is the action sector. During the seventies, securities markets underperformed inflation while tangibles excelled. So far, during the eighties, financial assets have provided a real rate of return whereas most tangibles show negative numbers.

If you wanted to dream a little about the impact of the disinflation thesis on financial assets, the valuation level for stocks is still in relatively low territory, viewed historically. Before you get too excited about stocks going to the moon, keep in mind that interest rates would have to decline to 4 percent, comparable with those of the early sixties. Japan and Germany, which have no inflation and 6 percent interest rates, enjoy much higher valuations for stocks than the rest of the Western world. Both governments are fiscally frugal, as are their constituents. Conceptually, stocks could sell at a 6 percent earnings yield in the United States. This is equivalent to long-term bonds yielding 6 percent. It would put us up to 16 times earnings—probably 1.5 times real book value—and take the Dow Jones Averages above 2000 without any earnings growth. We got very close to 2,000 by the summer of '86 and there was still no earnings momentum.

The concept of an upward bias to stock valuation is contrapuntal harmony to a downward bias for inflation and interest rates. The

TANGIBLES VS. INTANGIBLES

Compound Annual Rates of Return

	15 Years	Rank	10 Years	Rank	5 Years	Rank	1 Year	Rank
U.S. Coins	18.2%	1	15.1%	1	2.2	8	7.2%	7
Gold	15.2	2	10.5	7	(6.6)	13	9.2	5
Stamps	14.3	3	13.9	2	(2.0)	11	14.5	4
Oil	13.0	4	1.0	15	(15.4)	15	(48.8)	15
Diamonds	10.5	5	9.7	9	2.7	7	7.5	6
Chinese Ceramics[a]	10.4	6	12.0	4	1.5	10	1.5	12
Bonds	9.3	7	10.6	5	20.9	1	26.0	3
Treasury Bills	9.2	8	10.2	8	9.0	3	7.1	9
Old Masters[a]	8.5	9	10.6	6	7.7	4	4.8	10
Silver	8.5	10	1.9	14	(13.5)	14	(15.5)	14
Housing	8.2	11	7.8	10	4.1	5	7.2	8
Stocks	8.2	12	12.0	3	16.5	2	34.8	2
U.S. Farmland	7.4	13	4.1	12	(6.2)	12	(12.2)	13
CPI	6.9	14	6.8	11	4.0	6	1.5	11
Foreign Exchange	4.2	15	2.4	13	1.8	9	35.0	1

Inflation Scorecard (Number of Assets That Outperformed Inflation)

Tangibles	10 out of 10	7 out of 10	2 out of 10	6 out of 10
—Collectibles	4 out of 4	4 out of 4	1 out of 4	3 out of 4
—Commodities	4 out of 4	2 out of 4	0 out of 4	2 out of 4
—Real Estate	2 out of 2	1 out of 2	1 out of 2	1 out of 2
Financials	3 out of 4	3 out of 4	3 out of 4	4 out of 4

[a] Source: Sotheby's
Note: All returns are for the period ended June 1, 1986, based on latest available data.

crucial ingredient in the bull markets of 1920–29 and 1949–65 was the expansion of the earnings multiplier, not of earnings. It is exactly what is happening during 1985–86 markets. Wall Street's analysts have spent 98 percent of their time forecasting the market's earnings, its component sectors, and the individual companies, when their focus should have been on historic and comparative valuations in both deflationary and inflationary world scenarios.

Moreover, Wall Street missed the rewarding concept of the narrowing spread between stock valuations and economic value: the amount businessmen would pay to control the gross cash flow of a viable enterprise. There are hundreds of capital pools employed formerly for real estate acquisitions and natural resources, like the Belzbergs of Canada, who have moved down to Park Avenue offices and are shifting their focus toward publicly owned American companies. The Bronfmans are now taking a major position in du

Pont's affairs. It is more an oil company than a chemicals operation, these days. Yet, as we have seen, these moves seem to be a strategic error comparable with the Rothschilds' preoccupation with iron-ore properties just after the war.

We know that entire sectors of the market like oil and media, if not the market itself, are no longer a function of the ebb and flow of institutional or individual holders' interest. Moves in these groups reflect the entrepreneurial instincts of the entrenched managers or the protective measures of the custodial managers to repel predators by leveraging existing balance sheets. CBS and Unocal are examples of the protective buyback, Metromedia of the headman buying in the company for himself at a premium price. The Haas family, controlling shareholders at Levi Strauss, have come full cycle: from private enterprise to publicly owned, and now private again after a leveraged buyout. The cycle spanned less than twenty years. Operators like Steinberg, Riklis, and Lindner, who early-on were great promoters of their publicly held companies, were the first to opt for privacy, at premium prices for their equities held by the public. They sensed that it was better for them to reduce income taxes and utilize cash flow to build asset value; that it was silly to concentrate on the institutional investor's need to be gratified quarterly with a confirmation of earnings growth and periodic dividend enhancement. Even Exxon shrank its capitalization meaningfully. General Motors may be next. Its excess cash flow will build rapidly the next few years, and it has practically no debt on its balance sheet.

In an environment of steadily declining interest rates, the disparity between economic value and market value closes eventually, and then the market will reverse the process. The promoter who went public and then private will go public again with a percentage of his equity base. The stock market during 1984 and 1985 attracted approximately $100 billion a year in cash bids. During 1984, twenty-six of the S&P 500 stocks were bought out. At a time when it paid to "segment" more and more of your assets into specific market sectors, institutional investors zigged in the opposite direction. Index funds grew by tens of billions and could approach the $100 billion level during 1986. The top ten money-making sectors during 1985 and 1986 were concentrated in con-

S&P 500
PRICE EARNINGS MULTIPLES

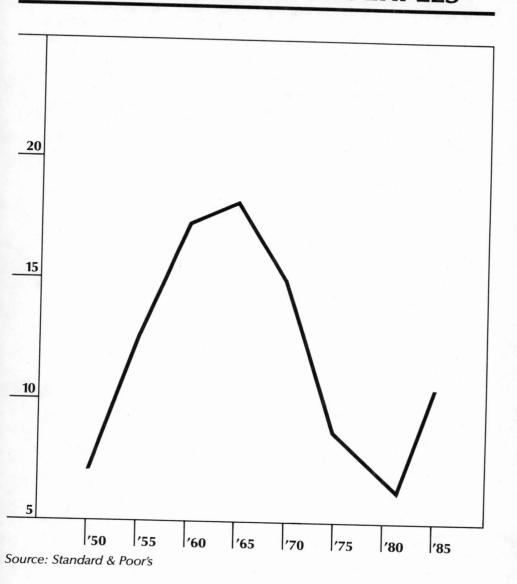

Source: Standard & Poor's

sumer-related businesses such as beverages, foods, and media operations.

Sooner or later, economists are right. In a deflationary environment, you should be selling assets and reducing debt because the rate of return on assets declines if you can't raise prices. This is true in the fixed-assets sector. You don't want to own a copper mine if it costs you 85 cents to produce a pound and the world price is 65 cents. But interest rates on acquisitions are low and tax deductible. So after you've written up assets in order to depreciate them more deeply, the United States of Leverage will go on. Because stocks and bonds thrive in a deflationary setting, the leveraging of financial assets by individuals and corporations still has a long way to run.

16   Red Highways of the Eighties

I REMEMBER Gerald Loeb in the late 50s, sitting in his tiny office at E.F. Hutton like a large puffy-faced Buddha. Loeb, a technician at heart, kept two hungry apprentices sequestered in an alcove where they were updating his daily chart books and feeding him the news off the broad-tape ticker. He clumped flat-footedly into his office at 7:30 A.M., wearing orthopedic shoes. By the opening bell, his office looked like a garbage dump. Pages torn from newspapers, chart books, and analysts' reports littered the carpet. Crumpled balls of paper that had outlived their usefulness were thrown away. By midafternoon, when Gerald departed, he was forced to kick his way through a sea of multicolored litter. At the far end of the twelfth floor at 61 Broadway, Barton Biggs and I comprised two-thirds of the institutional research department. In those days, we spent months pondering over our reports before we dared publish them.

The symbolism of Loeb's office was not lost on me, then or now. Each day was a new drama for Gerald, who traded the animals as they burst out of their cages from the opening bell until closing time. An idea often had a half-life of minutes, and information was used for instant gratification. The long term was a vague concept to fall back on to rationalize losses to your clientele. By 1960, Loeb, in his double-breasted navy blue suit, was an impeccably tailored anachronism, a throwback to the twenties, when there was either good buying (the insiders) or bad buying (the public). Nothing else—above all, security analysis—mattered. He knew the captains of industry and was particularly close to Chrysler. It was GML who told a story on himself, so he must have known the business was passing him by. Lunching with the president of Chrysler in the Chrysler executive dining room in Detroit headquarters, Loeb was perplexed by the erratic behavior of the chief executive, who kept bouncing up from his chair and excusing himself every ten minutes. Finally Gerald was asked if there was anything more management could enlighten him on. He said no, the answers to his questions were satisfactory. The photos of the new car line looked great. When Gerald landed in New York, there was a banner headline in the evening *World-Telegram: Chrysler President Fired*. The president's undisclosed ownership in an auto-parts company with which Chrysler did business had sent him to the showers.

For decades, Gerald was accustomed to processing insider tidbits. By the end of the fifties, he was caught on the outside looking in—an inferior position for a market operator. It could be seen in his mediocre performance, according to Shep Osherow, my partner, who worked some years for Loeb. While Loeb was floundering, investment research took off. Term papers written by the freshly minted Baker scholars from Harvard Business School pinpointed newly emerging growth companies like A.C. Nielsen, Dun & Bradstreet, and Haloid-Xerox. Loeb was still dictating tart letters on the Pennsylvania Railroad and Chrysler to his male secretary. Institutional trading was as yet under 5 percent of Big Board volume. There was then a public to sell stocks to when they were overripe. It was an age of technological discovery. I would walk over to Fairchild Publications on East 12th Street on Saturday morning to collect my copy of *Electronic News*. Otherwise it wouldn't reach my desk till Monday.

Twenty-five years and several billion dollars later, I was breakfasting with Henry Kaufman of Salomon Brothers in one of their intimate dining rooms on the forty-second floor of 1 New York Plaza. The building towers over New York harbor, and the symbolism is easy. The partners, including Dr. Kaufman, can watch their ships steam into port. At the highest or lowest echelons of responsibility, the day on Wall Street still begins at 7:30. Managing partners meet regularly for breakfast, and white-shirted traders with their sleeves rolled begin to dot the cavernous trading rooms, catching up on what has happened in the world while they slept.

Dr. Kaufman sensed that interest rates were headed up after the short respite in the fall of 1984. We felt that deflation was in the air and sensed the cost of money was headed down. It was time to beard the lion in his den. I had not been down to Wall Street in over a year. Henry, a frail, mild-mannered economist, spoke without emotionality about the damnation of the world. Trained at the New York Federal Reserve Board, he has a scholarly but inquisitional demeanor. It has earned him the sobriquet of Dr. Doom. While he picked at his scrambled eggs, Henry described to me the dialectics of the next financial panic.

"Why are economists so unsuccessful in predicting interest rates?" I asked him. The old days of projecting the supply and demand for credit each year no longer seemed to work.

"Ah, yes. You are on the right track," he said. "The old days are gone. Today the financial structure is too deregulated, too decontrolled, and, finally, too innovative. It is no longer possible to judge the credit structure of the country. You don't see all the credit below water: the currency futures, options, currency swaps, leasing, and all the intercountry transactions."

"You mean all the innovative financial instruments Salomon has introduced these past years—mortgage-backed bonds, for example?"

"We have done our share," Henry said.

"So what is the difference between you and a money-center bank?" I asked.

"There is an enormous difference. Salomon insists that its traders mark their positions to market at the end of every month. This is the ultimate discipline of a financial institution. But nobody wants to be disciplined these days. Do your children like to be disciplined?"

"So you're saying that the dull-normal banks remain in the throes of entrepreneurial anarchy. Banks rarely mark their loans to market," I said. "The banks' loans to Mexico are really twenty-year bonds and worth about 30 cents on the dollar."

We both sipped our breakfast coffee. Henry continued, "Under financial deregulation, when interest rates go up, everyone tries to grow his way out of the profit squeeze. Look at Citicorp. It is bad enough that they contaminated the banking system with the Latin American loans, they are now busy contaminating the insurance industry. Since they have run out of loan leverage, they are utilizing the underleveraged insurance business. Cigna will guarantee $900 million of City's Latin loans.

"And the regulators let them get away with this mufti-pufti?"

"The Federal Reserve is helpless. If it calls too much attention to Latin America, it creates the very panic it seeks to avoid."

"You mean the Federal Reserve is no longer independent?"

"I mean there is a movement in Washington that seeks to abolish the FRB. Jack Kemp wants to limit the powers of the Fed to controlling money-supply growth. The far right wants it gone."

Yes, I thought. We go back to nineteenth-century laissez-faire with a financial panic every decade to cleanse the system. Try and protect yourself against that!

Henry is warming up. "The key financing rate in the United States is not long rates. Except for the Treasury's sale of twenty-year bonds, nobody is operating there. Of the $28 billion in corporates this year, only $2 billion was long term. Think of all the adjustable-rate mortgages being written. The whole country is tied to short rates."

"Henry, you're telling me the Fed is helpless to control long rates. I accept that, but the implications are that they can control only the short rates. Doesn't it mean that the traditional economic cycle goes by the boards. It sounds as though cycles elongate."

"Yes, yes. Interest rates creep up for years while the credit excesses build, and then you have a big bang. Rates flare and the cycle ends."

"And all the bad loans are then marked to market," I thought. Yes, the private sector is too aggressive—floating-rate notes issued in the billions monthly, and Morgan Stanley just starting to underwrite and trade junk bonds. We are living in a country where any plausible corporate entity can issue hundreds of millions in bonds to eager institutional takers looking to nail down a little more coupon interest. The new-issue mania of the spring of 1983 had turned into a floating-rate-bond crap game late in 1984 that has lasted into 1986.

Dr. Kaufman continued his refrain. "No tax-reform measures will have any impact on 1985, and by then the dollar will start to weaken. As money leaves the country, interest rates will rise along with inflation." Maybe, I thought. (He was wrong.) "The exact timing is unpredictable, but it is out there on the horizon."

I have gotten answers to the questions that I expected to get when I came downtown. Twenty years ago I had breakfasted with Sidney Homer, Dr. Kaufman's predecessor at Salomon. I was then director of investment research for the Starwood Corporation, manager of assets for the Rosenwald family, cofounders of Sears, Roebuck. My first assignment for Edgar Stern, a board member, was to examine the capital structure of Sears to consider whether the company should fund $2 billion in short-term debt. Sidney sat surrounded with oversized cardboard charts on his windowsills. The economy was in a long phase of orderly growth, no excesses. Interest rates would remain in a narrow channel around 4 percent. There was no immediate need to go long term on the debt. Sears could save a quarter or half point on its interest expense.

Viscerally, I felt it was wrong to speculate to save 25 basis points, and we recommended that the board fund its short-term paper. Sears sold at 25 times earning at the time, and the board turned down our recommendation. It was a costly decision: hundreds of millions in interest expense could have been saved over the ensuing years. Sears now sells for 8 times earnings and spends its discretionary money buying control of brokerage houses like Dean Witter at 2 times book value. Dean Witter lost them tens of millions in 1984. Henry is right. Karl Marx was right! The dialectics of materialism contain the seeds of capitalism's destruction. Sidney Homer couldn't anticipate the Vietnam war, during which the politicians destroyed the orderly growth pattern of the economy. Argentina borrowed $45 billion from the banks, and more than half of it can't be found. There is some scrap iron on the Falkland Islands, but perhaps $25 billion exited the country for such productive use as Miami Beach condominiums. Meantime, Argentina's new president, Raul Alfonsin, won office on a platform calling for real wage increases of 6 percent in an economy with whirlwind inflation somewhere between 600 percent and 1,200 percent. Politics always seems to override economics. The richest man in the world may be Ferdinand Marcos, recently of the Phillippines and now in Hawaii. He denuded his underdeveloped country of somewhere between $5 billion and $10 billion.

In the money-management business, rates of return are measured against the yield on riskless cash investment. After all, why should anyone play with stocks or bonds unless the prognosis is for a higher return than T-bills? During the postwar years, the Big Board has delivered a real return of 5.5 percent per annum, or about 5 points above cash equivalents. Lee Cooperman of Goldman, Sachs argues that to remain attractive, stocks should keep at least this 5-point edge over cash, plus some premium for all the risks you take. So if T-bills yield 7 percent, the required return on stocks is over 12 percent. Remember, the typical multi-national dollar corporation is not structured to earn more than 15 percent on invested capital. It pays out 40 percent of its earnings in dividends and retains 60 percent for reinvestment, thereby affording investors a theoretical 9 percent internal growth rate plus 4 or 5 percent in dividends. I say "theoretical" because corporations can grow old and die. Rates of return on equity during recessions go down to 11 or 12 percent. Dividends can compound slowly. Only in hyperinflationary periods do rates of return rise much above 15 percent. Every serious discussion on what stocks are worth usually bogs down in theoretical gibberish. Price-earnings ratios, earnings yield, equity-risk premiums, price to book value, price to inflation-adjusted book value. No benchmark of value ever seems anything more than a working hypothesis. The market has overshot or underachieved theoretical valuation zones by 25 to 50 percent from cycle to cycle.

Why own stocks if the banking and savings and loan world were going to bid for money and sooner or later load up again with mini-Argentinas? I was beginning to feel as obsolete as Gerald M. Loeb twenty-five years ago. The stock market had become one giant instant-discount machine for interest rates. Even Dr. Doom admitted readily that you can no longer forecast interest rates. The players are no longer stuck in their traditional molds. A day after my breakfast with Henry, he rushed into print with a new forecast. Rates were going down for some months with the vital signs of the economy flattening: consumer credit, retail sales, inventories. It took just three days in August for the market to shoot up to 10 percent on a readjustment of its perception, that, after all, 15 percent interest rates (the Kaufman forecast then) were not at all just around the corner. While this was going on, I was caught in a traffic jam between Nice and Cannes.

A few years ago, I bought a seat on the Chicago Board of Trade for my twenty-two-year-old nephew. Tommy spends most of his time on the floor concocting neutral spreads on options and trading stock-index futures. He scalps eighths and quarters, and by the end of the day, his tan smock has been torn to shreds and his eyes cry for a bunch of drops. I have just asked our clients to permit us to use S&P 500 futures. There is no other way to deal with the market's volatility. The futures index market's daily open interest

S&P EARNINGS YIELD vs. INTEREST RATES

(1975-1985)

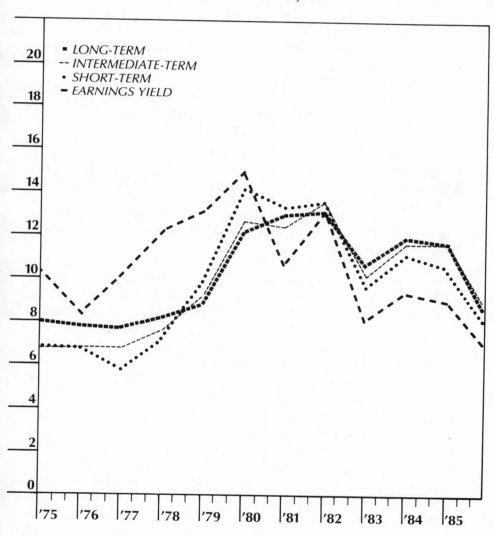

- LONG-TERM
-- INTERMEDIATE-TERM
- SHORT-TERM
- EARNINGS YIELD

now exceeds the New York Stock Exchange equivalent dollar volume. And because there are so many players, you can buy $1 billion worth of futures without moving the market more than 30 basis points. Tommy tells me we should be trading the S&P 100 options on the index and not the futures. It's where markets are even more liquid, with hundreds of traders killing each other minute by minute. This is an example of where financial deregulation takes us. There are futures indices on over-the-counter stocks, high-technology groupings—you name it. As Henry said at breakfast, "Nobody wants to be disciplined. Does your child like to be told what to do?"

By mid-decade, the markets finally sensed deflation. The Open Market Committee of the Federal Reserve Board sniffed the air in the fall of 1984 and found it a little heavy:

> Most believed that appreciably slower, but sustainable, growth with some pickup in the rate of inflation were probable, though by no means certain, prospects for 1985. Several observed, however, that uncertainties created by various imbalances and financial strains in the economy made forecasting economic activity and prices particularly difficult at this time, and less confidence should be placed in any particular forecast.

After looking for inflation under every rock since 1980, the board couldn't agree on a forecast of much more than 5 percent for 1985. In the fall of 1984, the Wholesale Price Index actually posted a negative rate. Early in 1986, when oil prices collapsed, the Consumer Price Index dropped below zero. The country had a negative inflation rate for the first time in decades.

I sent my computer boys back to their machines and asked for a color graph correlating interest rates with the earnings yield for the stock market. Although I knew that the market's earnings yield had to track long-term interest rates, I was amazed to find that the highest correlation was with short-term rates, especially with linked time spans of 2, 3, 4, and 8 years. Because of the enormous changes from the historic norm for real interest rates, I then sent them back to adjust the earnings yield for past inflation. If a dollar of earnings was worth less during hyperinflation, it was going to be worth more with deflation closing in. In the early sixties, when interest rates chugged along at 4½ percent, the market sold at 18 times earnings or an earnings yield of little more than 5, thereby matching bond yields. For the late eighties, this is the big dream. It has already begun to happen.

Not only had the Federal Reserve Board reached an inflection point where even the members had begun to discern deflation, but the market had to deal with an energizing concept of reductive simplicity. The quality of earnings was moving up while reported earnings momentum decelerated. (IBES gathers about 8,400 estimates for the stocks in the index.) IBES had estimated the Dow Jones Industrials would earn $139.14 for 1984. The actuality was $113.58. The $152 a share estimate for 1985 proved high by a comparable 20 percent. Early in 1986 the IBES earnings estimate for the S&P 500 was $19.78 a share. Our most optimistic projection is $17 a share for 1986. It looked like $16 by October. During May, analysts made 1160 upward revisions of earnings and 1818 downward revisions, suggesting that they had begun to waver in their optimism. There was no change on fifty percent of the analysts' estimates. It didn't matter. The market rose 20 percent as interest rates crashed down. Analysts' projections typically top out a few quarters after the peak rate of growth in industrial production. I sent our guys back to their scratch pads after they handed me a downward-revised 1986 projection for the Dow Jones earnings that still seemed too optimistic.

"Schmeiss your numbers on steel, chemicals, and the oils and then let me see it," I said.

The inner voice started yammering again. "Idiot! Less is more. Less is more, you fool. When are you going to wake up? There is a long cycle out there for bonds and stocks before the music dies. Forget earnings! The market is valuation driven."

One night my Washington contact telephoned. Ambassador Dobrynin was smiling broadly again, with his let's-make-a-deal face. For me, the mosaic finally was completed. Even the Russians needed some respite for their private sector. Arms control became a possibility, even with a hard-line president. Reagan had stumbled on what could be the most significant change in the Western world: the role of government was peaking. Federal budgets had grown steadily, reaching 50 to 60 percent of GNP in Scandinavia, the Netherlands, Italy. France and England struggled with double-digit unemployment and an industrial base that was losing its competitive status. Archaic state-countenanced work rules and

GOVERNMENT EXPENDITURES AS A % OF GNP

1973-1985

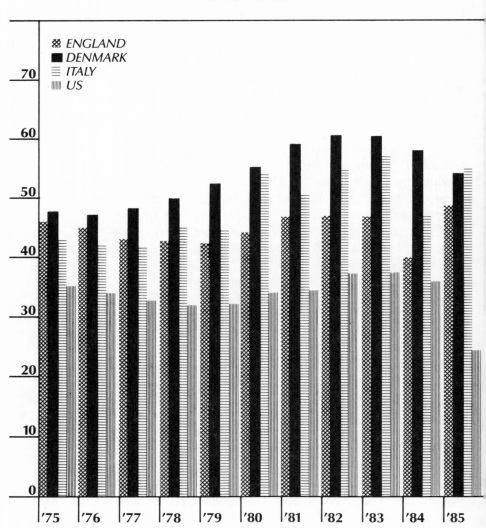

seniority systems, along with incompetent management, had taken their toll throughout Europe, and the Russians were adrift in the same boat. Why was wheat production diminishing each year? In the spring of 1986, the French socialists, under Mitterrand, lost to the conservatives. Chirac, the new prime minister, moved immediately to denationalize banks and other state-controlled industrial sectors.

On my last visit to Denmark, in downtown Copenhagen, there was a demonstration against unemployment by thousands of mute bicyclists who pedaled by in impeccable double files. I bisected their line and was awarded the finger by a gray-bearded Dane. Yes, I thought. You all live in neat whitewashed cottages with the windowpanes trimmed bright red. But the rooms are tiny, and the downstairs living room becomes a bedroom at night. This is the very best that enlightened socialism delivers. And the Japanese, for all their prosperity, lived in cracker boxes. No wonder the savings rate is three times ours. There is no room for anything you buy.

After a big up day in the market, I met my wife at the Museum of Modern Art for the opening of its exhibition, "Primitivism in Twentieth-Century Art." The curating by William Rubin was breathtaking in scope. The tribal masks and the wooden figures from all primitive cultures were adopted freely by the Western world's great names. Not only was Picasso enthralled with this work, imitating its conceptual reductiveness, but pieces by Matisse, Modigliani, Gauguin, Henry Moore, Miro, Giacometti, and comparable giants bordered on pure copying.

"My God! You can't trust anything you see," I said to Toni.

"Yes," she said. "I knew your business was full of sleazy characters, but who would have thought there were so many second-story operators in the art world?"

There are a half dozen more sophisticated market indices than the Dow Jones Averages, but none older, simpler, and more reductive of the market, in the public's consciousness. Television broadcasters don't know the Wilshire 5,000 or the Standard & Poor's 400. Even some professional investors assume that Dow Jones is a relic of the twenties, when there was nothing but basic industrials like U.S. Steel, Mack Trucks, and Victor Talking Machine. A closer look suggests that the Dow today is as good as

DOW JONES DART BOARD

Price Weighted Contribution

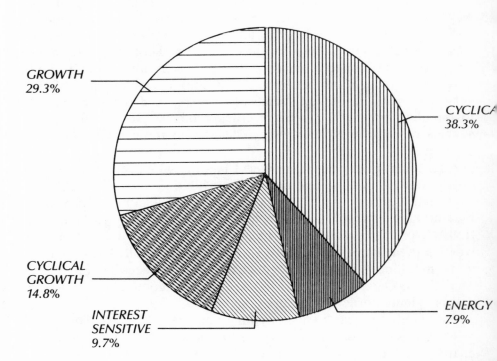

GROWTH
29.3%

CYCLICA‹
38.3%

CYCLICAL
GROWTH
14.8%

INTEREST
SENSITIVE
9.7%

ENERGY
7.9%

(The smart way is to throw at sectors, not stocks.)

Mask. Sira-Puna. Gabon. Painted wood. 12¼" high. Private collection.

Henri Matisse. *Portrait of Mme. Matisse* 1913. Oil on canvas. 57⅝" × 38¼". The Hermitage Museum, Leningrad.

any other index in reflecting the bias of the averages toward high-priced growth companies with big-market capitalizations. Industrials, if weighted by their low prices, comprise just 36 percent of the index, and the growth and countercyclical stocks dominate the index. The stock market can go up without U.S. Steel selling around $25 a share. But it can't rise without IBM, Merck, Eastman Kodak, and MMM, whose average price is closer to par. These four stocks, weighted by their price level, comprise 27 percent of the Dow.

It is from such reductive realigning that a useful hypothesis takes shape. Corporations with the highest returns on equity are worldwide operators like IBM and Merck. The enormous appreciation of the dollar had slowed them down. In a deflating environment, there is no pricing leverage. The dollar had to decline 40 percent or more just to relieve profit-margin pressure from foreign goods. This is what happened in late 1985 and 1986. Being a manufacturer in America today is crazy. Few were prepared for the 70-percent trade-weighted appreciation of the dollar over five years. Aside from IBM, few companies have enough efficiently positioned factories. It will take years to reposition such facilities. The pivotal variable is that the dollar slips some more because the disparity in real interest rates between us and the rest of the world has narrowed. Our corporate profits have no great elasticity in this environment, which may stretch through the eighties.

O, that I could project 3000 on the index or even a Joe Granville 500! (Granville stayed bearish for the first 1,000-point rise in the market from its 1982 low; he didn't turn bullish until February of 1986.) The market could go up only if the earnings multiplier rose, and that could rise only if interest rates had a downward bias. So pray each day for lower interest rates. That's all we need. Otherwise, there is no windblown boat on the horizon with a sail of gold numbered 3000. Unless interest rates stay reasonably low, two thousand years hence, when they dredge up the Statue of Liberty in 400 feet of mud, the historians will say there was no Trojan horse in the Western world's financial system: "They did it to themselves." Among economic practitioners, Karl Marx may prove himself the only reliable forecaster of long-term trends.

17 Goodbye, Tanzania

EAST AFRICA—a place of dwindling options. As our Beechcraft buzzes a dirt airstrip clogged with buffalo and wildebeests I think, "If we cannot chase them off, we cannot land." Nearby is a baby rhino with its placid mother rolling in a bath of dust. They have been around for maybe 60 million years. Later, we sneak up on a nursery of female hippos and their young sunning on a sandbank, a male submerged to his bulging eyeballs at the top of the deep pool in the river, guarding his harem. Dennis, our guide, stands up and discourses with the animals as we adjust our zoom lenses to frame this scene: "I say, gentlemen. Can you show me the best passage across your river?" There is a chorus of grunts, chest tones that resonate for hundreds of yards through the stillness, and then a staccato splashing of muddy bodies plunking into the brown water.

Later, we startle a family of elephants with babies not even reaching their mothers' bellies, the darkish birth down crowning their heads. The calves play in the mud, tossing watery clods over their shoulders onto their backs. The mothers fan themselves with their ears, one eye cocked on us, but smiling. By the roadside, a good specimen of a mature male baboon refuses to bolt, and he stares us down. Defiantly, he masturbates. It takes a few seconds, and then he savors the semen with smacking lips.

We scout two harems of impala from our Land Rover: two males reign over a dozen females each. There is an altercation. A doe leaves Harem A for Harem B, and Harem A's buck chases after her, snorting disapproval. A ritual show of horns between the two crown princes. The deprived stud lowers his head and butts the usurper, who gives ground. But the fickle doe dances away and scampers off joyfully to Harem B. Ginny and Toni laugh hysterically at the untoward outcome. Richard and I identify with the spurned lover who snorts away, wagging his horns in frustration. Toni, my wife, says, "Isn't that something! He does everything right and still loses the girl,'' and Ginny, "This is definitely not musical comedy, where the coward wins." The buck urinates over the defecting female's discharge. Where are our movie cameras?

Then we climb back into the two-engine Beechcraft. Fiona, our pilot, perhaps the best in East Africa, offers us coffee, tea, juice, and sourballs to suck on for the lift-off. We taxi over the red clay, and the lethargic buffalo shuffle off. Forty minutes later, we are back in Nairobi, where the streets are crammed with cars—Mercedes-Benzes, Volvos, Escorts. The city's meter maids, in pastel uniforms as *de trop* as their cousins in New York, sport outlandishly peaked caps. Downtown, fifteen-story office buildings are sprouting up, the developers, consortiums of Europeans, Indians, and Anglo-Saxons. Nairobi is reminiscent of a thriving midwestern city, except that everyone is black; the men dressed in pressed slacks and fresh white short-sleeved shirts, the women a touch frumpy in cotton housedresses. The ambiance is quiet politeness, a touch of loudness, affability, and accent.

Richard reports on the rounds he has just made at the middle-class "white" hospital in Nairobi. (The Blacks go to a lesser institution.) They are back in the mid-fifties in terms of surgical procedures and medical technology, and he has promised his counterpart, the ob-gyn chief, a care package of new equipment, including adjustable head lamps for the O.R., an unheard-of amenity. Dennis is taken aback when Richard informs him that the painful prostate procedure he had undergone has been long obsolete, simplified and quite painless today. In medicine, at least, there is progress.

The dark, densely grained Maconde sculpture that we haggled over in Tanzania we find marked up 1,000 percent in Nairobi's principal *objets d'art* outlet. Hard currency talks. The dollar is preferred everywhere. I remember our experience in London on the eve of the Nixonian dollar devaluation—ten years ago? We were dining in the Dumpling Inn on Gerrard Street in Soho, and the couple on our left had run out of pounds. The proprietor demanded a 20 percent haircut for their dollars, and I was so outraged that I sold them currency at the bank rate of exchange.

We grab a Paris *Herald-Tribune,* the first in twelve days, and the stories are uniformly bleak. The Iranian president and prime minister have been blasted into eternity by the outs. The Americans are blamed. The stock market has slumped another 50 points. I am poorer by $1.5 million, but feel no pain. The Hang Seng index in Hong Kong is sympathetically lower. Money rates are pushing up all over the world. Gold rallies. Interest-rate futures make new lows, and the Nippon Dow Jones drops 70 points a day—about 1 percent. In France, the franc is six to a dollar. It had been four to one. Mitterrand is elected on a platform of wealth distribution. Higher taxes for higher brackets. Escalating social welfare spending, nationalization of banks, and more job creation. Three years later, the franc is 10 to a dollar. Cyclicality, endurance, it will take a hundred years more before even Venice sinks back into the mud. Every time we have entered Italy there has been an airline strike and a work stoppage on the railroads, but the pasta comes forth from the ovens bubbling hot, and the Tuscany wine tastes the same. The chart on inflation spells out, finally, the turn away from fiscal stimulation for the Western world during the mid-eighties.

Even in the Western world, progress has become a nostalgic concept. Back home, in 1982, Reagan wrestled with his accelerating defense budget in the face of a budget deficit going past $60 billion, not the projected $40 billion. We headed toward $200 billion by the mid-eighties. The assumptions of the Council of Economic Losers were as outlandishly ineffective as an ostrich hiding from its enemies, its head lowered to ground level. The council had projected 5 percent economic growth and a debt service cost declining to 6 percent for Treasury bonds by fiscal 1984. The actuality: long Treasuries hit 14 percent in the spring of 1984. Meanwhile, the president of General Motors was tearing his hair out in 1981. Production schedules were cut back, and the General Motors dividend, heretofore unassailable, looked shaky. We were building fewer homes in the U.S. than in Japan. Negative GNP growth was a common denominator for the Western world during 1981. By the spring of 1986, the world's economists still awaited a meaningful acceleration.

On Wall Street, Henry Kaufman, Dr. Doom, croaked like an old toad: "Monetizing the debt is inflationary. The federal government is crowding everyone else out of the bond market. Interest rates are headed irregularly higher until the budget comes closer into balance." Bullshit. Long bonds fell to 10 percent by mid–1985 and 8 percent early in 1986. (But Kaufman had been right for a long time.)

MAJOR INDUSTRIAL COUNTRIES

Average Inflation Rates and Their Variation Across Countries 1980-86

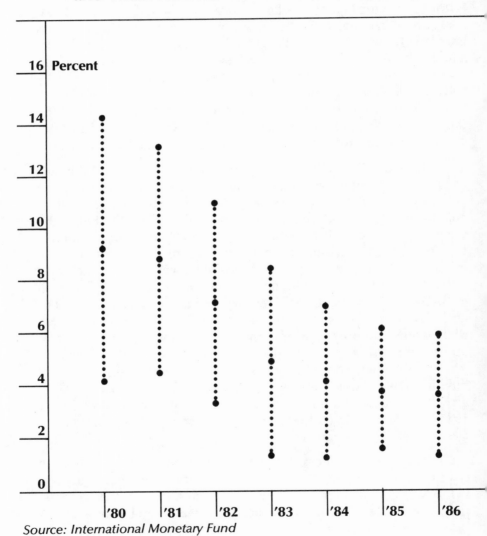

Source: International Monetary Fund

Ten years ago, the game parks were thickly populated. The white hunters had to thin out elephant herds by the hundreds. Poachers hadn't bought their helicopters yet, and rhino horn was selling slowly as an aphrodisiac in Hong Kong. After OPEC, Arab teenagers demanded rhino-horn handles for their daggers. It is another variant of sexual insecurity. In the early sixties, from his zebra-striped plane, Michael Grimzak logged fifty-nine rhino in the Ngorongoro Crater. Twenty years later we spotted five, and two were calves. Soon the only rhino will be in the zoos of the Western world. This lethargic, nearsighted beast is overmatched against well-capitalized poachers who hunt from helicopters. Dennis, the cold-blooded realist, looked at the problem on a higher level:

> Poaching created a middle class in Nairobi. We exported tens of millions in ivory and rhino horn, and in a few years it will be all gone. The money has been reinvested in local businesses. Game parks must be transformed into grazing land and farms. Primogeniture has shrunk down the subdivisions of arable land to uneconomic units, and the desert encroaches inexorably. The blacks will not stand by and allow their cattle to starve so we can watch elephant and rhino. Enjoy it while you can.

We arrived at the Crater Lodge just in time for the evening meal. The dining room is a melting pot of Indians, Germans, English, and Blacks. Wildebeest steak is our entree, but it is so gamey and tough that one bite is enough. Ginny cleans her plate gamely, but the next night she bypasses the zebra steak for a pork chop. A bottle of Tanzanian red wine is ordered up, the label bereft of any information. It is highly tannic, barely potable. Where are the friars Dom Perignon and Dom Ruinart? The residue of an English protectorate which stretched over fifty years is the table service, which is punctiliously deft. Clear soup to start and then a dish of Nile perch, tenderly overcooked. The wildebeest is served up with cauliflower and glazed carrots. Dessert is flan, and it is cook's best. Dennis lectures the wine steward as if he were a twelve-year-old boy. Unless there is a written receipt forthcoming, Dennis will not pay. He is firm but pleasant. The old Black is confused, and he calls over the maître d' who tells Dennis, in polished English, that the wine will be put on the room bill. Dennis upbraids him. There was supposed to be a birthday cake for Ginny—with candles—and there is none. There is no frame of reference to deal with a birthday-cake order in the Crater Lodge, so it is ignored. Asleep in our cabin, we are startled by a buffalo scratching his horns against the plywood wall. He is dozing outside our window in peaceful coexistence.

Aside from Ngorongoro Lodge, which sits on the rim of a steep-sided natural bowl nine miles in diameter, the other lodges in Tanzania are politically made mausoleums. Wherever we stayed, there were no more than a dozen occupied rooms out of 150. The swimming pool at Lake Manyara, which I remembered fondly, ten years previous, when it was bubbling with chattering Germans, mourns rippleless, its waters an opaque inky green. Two pretty Parisiennes prattle away at the pool's edge, but the opaque water is too foreboding for anything more than toes. At dinner, there are more staff than guests, and five white-frocked waiters fuss over our wine bottles. They probably haven't opened a dozen throughout the season.

One runs out of amenities at the Seronera Lodge on the edge of the Serengeti plain. The hot water there is turned on for one hour at 8:00 P.M., the dinner hour. Obviously, management believes we should either eat and remain filthy or starve and be well scrubbed. Electricity is off for the night at 11:00, and after breakfast, the generator shuts down. No cold water, no toilet flushing. The petroleum pipeline does not extend this far. There is nothing to drink at night. No beer, no bottled water—only lemon squash, which the locals dilute with water. We buy a bottle of concentrate but are afraid to dilute it with the water; we brush our teeth and use it for a mouthwash. Later, Fiona's plane flies in a CARE carton of vodka, tonic, passion-fruit juice, and Grand Marnier. We have moved to a campsite and dine outside, our tents pitched on the edge of the Serengeti plain that fans out to the horizon. It is like looking out on the world. Richard has built a campfire, and as the lion roars miles away in the resonant blackness of the bush, we sip Grand Marnier. It's a long way from the East Bronx.

The Hemingway stories flow effortlessly from Dennis. How Dennis spent six months fishing off Cuba on the *Pilar,* a tub of a boat. Hemingway would devour books all day while Dennis watched the bait skipping over the water. They fished for months and caught but a few blue marlin. The old man downed two bottles of booze per diem and was already into his final depression. It is a mellowing coda to a full day of game viewing. The more we saw, the more we compared animal behavior with our own—the two-year-old jealous lion who tried to please his mother by stalking a wildebeest by himself, the mother oblivious to him but engrossed with another cub; the defiant baboon who faced us down in our Land Rover and masturbated. Fragile novelties.

The border between Tanzania and Kenya is a mess of red tape. Since the financial debacle of East Africa Airways years ago, tourists cannot move readily between the two points but must enter and leave through a third country. It is not so different than the mideast years ago, when you couldn't fly directly from Jerusalem to an Arab country. Our travel agency has made out business cards for us, and we are posing as travel agents. Aside from two Indian merchants, two Catholic sisters in white muslin, and a few backpackers, we are the only tourists at the border town. The customs men are stubble-bearded, sullen, more like vagrants than government officials. There are two canary-yellow Mercedes 280s parked in front of police headquarters: the president's cars. We see them again at the Arusha Airport, along with his entourage of bereted soldiers in camouflaged fatigues, shouldering rapid-firing, Russian-made carbines. The men have big spaces between their four upper incisors. Orthodontia exists only where there is a middle class. It is hard to say which is the anachronism: the spiffy limos with the tiny presidential flags fluttering, or the tin-roofed shanties from which the hawkers thrust at us beaded necklaces that are as broad as Elizabethan ruffs. The Masai are decked out in them.

We rotate from desk to desk, signing in on the police blotter, a crudely hand-ruled paper, the column widths bearing no relationship to the length of one's proper name. And the president's photograph smiles down benevolently from the roach-powder walls, Nyerere's teeth filed down to diamond-shaped points. The photograph is omnipresent in public buildings, the sole wall hanging, a 24″ × 24″ black-and-white lithograph framed in dark wood. Besides the Mercedes, it is the most pervasive object of demagoguery.

Unexpectedly, there is a stretch of road from Namanga to Arusha that is surfaced in asphalt. Not much wider than a footpath with many manned checkpoints, it turns to dirt an hour out of town. A few motor lorries churn up dust, some bicycles, then a half-ton jitney crammed with good-natured Blacks hanging off the fenders and from the tailgate. In Tanzania, when you walk, you fight the road dust that turns your hair into steel wool in seconds. Roadside loungers, waiting for a jitney, are wrapped in capelike outer garments, sleeping like mummies. The iconography of the country is lassitude. Tanzania lies gasping for air. There is no hard currency to buy diesel fuel. We transport huge canisters of gasoline in our minibus.

And the contrasts. Well-scrubbed schoolchildren in their green cotton shirts and shorts wave us on, while the Masai boys prod their pygmy cattle expertly onto the roadbed.

Tanzania is supposed to be a venture in socialism, but everyone we meet is entrepreneurial. American currency brings double the official rate of exchange. We use it sparingly. Outside the Lake Manyara Lodge there is a cluster of al fresco peddlers with a selection of Maconde sculptures made from an ebonylike oily wood. Bargaining unmercifully, we scratch out bids with a bent nail on the dusty black inner forearms of the offerees, crossing out their numbers and writing in ours, down 50 percent or more. One young crook wants $40 and my bush hat for a semirepresentational free-form carving. It looks like a mass of gymnasts pyramiding themselves, linked in gracefully contorted nude torsos. A gaily colored beaded belt catches my eye, and my new friend wants my wife's sunglasses and the tennis shirt off my back. Later, I return with three dirty T-shirts and get my belt. Our driver tells us that these rags will be resold that day for more than 100 shillings ($12 each). Nobody in Tanzania is making T-shirts. Today someone there is sporting a green T-shirt that displays the American Ballet Theater Company in *Giselle*. I bought it for $6 five years ago at a Lincoln Center performance. Next time, I will bring a dozen Timexes and buy up half the country.

Back in Nairobi Airport, East Africa's linkage to the Western world, British Airways has overbooked its twice-weekly 747 bound for London. There is an hour's hassle with over fifty bumped travelers. A twelve-year-old Indian boy headed for public school in England has a seat, but not his father, and they are losing an argument with the dispatching clerk. The mournful reproaches of the middle-aged father resonate throughout the cavernous waiting room. Nobody looks up. The father may not get out for a week. Later, a bereted soldier slides his hands down my flanks and brushes over my private parts. Toni has her left breast squeezed by a matron dressed like a meter maid. We are as yet a step away from the developed world. Later, we adjusted our sleeper seats until they were stretched out to barber-chair proportions. As we lift off, I see a grass fire burning 500 yards adjacent to the runway. It is the symbolism of East Africa. Controlled or uncontrolled, the grass fires burn off the protein-deficient dried grass so new green shoots may sprout from the depleted soil. Meantime, the desert moves like a slow, undulating tide across the plains sizing down the grazing cattle. A Masai herd encountered in the Serengeti was the size of collies. Our cicerone, Dennis, ex-British army captain, white hunter, chief game warden, and now citizen of Kenya, paries any hopes we have for the longevity of primeval Africa:

> Just as your bison on the Great Plains disappeared in the nineteenth century, our wildebeest in the Serengeti will be shot for meat. The ultimate reality is that only 15 percent of the land is arable, and the pressure for grazing rights and food will lead to the plowing up of the game parks. The arithmetic is too simple for the politicians to oppose. Nobody really cares about tourism anymore. How can you blame them when 40 percent of foreign-exchange earnings goes for petrol imports? Here they would rather be poor and independent than better off and dependent. Your concept of progress doesn't exist in the African psyche.

"But what will happen to these countries?" I ask, knowing that Dennis is about to administer his factual coup de grace.

"They will turn back to tribal rule, and God only knows they may be better off. Infant mortality in the bush is still running at a 70 percent rate the first year, but the population gain is put at 4 percent per annum." He looks at Richard. "You go try to sell birth control to a mother and father who don't see more than one or two of their six babies grow to maturity!"

Before the plane lifts off we play catch with hot washcloths. The sleepers from Johannesburg are unamused and squirm restlessly in their barber chairs. They have been on board for eight hours, and there are eight more hours to Heathrow Airport in London.

"Ah, if only your grandmother could see you now," I whisper into Toni's ear. "The goblets of champagne, chablis and Brane Cantenac lined up on your tray." Grandmother was a congenital sender-back of burnt toast and moist lettuce. It had to be toweled off. Were the East Africa game parks just another amenity? We had our 25 packets of Ektachrome slides. The Tanzanian citizens had little but the encroaching desert, and their politicians cruising by in yellow Mercedes-Benzes. We overhear the man next to us telling his female companion how he couldn't have enjoyed the trip with another woman. For months he has debated whether he could make a lasting commitment. The abrasive neuroses of New Yorkers are seeping back into the cramped Concorde cabin. Out of the corner of my eye, I note the tears running down the wife's cheeks. Like Tanzania, she had nowhere to go.

After fifty, it is hard to hold onto a growth concept. Dennis lives alone and has not seen his grandchildren in London. The prostate problem enforces a slim ration of alcohol. Fiona's husband turned paranoid and tried to shoot her. She is divorced. Earlier, the foremost fertility specialist in London could not help her conceive. The African sun has deposited crow's-feet on her upper lip. For Richard, the reality of his hospital is a hundred overachieving middle-aged doctors cutting each other up. There are too many doctors who want to be on Park Avenue. And I contend with an unruly stock market that will ebb and flow, short-circuiting some of my self-esteem if I am fallible. Toni still yearns for an acting career that was a challenge in her twenties.

We are jarred by the Concorde as it smacks the fogged-in runway at Kennedy with a *khrumpt* that resonates in our eardrums. The steward, who is perched on his jump seat, exchanges looks with me, his eyes terrorized. It was the hairiest landing of his experience, he told me later, a combination of the 100-foot ceiling, a strong tail wind and an aircraft with a high landing speed. We had consumed all of the runway right to Jamaica Bay. The pilot—all of us—had run out of options long before landing—just like Tanzania.

At mid-decade, two unrelated events underscore a point at which the professional investors' heads were turned. What is better, hard assets, or soft loans? New and very large oil tankers were slipping out of their dry docks and heading toward Korea, where they were to be blowtorched into heaps of scrap. VLCCs that cost $80 million to construct a year ago were valued at $6 million as scrap. Saudi Arabian oil production declined to 2 million barrels a day, down from 10 million barrels at the peak of the oil crises in the early 1980s. The Saudis had slipped from a budgetary surplus of tens of billions to a deficit. They had two years of dollar reserves left. The Persian Gulf, for which the tankers were designed, was not yielding much oil trade.

Meantime, the broadcasting trade press was nipping at my heels. Why did we own so much CBS for our clients? Was Larry Tisch really going to step up and buy it all? Isn't Tisch, a hard-asset player, acting out of character? Is he imitating his friend Warren Buffett, another value player, who has gone outside his discipline with a major investment in the ABC buyout by Capital Cities Broadcasting? (Larry became Acting President of CBS in 1986.)

There is always a new underwriting that encapsulates the financial history of the country cycle to cycle. In the late fifties, the public passed the baton of speculation to professional money managers who have run with it for twenty years without setting any world records. Twenty-odd years later the Manhattan Fund topped out the era of professional speculation. Today the modern corporation and its ilk has the stick in its hand and is leveraging itself with company buyouts that are closing the gap between economic value and market prices. This is exemplified in the leveraged buyout of Storer Communications by Kohlberg, Kravis, Roberts & Company (KKR), underwritten by Mike Milken and his company, Drexel Burnham Lambert, which beat out Merrill Lynch and the Bank of Montreal, although their offer on paper seemed higher. It was a $2.5 billion deal, but there have been bigger ones. What is so telling in the Storer LBO (aside from good old Citibank's and Manufacturers Hanover's participation of $740 million in financing) is the nonexistent coverage of the interest on the debt created to do the deal.

Storer was one of the first companies to enter the television business in 1948, and now reaches 9 percent of all television households with its stations. It is also the fifth-ranked cable-television operator. The newly formed holding company shows 10 percent equity against $2.3 billion in long-term debt. In a footnote to the summary of pro forma financial data, it is noted that there is a shortfall of combined fixed-charges coverage and preferred dividends of $284 million for 1984 and $127 million for the first six months of 1985. Without a sizable disposition of properties, there is no way that cash flow can be covered from the operating results of the broadcasting properties. During 1985 and 1986 the bidding up of media and broadcasting properties reached feeding-frenzy proportions. Even The New York Times, Gannett, and the Washington Post Company releveraged their balance sheets to buy broadcasting and newspaper properties. In June 1986, John Kluge was selling off his cellular radio operations, having already disposed of his Metromedia stations. Perhaps Kluge's all cash position was a signal that the industry had closed the gap between market value and economic value. Maybe, . . .

Herein lies the total polarity of the investment setting. VLCCs steam toward Korea and Taiwan to be turned into washing machines and typewriters. Wall Street's most voracious operators vie to buy, for 10 percent down, a broadcasting franchise that will have a quarter-billion-dollar cash-flow deficit from day one. Hard assets go for 10 cents on the dollar and soft assets go and go and go. The players justify both their investments as inflation hedges. They are absolutely right if inflation prevails. In a deflationary setting, I tire of switching off my children's TV receivers tuned to the Sports Channel. Then I cancel my subscription. The Rangers still play hockey, but the kids sleep longer. More tankers are chopped into slabs of steel earmarked for recycling. The cattle in Tanzania forever stay the size of collies in the Masai herds. For them there are no economic cycles: only for us.

18 Silent Investor, Silent Loser

WHEN the 747 banked into its final turn to Kennedy, the pilot switched on his intercom: "Ladies and gentlemen, we have been rerouted by air traffic control to a southern landing approach. Those of you on the left side of the plane will obtain a rare daylight view of the New York skyline as we fly over the Statue of Liberty and then parallel the building facades of Wall Street and midtown Manhattan before turning toward Kennedy."

And what about those of us on the right side of the plane? I thought. I am in an aisle seat on the right side of the plane, and I can see nothing; the dreary grids of Queens, the rows of two-family hutches in Flushing. "Those of you on the right side of the plane will see nothing," I said out loud.

Twenty-five years ago, when I was in my twenties with $500 to my name, I was a junior analyst covering the electronics industry. It was just beginning to spit out transistors for military transceivers and computers. I took my $500 and bought 25 shares of International Telephone & Telegraph because I had heard from friends who were reporters in the Washington bureau of a newspaper that IT&T was going to win a multibillion-dollar defense contract. The company won the contract, and years later, I met the treasurer, David Margolis, a former securities analyst. I told him how I had scalped 5 points on some good inside information. (Today I could be put in jail for this by the SEC.) David laughed and told me how lucky I was to make $100. International Telephone wanted the $4 billion contract as a learning experience and to cover overhead. It was destined to lose money. There was no way the contract could have been construed bullishly for the company.

If you are what you eat, a corporation can be judged by what it earns, reinvests, and pays out in dividends. Securities analysts deal with corporate micro-factors. Then they develop a pecking

261

order for all the companies within an industry and then within a broader sector of common characteristics—consumer driven, capital-goods oriented, natural resources—or sensitivity to interest rates. What's missing is historical perspective. What does it mean that Ford can earn $10 a share one year and lose money the next year? Do you average both years? Do you compare a Honda sedan with an Escort, pound for pound, dollar for dollar, or do you just assume that the quota system for Hondas remains? Ford then learns how to build Honda-Escorts or buys a piece of Honda and has them build Escort-Hondas. Today, Ford sells in the marketplace for 4 times earnings. No stock sells at 4 times earnings for very long. It either doubles in price and sells at 8 times earnings, or its earnings collapse and it nearly goes out of business.

By mid–1986 the marketplace was betting that Ford's earnings would decline substantively during 1986–1987. There were those on the right side of the plane who saw clouds, and those on the left side of the aircraft who saw blue skies. By mid–1986 we knew we were happy occupants of the left window seat. It takes about a year for a contrarian position to prove itself, or, stated from the other side, for the market to catch up with the newly emerging facts that would rearrange the consensus. If Ford would sell at just 8 times 1987 earnings, the stock would double over the next twelve months.

But the market is never especially stupid for very long. Ford's record over the past ten years had been undistinguished. If the company reverted to trend, it would earn 10 or 11 percent on its equity—about $4 or $5 per share—and sell somewhere between $40 and $50 which it had done for many of the past ten years. Ford, then, is no different than many other of its brethren. If a corporation cannot deliver much more than a 10 or 11 percent rate of return on its net assets during a period of troublesome inflation and interest rates of double-digit proportions, there is no way the stock can do more than go through interim fluctuation within a narrow band of valuation. Stated another way, if interest rates on five- to twenty-year Treasury notes range between 13 and 14 percent, there is no reason to own stocks with rates of return on assets of less than 15 percent. Even in a recovery year, 1983, only seven of the largest twenty industrial enterprises in the country cleared more than a 15 percent rate of return on their equity. There were more which delivered less than 10 percent.

S&P 400

1947-1985

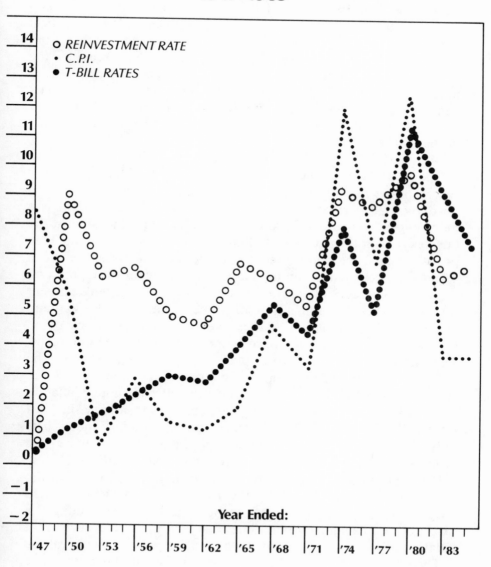

o REINVESTMENT RATE
· C.P.I.
● T-BILL RATES

Year Ended:

'47 '50 '53 '56 '59 '62 '65 '68 '71 '74 '77 '80 '83

Ask yourself why anyone should invest in a major industrial's equity if it delivers a subpar return. The answer is that you invest only for a short cyclical burst. General Motors went from a deficit in 1982 to a rate of return on equity of 18 percent during 1983. From the dog days in the summer of 1982 to the spring of 1983, General Motors nearly doubled in price, but the stock was substantively lower a year later. Eliminate the capacity to buy cyclical stocks when they are reporting deficits because they might go out of business, and you have eliminated a good 30 percent of the market. If you X-out natural-resource issues because you believe inflation will remain low, another 20 percent of the market's valuation is gone. Not only is it nice to know where you shouldn't put your money, but why you may or may not have made money in the market.

The chart on 263 plots the plight of the major industrial enterprises in the country: the index of the Standard & Poor's 400. The reinvestment rate for a corporation is the rate of return delivered on reinvested earnings, i.e., earnings less dividends paid. It is a more cogent indicator of profitability on capital reinvested in the business. After the early burst of high profitability in the immediate postwar years, the reinvestment rate fluctuated aimlessly between 4 and 8 percent. (If an industrial earns 10 percent on equity and pays out 40 percent of earnings in dividends, it has a reinvestment rate of 6 percent.) Nothing to write home about. Until the Vietnam war induced the inflation of the seventies with the shock of oil prices trebling in 1973, the reinvestment rate remained quiescent. The chart overlays the two critical factors of interest rates (the risk-free return) and inflation in the form of the Consumer Price Index. Until the mid-sixties, the reinvestment rate gapped inflation and T-bill rates of return. During the Johnson presidency, interest rates and inflation overshot the corporate profitability index. The only time you make easy money in the market is when the reinvestment rate soars above interest rates and inflation.

It is easy to understand why so much money was made in the early postwar years. Yet, by the late sixties, the game turned rough. Not only did you have to be a genius in projecting the profitability of major corporations, but you had to factor in what inflation and rising interest rates would do to price-earnings ratios.

The chart on 265 traces the collapse in price-earnings ratios as soon as interest rates and inflation caught up with the political

S&P 400

1947-1985

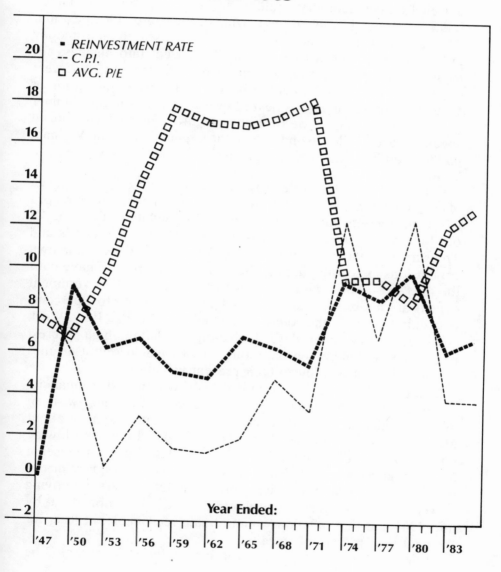

realities of Johnson's guns-and-butter policy. The market's near-term insensitivity to political change should not be discounted. It took the bond crowd and stock practitioners the better part of the sixties to wise up. Price-earnings ratios remained high for three to five years longer than one could explain today. Perhaps it was disbelief that the country could go to hell so rapidly. This Greed Index never again reached the heights of the end-of-1968 position. At that point I resigned as director of research and money management for the Rosenwald family. I went into business for myself in an investment partnership, where the fee was 20 percent of the profits. The stock market peaked out early in the spring of 1969. The Greed Index was never lower than it was in the summer of 1970. Quite simply, we also got caught up in professionalized speculation and failed to understand the implications of the Vietnam buildup until it was very late in the day. That's all you had to know.

Before we completely destroy the case for investing in a piece of corporate America, it is fair to mention that the long-term record of financial assets has at least outperformed inflation. For most of our lifetimes, equities have delivered this much while bonds and Treasury bills have consistently failed to do so. Draw your own conclusions as to what impact the political process will have over the next five-, ten-, and twenty-five-year intervals. If government deficits are not brought down from 4 percent of GNP to 2 percent, in twenty-five years the country may look and feel like Italy. Work stoppages every other day, double-digit inflation, high interest rates, and debt-heavy corporations. Stocks would sell at 4 times earnings—about one fourth their present valuation.

If the political drift is too hard to call, why invest in financial assets at all? One evening in London, we were dining with an illustrious dealer in Old Masters. I just wanted to talk about Massaccio and Leonardo da Vinci. He wanted to discuss worldwide interest rates and inflation. Aside from the few pieces of museum quality that he sold, our dealer friend purveyed secondary pieces to well-heeled investors who worried about preserving buying power. When I suggested that world oil prices had topped out by mid–1984 and that inflation would remain reasonable, at least for the next year to two, his face fell.

"I am ruined. I have all my working capital in inventory," he said.

EQUITY, DEBT & RISK-FREE RATES OF RETURN

Outperforming the Consumer Price Index
(5,10,15,20 & 25 Year Time Intervals)
1926-1985

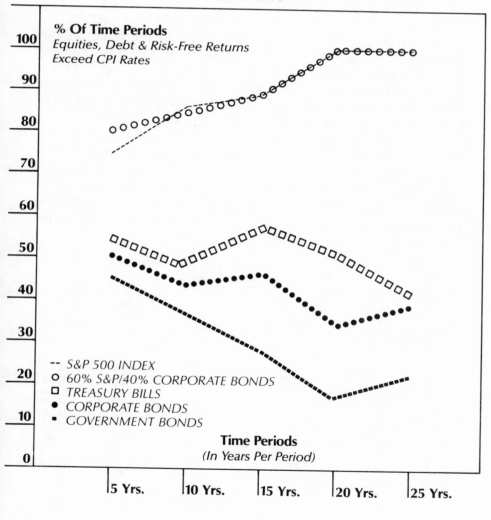

% Of Time Periods
Equities, Debt & Risk-Free Returns
Exceed CPI Rates

-- S&P 500 INDEX
o 60% S&P/40% CORPORATE BONDS
□ TREASURY BILLS
● CORPORATE BONDS
▪ GOVERNMENT BONDS

Time Periods
(In Years Per Period)

5 Yrs.   10 Yrs.   15 Yrs.   20 Yrs.   25 Yrs.

"Don't worry too much," I said. "If the dollar stays buoyant, Americans will buy your goods with appreciated currency."

"Ah, but I sell to doctors on Park Avenue and furniture manufacturers in Grand Rapids. They all worry about inflation. If they are not afraid of inflation, they won't buy. After all, they are not collectors."

"You may have a problem for the next year or two, but don't despair," I said. "After all, we have yet to deal with the out-of-hand deficits in America."

"I will pray for Jesse Jackson to win in 1988," he said.

"First you should pray for Reagan to lop off some military spending," I said. And then I thought of my own financial insecurities. When I was earning $100 a week as a copy editor in my early twenties, I stocked half a dozen banjos in the closet. Whenever I needed a hundred bucks, I would pawn a few banjos, but never the case instrument. That's all I needed then.

The precariousness of stock-price stability for even the broadest-based capitalizations is shown in this table on institutional ownership. It suggests that the investment consensus on specific issues determines stock prices. Almost every major corporation in the country has from half to three-quarters of its shares controlled by professional investors. At the first whiff of fish, they bang out the goods and go on to something else.

S & P 500 TOTAL RETURNS

5-Year Period Ending	Avg. Annual Total Return	Probability of Earning 13% or More	5-Year Period Ending	Avg. Annual Total Return	Probability of Earning 13% or More
1960	8.9%	39.7%	1973	2.0%	24.5%
1961	12.8%	49.6%	1974	−2.4%	16.9%
1962	13.3%	50.8%	1975	3.2%	27.1%
1963	9.8%	42.1%	1976	4.9%	30.5%
1964	10.7%	44.4%	1977	−0.2%	20.3%
1965	13.2%	50.8%	1978	4.3%	29.5%
1966	5.7%	32.3%	1979	14.8%	54.4%
1967	12.4%	48.4%	1980	13.9%	52.4%
1968	10.2%	42.9%	1981	8.1%	37.8%
1969	5.0%	30.9%	1982	13.9%	52.0%
1970	3.3%	27.4%	1983	17.0%	59.9%
1971	8.4%	38.6%	1984	14.7%	54.2%
1972	7.5%	36.7%	1985	14.5%	53.6%
			Average	8.8%	40.3%

Source: Goldman Sachs

INVESTMENT CONCENTRATION BY INSTITUTIONS

Rank Company	No. Of Inst.	Shs. Held	% Shs. Outstanding
1. Int. Bus. Mach.	1,569	303,075	49
2. Gen. Electric	1,041	225,995	49
3. Exxon Corp.	947	266,572	31
4. Gen. Motors	967	114,438	37
5. Stand. Oil Ind.	773	151,148	44
6. Atl. Richfield	883	129,705	51*
7. Schlumberger	871	122,265	42
8. Stand. Oil Cal.	695	151,148	44
9. Eastman Kodak	858	82,885	42
10. 3 M	696	71,051	60*
11. Philip Morris	636	77,524	63*
12. Sears Roebuck	588	167,831	47
13. Hewlett-Packard	600	124,831	47
14. Am. Home Prod.	694	79,973	50*
15. Mobil Corp.	689	151,689	37
16. Ford Motor	689	104,605	57
17. Digital Equip.	547	43,778	76*
18. du Pont	597	81,975	34
19. Merck & Company	661	43,068	58*

* Institutions owned over 50% of these companies.
Source: Standard & Poor's *Outlook*.

The investment dilemma can be stated another way. If the biggest and adequately capitalized corporation can't deliver a consistently high return for any five-year period in recent history, you'd better own them only when profit margins are about to reaccelerate. This is the earnings-momentum school of money management. You'd also better be able to forecast interest rates. If intermediate-term government bonds are yielding 13½ percent, as they were in the summer of 1984, stocks had scant probability to outperform bonds. This explains why we remained 25 percent invested and looked principally to the bond market for a cue as to when market erosion might end. The on left table demonstrates dolefully that it pays to know what you're working with. The largest capitalization stocks have no dreams attached to them except in the minds of the institutional investors, who rely on their capacity to project earnings better than their competition. The record suggests no one can do this consistently.

If the well-heeled American Corporation can't make money consistently because of its limitations (rarely making more than 13 or 14 percent on its equity base), why not just buy a bunch of Persian carpets and put them in a warehouse for ten years? Well, carpets don't pay you interest, nothing like the 13 or 14 percent on unrated bonds. If inflation remains low—5 to 7 percent— collectibles will not appreciate more than the inflation rate. So, owning Sarouks, you have made an inflation and interest-rate forecast just as much as any professional securities investor. You definitely have reduced your liquidity. The ability to buy and sell Persian carpets at will is questionable. I can make three phone calls to government-bond traders and buy or sell a billion dollars' worth of paper within 15 minutes and not move the market $\frac{4}{32}$s of a point.

Every investment must earn its keep relative to a clearinghouse rate of interest. If you can get 13.5 percent on two- to four-year government paper, stocks don't exceed the clearing rate unless there are some catalytic forces at work that could push up the rate of return on equity. One way to go is to change the capital structure of a corporation. Instead of putting all the company's cash flow into a new paper mill, maybe International Paper and its brethren could buy back 10 percent of its capitalization. After all, IP averages only an 8 or 9 percent return year after year. Unfortunately, most major corporations are more interested in preserving their bond ratings than in making money for shareholders. Conversely, I have never found a management with a majority stake in the equity of its company that would willingly dilute itself.

Now that we have destroyed the case for investing in corporate America most of the time, what can one do to develop a coherent investment viewpoint that is something more than a hair shirt more years than not? Keep in mind that the years when the S&P 500's price appreciation has been lower than cash equivalents, no more than 10 or 15 percent of the index outperforms cash. In other words, you can't win unless your stock-picking capacity is equivalent to your being a chess master.

"I know what you do," Bob Kobel, our director of marketing, said to me one day. "I've watched you for years, and now I understand it."

"What do I do? I'm not sure I know what I do anymore," I said.

"Well, the first thing is you find a company with position on the board. It could be The New York Times, Dow Jones, even Boeing. The company has to have market primacy," Bob said.

"The first stock I ever made any serious money in was Electrolux," I said. "More than twenty-five years ago, I liked the machine and read in *Consumer Reports* that they raised prices every other year. The stock was over-the-counter at six times earnings," I said. My first wife insisted that I buy her this damn expensive machine. So I got even with her and bought the stock.

"That's another point. The stock has to be relatively cheap and undiscovered," Bob said. "You never bought Dow Jones despite its proprietary position in newspapering. The price-earnings ratio was always too high."

"So how many great companies are there that sell on the cheap?" I laughed and put my feet up on the round marble table in my office. "You can count them on one hand from cycle to cycle."

"There are other variables," Bob said. "Look at Salomon. Enormous operating leverage in the commodities sector and in the brokerage business. The savings and loans, the same thing. At the bottom of the cycle in 1982, they were virtually bankrupt on paper—and then interest rates turned. Chrysler, the same way. From a deficit to enormous earnings when the cycle turned."

"Salomon is a good example," I said. "Look at the proxy statement and you will find twenty overachievers with a big stake in the company. It's like having a hundred doctors at Mount Sinai looking after you. In a mediocre year, Salomon earns 20 percent on its equity, maybe 40 percent in a great year. It is simultaneously an inflation hedge and a call on the stock market. What difference does it make if interest rates go to 15 percent if their clearing rate on reinvested capital is 20 percent or more? At the bottom of the cycle, you could buy Salomon at book value and at a valuation lower than the market."

"And what is the rationale for Caesar's World?" Bob asked.

"Ah, that is a gambling ticket of a different kind. There is the operating leverage as gaming recovers in Las Vegas. But then there is the magnificent gross plant there. It is not reproducible at anywhere near the price the market is valuing the capitalization. You are buying enormous swimming pools and tennis courts at a discount, and they should begin to earn a good return."

"How do you buy managements?" Bob asked.

"I am always looking to buy the owner-managers who want the price of their stock to move up for solid reasons. I bought Steinberg and Singleton and Larry Tisch. We still are buying Larry and the neurotic overachievers at Salomon. Rising returns on equity, increasing net-free cash flow, utilizing the balance-sheet strengths whether buying in stock, exchanging assets with low returns, whatever."

"And what about The New York Times people?"

"Walter Mattson is a good professional manager, but he doesn't control the destiny of the company. There is still too much 'Our Crowdishness' in the Sulzberger family dynasty. They aren't hungry enough."

"The Sulzbergers should have taken the company private?" Bob asked.

"Yes, but they don't think that way. Instead, the trust was a seller early-on in the recovery cycle."

"But the Times as a stock is priced more efficiently today than ever before. It sells at the same price-earnings multiple as Times Mirror ands all the other well-situated media conglomerates," Bob pointed out.

"It's true," I said, "but look at the net-free cash flow of the company per dollar of market capitalization. It is still significant. And, despite the move in the stock, the market's capitalizing the Times below its economic value. You could sell off the regional newspapers and CATV system for the price of the stock today and have the metropolitan daily for nothing."

"So you are still buying assets at a discount?" Bob asked.

"We'd better be. A couple of million pieces are in the accounts."

"And don't forget Metromedia," Bob said.

"Kluge did it all," I said. "A perfect casebook study for Harvard Business School. First he traded up his TV station properties, and then he started to shrink the stock and leverage the balance sheet. Don't forget we discovered Metromedia when the computer spat out a 40 percent reinvestment rate for the company and a price-earnings ratio of 8. Kluge started off owning 10 percent of the company and by the time it was all over with the leveraged buyout he had about 80 percent and was using bank and insurance money to take out his shareholders. There are very few Kluges in the world. They end up owning their companies. Some of them want to own the world. Driven men. I want driven men working for me twenty-four hours a day. The guys in white shirts making $600,000 a year and $37,000 invested in their multibillion dollar asset bases—that's for the public. Let the public immobilize its money there."

"So the cards are stacked against the public?" Bob asked.

"The cards are the cards," I said.

There is more than one way to invest in securities markets. There are growth-stock players and emerging-growth players. Most of them get caught up in the overvaluation and hysteria that bubbles up during each cycle. Some guys always know when to step up to bat when the industrials all look as if their factories are going to turn to rust. And then there are the asset-value buyers. They will buy any kind of stock if it is 40 cents on the dollar. Maybe a few people in the world can project interest rates with any certainty from cycle to cycle and play the yield curve on bonds. I don't know any of them. Very few money managers, economists, or presidents of banks are worth $100 million or more because of their investments or interest-rate forecasts.

The only broker I know who has made serious money is Mike Milken of Drexel. Mike trades junk bonds and delves into bankruptcy reorganizations. You can tell a broker by his customers. Tisch, Steinberg, Lindner, Riklis—they all deal directly with Michael. He underwrites billions of dollars in unrated bonds and some unseasoned equities. Some of the less-than-fundamental equities don't do very well, but a junk bond can only lapse into receivership or get better. From the bottom of the cycle, you could have made more money in Chrysler's preferred stock than in the common equity. Institutional investors can't buy unrated bonds for their clients, so the field is left to the wealthy lone wolves of the world who buy and sell billions. An unrated bond, International Harvester Financial, the company's credit subsidiary, yielded over 20 percent, and its floor inventory was worth much more than the bond sold for in the marketplace. The insurance companies had to clear this paper off their ledgers for cosmetic reasons at the bottom of the cycle. Harvester survived, and Mike's clients got a little richer.

There is another way money is run that is the reciprocal of what we try to do. Instead of looking for energized managements, the dividend-discount-model players look for demoralized markets and industries. The last thing such investors want to own is a well-recognized company with good management selling at a premium to the market. Rather, they want to trade on the fears and insecurities of investors—the public and other professionals. Many serious money pools ranging over $10 billion are run this way. "So you are afraid of Manufacturers Hanover Bank because of its concentrated lending in Mexico? Good. I will take it off your hands at 3 times earnings when it is yielding 12 percent," they say. "You are afraid of IBM becoming just another commodity company? I will buy IBM from you at 8 times next year's earnings because we think IBM will sell at its historic 125 percent of the market's valuation next year or at 12 times earnings." Early in 1986, these guys started to buy the oils after spot prices dove from $28 a barrel to twelve bucks.

There is merit in this brand of contrarian thinking which says that almost everything comes back to a historic relationship to the market before long. The only good stocks are cheap stocks. The only markets worth playing are undervalued ones. If the dividend-discount practitioners have credible track records over time, it is because the economic cycles have not been too extreme. When a depression hits, corporate equilibrium cannot be restored—except by innovative political changes in the system that leave many industries with little residual equity after their reorganization. So far, creative accounting, approved by the regulatory authorities, keeps the banks and utilities afloat. Occasionally, shareholders must sit for haircuts: Continental Illinois, Long Island Lighting. The dividend-discount boys understand this phenomenon well. Their rationale is that industries have good years and bad years, and the pendulum of sentiment generally swings too far at the extremes of each cycle. If the country plunges into a Great Depression, all bets are off, the model self-destructs, and all equity-valuation yardsticks are meaningless. The money invested is sucked down the drainpipes.

The S. C. Bernstein dividend-discount table is reproduced herein. Minus an MBA and a stretch on Wall Street, its interconnecting variables make your absorption in one sitting problematic. The model makes many forecasts before it reaches its conclusion as to the market's valuation. The economic cycle for Bernstein stretches from 1982 till 1988, with returns on equity for corporations averaging 16.5 percent—somewhat higher than in previous cycles. Normalized earnings compound 7.4 percent in an environment of trendline growth for the economy of about 3 percent. A critical derivative is the valuation structure for the market. It is based on a 40 percent dividend-payout ratio and a bond rate of 9.5 percent during the cycle, with inflation ticking away at 4 percent per annum. Under such conditions, price-earnings ratios would move up almost 50 percent from the mid–1984 level of 8. By mid–1986 this is exactly what happened. Interest rates and return on equity are then adjusted downward for inflation to provide a real bond rate of interest and real return on equity.

There are so many political and economic cycle predictions involved in this interlinked forecast that slippage could take place anywhere, and last for a year or more. An iron will, belief, and the strictest discipline are obvious prerequisites for playing so intellectual a game. There are many what-ifs. How much pressure can a money-management organization take if its forecast on interest rates and corporate earnings are wide of the mark? Inflation can be induced politically and therefore be unpredictable. Oil prices tripled in 1973 and then tripled again over the next several years. Deficits can be induced by wars or Great Society practitioners. When does a Jesse Jackson ever attain the presidency? Wall Street always believes that the Republican boy is gonna win big for them. The dividend-discount model works in an orderly economy of trendline growth, but it is a sterile document in a time of radical political change, abbreviated economic cycles, and aberrations in Federal Reserve Board policy. The market is the country—its fantasies and its reality intertwined with an enormous capacity for mutational eruption.

On a mellow summer evening we drove along the crescent-shaped shoreline near Cannes. Offshore, an oversized white yacht sparkling with lights revved its motors of thousands of horses in deep-throated resonance. Somehow an Arabic prince had convinced the township of Cannes to approve his road, cut on the right side along the Boulevard de la Croisette. A bulletproof wall at least twenty feet high masked his beachside villa. Farhi, the sculptor, pointed out that it was the only monstrous exception on the coastline of the Côte d'Azur.

"And for an Arab."

VARIABLES INFLUENCING EQUITY VALUATION
(Standard & Poor 400)

Period	ROE	Normalized EPS Growth	Actual Dividend Payout	Potential Dividend Payout	Mean P/E Ratio
1952–57	13.7%	5.7%	53.0%	58.4%	11.9x
1958–60	10.6	5.8	59.4	45.3	17.5
1961–66	12.1	5.6	54.9	53.7	17.4
1967–69	12.5	7.6	52.4	39.2	17.3
1970–73	12.3	8.6	49.5	30.1	15.1
1974–79	15.4	11.0	40.4	28.6	9.2
1980–81	15.9	12.6	41.1	20.8	8.5
30-Year Average	13.2%	8.1%	50.1%	39.4%	13.8x
10/13/82 (Bond Mkt. Peak)	16.5N[2,3]	9.0	54.0	45.5	7.8[2]
5/30/84 (Bond Mkt. Trough)	16.5N[2,3]	7.9	44.5	52.1	8.0[2]
4/25/85 (Current)	16.5N[2,3]	7.9	44.5	52.1	8.9[2]
1988E (End of Cycle)	15.5N[3]	7.4	40.0	52.3	11.4

1—Equity risk premium *equals* total equity return *minus* bond rate.

2—P/E of S&P 400 based on *normalized* earnings as follows:

	Book Value	Normalized ROE	EPS
10/13/82	$118.00	16.5%	$19.47
5/30/84E	129.50	16.5	21.35
4/25/85E	139.00	16.5	22.95

3—ROE is expected to average 16.5% during the 1982–1988 cycle. By 1988, however, normalized ROE is expected to have diminished somewhat.

Source: Standard & Poor's Corporation, Department of Commerce, Federal Reserve Board and Bernstein estimates.

"My God! The wall is hundreds of feet long. Is this what money buys? *Les murs ont des oreilles,*" I said.

We were two couples returning from a three-star degustation in Mougins that Roger Vergé had cooked for us. Farhi was at the wheel of his 1947 Chrysler Town and Country, a red convertible with a honey-colored wooden body and huge white sidewalls. At every pedestrian crossing, a spontaneous round of applause greeted

CHRYSLER CORPORATION

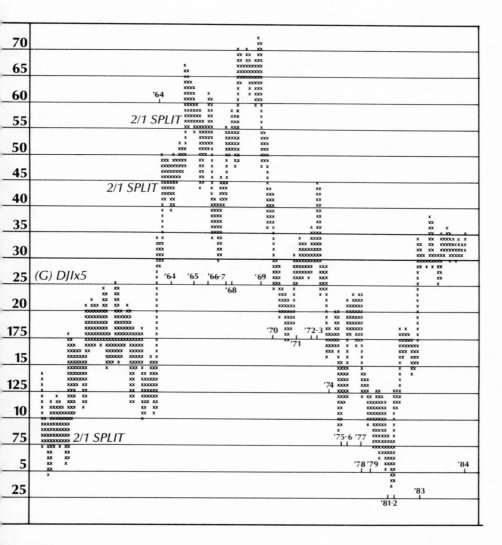

Source: Market Charts Inc.

the vehicle. It was a full cycle for me. More than thirty years ago, a buddy at college had driven around New York in the same wheels, maybe the identical heap.

"There are only twenty-six left in the world, and this is the only one in Europe." Farhi was saying. "It came with a five-hundred pound sack of spare parts. She rides beautiful. Yes, Martin?"

"Farhi, you are a crazy perfectionist," I said in French. The car was bought for $65,000 from some maniac in Detroit.

"In France there is nothing left but the good food and the good wine. Yes, Martin?"

"*Je suis très heureux,*" I said.

"Air Roz," Farhi said. "You don't use your lips sufficiently. The S like a Z. His head tilted up for the *Air* and down on his chest for the *Roz*.

"I will never be able to say 'happy' in French," I shouted. "Air Roz, Air Roz, Air Roz."

"And you, Toni, are *heureuse*. Air Roza."

Toni was smart. "Forget it, Jean Claude," she said in English.

And the spiffy American anachronism coasted along the road by the sea in its serene fluid drive, secure in its world of motive power and unaware that its maker, Chrysler, had seen a woof-woof at its door and then had come back to earn billions. In the practitioners' chart books, since the late thirties the stock had traced an enormous 10-gallon hat.

Is that what my years and years on the Street symbolized? I traced the line of the Stetson with my index finger. There were shimmering stars and fallen stars, but never the certitude of pure clarity.

Epilogue

IT is April 1986, and the Big Board is delivering zippy 30 and 40 point up-and-down days. Spot prices for oil had collapsed to a sawbuck per barrel, and year over year had snuffed out any inflation left in the system. Bond rates broke to 7.5 percent. The central banks of West Germany, Japan, and the United States synchronously were lowering their discount rates. The bond market, as usual, had anticipated this action months before. Was the deflationary dream coming true? The economy seemed becalmed by flattish automobile sales. IBM's new computers sold slowly. Corporate earnings were yet to bloom, but the valuation of the market rose reciprocally as interest rates simmered down. The best recipe for all bull markets is always the hope you are buying earnings on the come.

I phoned Mike Milken and told him we wanted to take our money-management company public. "Look, Michael. Dreyfus sells at 20 times 1986's estimated earnings. All their growth has come from the influx of money into their government-bond funds— billions of dollars the past two years. That's not going to last. Our earnings are much higher quality. We have a broadly based client list. Good performance. You know what we do." On Wall Street there are no absolutes. Only relatives. This is to this as that is to that.

"I hear you, I hear you," Mike said.

"I want to go public at 20 times earnings, and I want to raise debenture money. I want you to do a $100 million convertible with a six and one-half percent coupon and a breakeven time of three and one-half years. Up 25 percent, Mike. I want it now."

"It's not a problem," Michael said.

"Put your best corporate-finance man on this as of yesterday," I said.

"Okay okay," Mike said. "I'll call New York. Let me go to work."

279

I heard the usual cacophony of traders screaming junk-bond quotes on the wires to their customers as Mike's voice trailed off. Now all I had to do was convince my people that we should sell some stock to the world.

"We are in an era when financial assets beat everything. Paper is supreme," I said. "Drexel will raise us a hundred million dollars. It is nondilutive from the arbitrage profit on the proceeds. We can take six and one-half percent money and put it to work at 10 to 13 percent."

"You are going to drive us crazy," they said. "We are going to earn $17 million this year, maybe $25 million next year. That's $15 million for you and the rest for us. Nobody in this country makes that kind of money." The eyes darted around the black marble table. "We don't want to give that up," X said. "I don't see why you want to give up $15 million a year. It's serious money, even for you."

"Look," I said. "All we are doing is changing the form of the money. You give up ordinary income for capitalized value in the stock. The valuation for the company is $140 million."

"I can count," Y yelled. "I've been waiting all my life to make a million bucks a year, and now you are taking it away. Well, up yours. I want my monee. I'm looking at a coop overlooking the park. They are asking two and a half million."

"Fuck your housing problems. Get a mortgage," I said. "It's tax deductible. I'm tired of listening to how poor you all are."

"What in hell are we going to do with a hundred million dollars?" X asked.

I sensed he was a little more receptive to the concept. The voice had lost its flintiness.

"I haven't the faintest idea what we're going to do with the money," I said. "But if the market tanks, we will have a bankroll ready to buy things on the cheap."

"You of all people know how hard it is to buy companies right," X said. "This is insanity. You are taking dog biscuits out of my mouth for some crazy dream. I'm going to fight you, Sosnoff."

"Fight me, fight me." I flung a red plastic container filled with ball-point pens against the wall. "The numbers are going to govern this situation," I screamed. "If the arithmetic parses out, we are selling equity to the public. This is America. I want to control one percent of GNP."

" I'm not going to listen to this insanity," Y said. He drained his soda glass and stormed out.

The difficult problems are the problems of success. How many stocks do you buy and watch double or triple before you grow bored with tacking on zeros? It was time for us to build a company.

When Franklin Roosevelt wanted a tough cop to run the SEC, he tapped Joseph Kennedy, one of the great operators on the Big Board. Kennedy knew all the tricks and cleaned up the exchange in six months. The only way to embarass Corporate America into delivering higher rates of return to their investors is to unveil their self-interests and multiple stupidities. We need an SEC chairman like Billy Conn to carry the fight to the establishment. Maybe you get knocked out in the thirteenth. Maybe you don't. I sensed a raised consciousness on the Street. You can no longer easily get away with greenmail. Corporations are embarrassed to pay it, and even Saul Steinberg is too embarrassed to take any more of it. The rates for officers' and directors' insurance have gone through the roof. All the double-breasted boardroom crowd is afraid not to act in the public interest and want to be indemnified if they are challenged by outside shareholders.

After many confrontive sessions, Atalanta/Sosnoff Capital was underwritten by Drexel Burnham Lambert. It was the first underwriting of a privately owned money-management company that was not in the mutual-fund business. The valuation placed on us was $140 million. We owned no hard assets except for a few round granite tables, a Hewlett-Packard computer that sat in an air-conditioned room, and a seat on the New York Stock Exchange. There were no steel mills belching black smoke, nor was there a cavernous factory filled with workers in white smocks who riveted at their work station subassemblies that progressed along overhead conveyors to become television sets, washing machines, Broncos, Blazers, Pintos, and assorted four-wheeled beasts. Here were a handful of guys sitting around the table mumbling at each other that nobody knew what they were talking about. I was screaming at our director of research, Eric, a brilliant twenty-seven-year-old. "You have the brain of an ant, the perspective of a mole, and the courage of a sheep." And I laughed to myself. With all our mistakes, we are pretty good manufacturers of money. After all, Texaco bought Getty at the top of the oil market. U.S. Steel is still writing off blast furnaces, and Manny Hanny owns a piece of Mexico.

On a sparkling clear day in June we went public. The market declined 46 points, its biggest point decline in history. A handful of our friends stood up and bought our issue. The Street's brokers flipped a half million shares within 48 hours. Our competitors, the institutional investors, wouldn't take a share. Everyone wanted the convertible. At an evening dinner meeting for Simon Wiesenthal I met Fred Joseph, the President of Drexel Burnham Lambert.

"Thank God for American capitalism," I said. "It works like a Turkish bazaar. If you want the beautiful white angora goat, you must buy the mangy gray one."

"No! No!" Fred said. "Thank God for Mike Milken."

It was the end of a long day for us and the guys on Wilshire Boulevard who decided we should get some money.

INVESTMENT METHODOLOGY

1

Government Spending Emphasis.
Federal Reserve Policy Emphasis.
Analysis of Critical Economic Variables.
G.N.P. Analysis of Demand Momentum.
Review of Inflation Momentum.
Interest Rate Forecast.
Capital Formation Environment.

2

Balance of Payments Trends.
Rate of Change in OPEC Surplus.
Price Changes in Precious Metals.
Interest Rate Review by Major Countries.
Inflation Review by Major Countries.
The Dollar vs. Other Currencies.
Geopolitical Changes.
Equity Valuation Comparison.

3

Current and Projected Institutional Cash Flows and Asset Allocation.
Analysis of Institutional and Corporate Cash Flow and Asset Allocation.
Total Value of Equities to New Issue Supply. Dollar Value to New Issues to Cash Flow.
Speculation Analysis; (Margin Debits, Low/High Price Ratio) Turnover, Volatility of Low-Price Stocks.

4

Analysis of Riskless Return to Our Required Attractive Return.
Analysis of Intermediate Bond Yields to Riskless Rate.
Analysis of Long-Term Bond Yields to Intermediate and Riskless Yields.
Determination of Alternatives to T Bills Relative to Yield Curve.
Analysis of S&P-500 Current and Forecast Earnings, Yield and Rate of Return on Equity.
Projected Range of Price/Earnings Multiple for S&P-500.
Total Return Analysis Equities to Various Bond Sectors.

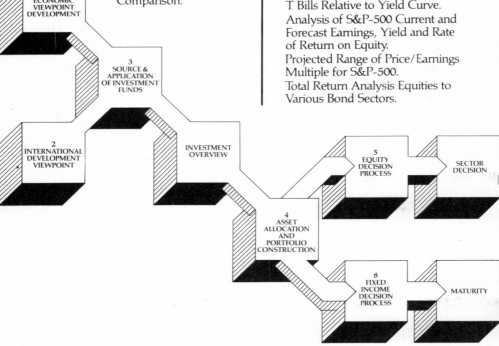